LI___S
AT 50

A HANDBOOK
FOR CREATIVE
RETIREMENT
PLANNING

By Leonard J. Hansen

BARRON'S

New York • London • To___

All inquiries should be addressed to:
Barron's Educational Series, Inc.
250 Wireless Boulevard
Hauppauge, New York 11788

Library of Congress Catalog Card Number 89-15009

International Standard Book No. 0-8120-4329-4

Library of Congress Cataloging-in-Publication Data
Hansen, Leonard.
    Life begins at 50: a handbook for creative retirement planning/ Leonard Hansen.
        p. cm.
    Bibliography: p.
    Includes index.
    ISBN 0-8120-4329-4
    1. Retirement—United States—Planning. 2. Retirement income
United States—Planning. I. Title. II. Title: Life begins at 50.
    HQ1063.2.U6H36   1989
    646.7'9—dc20   89-15009

This book reports on many concepts in all areas of human life and retirement years planning. It is not meant to be a substitute for professional practitioners of law or medicine in any of its references or intent.

References and research are believed accurate at the time of publication, but are, of course, subject to change.

Readers may address the author as follows:
        Leonard J. Hansen, Writer/Speaker/Lecturer
        Life Begins At 50
        Post Office Box 90279
        San Diego, California   92109

PRINTED IN THE UNITED STATES OF AMERICA

9012 800 987654321

This book is dedicated to the mature adults around the world who have taught me its principles . . .

. . . and to you, the mature adult reader, who may learn and adopt into your best life forward what is presented here.

ACKNOWLEDGEMENTS

It is very special when a request and a deep desire coincide. Such made this book possible when Grace E. Freedson, Acquisitions Editor for Barron's Educational Series, asked this journalist to recommend a writer for the first book in a new series to serve mature adults. I had the long and burning desire to write such a book but Grace had the idea and the publishing company to make it happen.

John Berseth, my editor from Barron's, earns the Ultimate Patience Award, as I jumped over distraction hurdles and bent deadlines.

Jim Gaffney of New Orleans, one of the very best of mature market newspaper editors, served as Devil's Advocate and with ongoing critique, and as ego deflator when he considered it necessary.

I acknowledge and thank my family for endorsing and supporting my cloistered times of research and writing—wife Marcia, sons Barron and Trevor, mother-in-law Helen Rasmussen, father-in-law Charles Rasmussen, and my mother in San Mateo, California, Margie Hansen.

I thank the thousands of interviewees who have enriched my knowledge and writing these past forty years, and particularly the mature adults of the past twenty years who have taught me that life really does begin at fifty.

And I acknowledge and commend you for choosing this book because of the promise of its title. You are more wise than most people in considering a plan for your retirement years, with a goal of making it the best time of your life.

Leonard J. Hansen
San Diego, California

CONTENTS

FOREWORD

By United States Senator Pete Wilson

You have a great opportunity for your best living in your mature years. Retirement is no time for you, for government, or for anyone else to put you on the shelf. No, retirement may be the very *best* time of your life, allowing you to move in new directions and to find new satisfactions.

This book, *Life Begins at 50*, will provide you with a wealth of creative ideas for planning your own retirement. It will put *you* in charge of your retirement years—able to assure your own health and financial security. It will challenge you—and prepare you fully—to participate in and even lead your community. It will encourage and enable you to be your own advocate and actually change the governmental processes that affect you.

The author, Leonard J. Hansen, is no "Johnny Come Lately" to writing about the mature years. He is, in fact, the pioneer journalist in the mature market field. His writing and commentaries have not only informed and entertained mature readers for eighteen years, they have also instructed those of us in government and public service. He created, edited, and published the first of the nation's mature market newspapers, *Senior World*, in San Diego, California.

I had just become Mayor of the City of San Diego when I met Len Hansen and formed what was to be both a lasting friendship and an invaluable learning experience. First, I read his investigative reporting in the fields of fraud, housing, insurance, and life-care residential contracts. Then I saw the results: successful prosecutions of the fraud perpetrators, the development of new housing concepts, the rewriting of state insurance laws around the nation, and new life-care protection for senior citizens in a score of states. His work is incisive and practical. It has won countless awards and commendations.

As Mayor of San Diego, I called on Len to serve as one of the city's first Crime Control Commissioners. Through his articles focusing on the special vulnerability of the elderly to crime, he was instrumental in the development by the San Diego Police Department of its "Adam 65" program— the first in the nation.

For five years he was a leading member of my Advisory Council on Senior Citizens, and served in a host of other community leadership roles. Len and his newspaper worked with city government in advancing what has been called one of the most innovative housing concepts for senior citizens in the nation—the private-sector development of senior housing on city-owned land under long-term discounted lease, with bonus density zoning that allowed efficient delivery of ancillary services to seniors in a pleasant congregate setting.

Len was also a vocal and effective advocate of the city's locally operated senior nutrition programs, which provided seniors discounted hot meals through the public grammar schools. The program provided many needy and otherwise isolated elderly citizens with both their only hot meal of the day and, perhaps equally important and nourishing, their only social sustenance of the day.

Since my election to the United States Senate, I have watched with pleasure and pride as Len Hansen's writings and investigations, his ideas and advocacy, have become more and more widely accepted and quoted nationally. Since coming to the Senate I have been privileged to serve on its Select Committee on Aging. Len Hansen's recommendations for programs for the protection of mature adults from crime have been sought by that and other legislative committees. Increasingly, his opinions on the whole range of concerns that affect aging are sought and valued by policymakers like President Ronald Reagan, who honored him with appointment to the 1981 White House Conference on Aging.

This book is a rich and valuable resource to guide you through the best possible retirement years. Len Hansen respects you and your right to choose your own direction—but in *Life Begins at 50* he has made your choices much easier, offering concrete ideas and options as well as sharing his expertise.

I congratulate you, if you have already made the decision not just to exist passively but to make the most of retirement. Only you can make it all that it can and should be.

It is not the job of government at any level—or the job of anyone but you—to make or direct your choice. We Americans are a nation of people who prize individual freedom. We jealously guard our right to make our own choices in life. And unless we have lost the ability to be self-sufficient, it is both our individual responsibility and our joy to make those choices and decisions.

Perhaps no other time in life will offer you as much freedom or as much fun as your retirement years. They are precious, so don't waste them!

I congratulate you upon the proud accomplishments and the years of hard work that have brought you to the point where you may consider new options and new opportunities in retirement. Whether you are already retired from the workforce or are making plans for this great adventure, you have many wonderful options and directions open to you. Len Hansen's wise and practical book will be of great value to you in exploring them and making wise choices.

May you enjoy long, healthy, and satisfying years, full of the rich rewards of contributing, of participating, and of leading the fulfilling and creative life that can and should be yours in retirement.

United States Senator Pete Wilson
Washington, D.C.
August 1989

PREFACE

Welcome to the better side of age fifty.

Forget everything you have heard about age or aging. Forget the taunts of your colleagues on discovering gray or white in your hairline.

Forget those stereotyped assumptions you have heard about debility, about poverty, about losing the abilities and senses you have.

Cast off any assumption that your best years are behind you or that life, from here on, is downhill. Because it doesn't have to be that way. Those stereotypes, those assumptions, those negatives that you've been taught, are wrong. The people who repeat them are wrong—and you are similarly wrong if you believe them to be true.

- Your health can actually be better now than ever before, if you make it so.

- Your wealth and discretionary income can be measurably better after you've reached the fifty-year mark than in your earlier years.

- Your activity and ability to achieve goals can rise to new levels if you choose that to be your direction.

- Your relationships and romance can be better, more satisfying, more rewarding, and more secure than ever before—if you let them happen.

- Your mind can actually be sharper, your senses keener, your perceptions even more focused in the years after your first half-century.

- You many choose new directions; you may climb new mountains; you may achieve more now than ever before!

Such is the subject and the dedication of this book. We will identify and destroy with fact the false assumptions, the negative stereotypes, and the foolish claims that age is all downhill. But our overall direction in this handbook is to look at the opportunities you have in your mature years. Read this book for discovery, and then go back and mark the information, the concepts, and the plans that can become yours if you so choose.

In these pages you will find that life really does begin at age fifty—and you have the ability to continue living to the fullest in your sixties, seventies, eighties—and even nineties.

Welcome to the best years of your life. It is all possible if you choose to make it so.

INTRODUCTION

You are a special person as a mature adult.

You have come to this age with accomplishment, having survived devastating wars and painful conflicts, the raising of children, the economic crises of recessions, inflation and stagflation, all the while developing a career, economic security, a distinctive lifestyle—and more.

You have a work ethic that is more highly developed than that of younger generations. You still report to work more predictably, take off fewer days for illness or other reason, and serve with more loyalty to employers and associates than younger counterparts.

You have contributed to the building of your community and its services.

You vote more regularly than any other age group in our society. You read more, think more deeply, and discuss public issues more frequently than any other age group.

You control three-fourths of the wealth and more than half of all discretionary spending in the United States. For the most part, you weren't given this money. You earned it by working, investing, and saving, again more than any other generation in our society.

You buy most of the better quality clothing and toys for your grandchildren, and for yourself, travel more, more frequently, and farther afield than any other age group.

Your money comprises 70 percent of that invested in savings and loans, allowing those institutions to lend to younger buyers for homes and autos.

You are at an age where you can reexamine your future and determine how and what you want it to be. At age fifty, fifty-five, sixty, sixty-five, seventy, or even seventy-five-plus, you can still redesign your own future.

In this book you will meet some remarkable people—some famous, some not famous at all, but each offering an important example for you to consider in your creative retirement planning.

In this book you will learn of your options and opportunities in these mature years, your rights and entitlements, and what you may expect and what you may reject.

This handbook presents hundreds of information briefings, ideas and suggestions, all cross-referenced so that you may refer to them actively in creating your own retirement plan. You will also find charting techniques that will help you adapt general rules to your own needs.

Here is your handbook for planning your future, for retirement living at its fullest and most satisfying.

Here's a test to see if
       your mission in life is over.
If you're alive, it isn't.

From the Messiah's Handbook in
"Illusions"
by Richard Bach

<table>
<tr>
<td>

CHAPTER

1

</td>
<td>

YOUR NEW WORLD

</td>
</tr>
</table>

What are you supposed to do in your mature years?

You are not "supposed" to do anything. You can do or not do anything you want, at any time, any place and in any new direction.

How many times have you heard someone say, "Act your age!" Have you felt then that you should be more sedate, more passive, more limited? And if so, why?

Age is really an illusion, generally being the assumption of limitations or debility or other negative characteristics. And old age can happen or not happen to anyone. An active life may span forty or fifty years, or eighty, ninety or one hundred birthdays, depending on the individual.

Baseball player and earthy philosopher Satchel Paige mused, "How old would you be if you didn't know how old you were?" I have seen people "old" at forty or fifty, and other people who were never "old" in their nineties. How "old" are you?

A line claimed by many people—from philosophers to stand-up comedians—is: "Age is basically mind over matter. If you don't mind, it doesn't matter."

Rather than the word "age," assumed in today's society as a negative, let's refer to this positive program in maturity as "aging." We'll not use the word "old" as a negative but as a recognition of a more mature point in the process of living.

Proper aging is a sign of maturity in fine wines, and for human beings the catalyst for richness and achievement in mature living.

Proper aging means taking care of the assets we have—our bodies and minds, financial and legal affairs, personal relationships, property and other physical assets, our role in the nation and our individual communities, and our relationships with families and heirs.

The assumption that anyone older is on a downhill path is not just one foisted on us by a youth oriented society. The respected psychologist Dr.

Ken Dychtwald addresses professional groups of gerontologists—professionals who work in the field of aging services—and as part of his presentation, asks questions of his audience.

"How many of you believe that the best ten years of your life are yet to come?" he asks. Typically, only a few hands are raised. Then, "How many of you believe that you are experiencing the best ten years of your lives right now?" This time a few more hands are raised. "And, finally, how many of you believe that the ten best years of your life are already behind you?" Most of the participants raise their hands.

When Dr. Dychtwald asks his audience their ages by groups, he finds that most are thirty-five or less! These professionals believe that the best years are gone, that life is on a downhill track, even at age thirty-five.

Dynamic and animated, Dr. Dychtwald exhorts his listeners to change their attitudes and assumptions—or to move to another business. He has taken this survey many times among professionals in gerontology and geriatrics—the latter being medical specialists in aging—and has found the results to be generally the same. Perception is the problem. Their expectations are negative; their assumption is that the road of life in maturity is without hope. And that is all wrong: None of their fears can be supported by fact; none of their attitudes recognize the success of today's mature adults.

Letters to my newspaper columns have asked, in all seriousness, "When I become a senior citizen, how do I overcome being sick and poor?" My reply has been: "Be a senior citizen for the discounts, and forget about being sick or poor unless you really want to be sick and poor, using age as a justification for those conditions."

"But what about nursing homes?" asks another reader. "I'm concerned that I won't like it in a nursing home, and as a senior citizen that's where I will be."

"No you won't," I reply in the column. "Less than five percent of mature adults—even at age sixty-five—are institutionalized in any way. So, unless you have an advancing chronic condition so that, predictably, you will not be able to take care of yourself, don't assume that you'll ever be in a nursing home. The odds of institutionalization increase only after age eighty-five, at present, and may actually be reduced—rather than increased—in the future if mature adults make positive lifestyle changes so as to stop or reverse the cause of most illness in older ages."

Those with experience in sales know that the key to success is identifying and then responding to and removing a prospect's real and hidden objections. In discussing people's roles, directions, and opportunities in mature living, there are stereotypic statements and assumptions that, similarly, should be identified, so that we might respond to and remove them, based on fact.

Some Stereotypes of Aging

Senior Citizens Are Poor. Untrue. Mature adults control 75 percent of the assets and more than half of the discretionary income in the nation. About 70 percent own their homes, 80 percent of them are mortgage-free!

Mature adults have, in the main, created estate values higher than all other generations combined. Most mature adults have been more careful in spending and more active in saving than any other generation. Most of today's mature adults will reap the benefits of this planning in their retirement years.

Mental Ability Declines With Age. Wrong. Mental ability is remarkable. The mind increases or decreases in ability, not because of age, but because of actions and personal attitude. A properly nourished and exercised body goes hand in hand with an active mind—at any age—whereas a reduction in nutrition, activity, blood flow, and oxygen often will lead to a deterioration in mental functioning.

Some of the best and brightest students in universities and colleges today are mature adults who have returned to fulfill their dream of a college degree, because their original intent was hampered by economic considerations or family responsibilities.

Many of the world's greatest inventions, ideas, and books have been produced by people over sixty. In politics people like Winston Churchill and Charles DeGaulle had their finest hours after our "normal" retirement age of sixty-five.

All Senior Citizens Become Senile. Wrong. Fully 95 percent of mature adults never experience senility; and even then, most senility is correctable or avoidable. Senility was a misguided assumption of the medical profession for years, so that any unusual behavior or memory lapse was misdiagnosed as such.

Other medical direction to "go home and rest" and "don't dare do any exercise" for diagnosed heart ailments, arthritis, and other problems actually catalyzed the symptoms of senility, by reducing the blood, oxygen, and nutrient flow in the body. Today's medical research shows that proper nutrition, exercise, and activity are vital and productive in dealing with most chronic conditions.

Most Seniors Are Chronically Ill. The statement is untrue in its intent. A federally funded study in the 1970s claimed that 85 percent of persons age sixty-five and over were chronically ill. The image was one of tragedy and disaster for older adults, hobbled by disability and pain. The medical establishment rushed to get more federal funding, and hospitals asked for more beds and facilities.

This particular research was seriously flawed because workers did not interview older adults themselves, but instead interviewed third parties

3

who were asked if they thought their senior neighbors suffered from any of a list of chronic afflictions. Then this error was compounded by the "chronic" problems, which included not only arthritis and heart disease but also hemorrhoids, ingrown toenails, a cold more than once a year, wearing of corrective lenses, and the like. There was no question asking if this broad base of chronic ailments seemed limiting or serious to the observer. So, the world was told that "senior citizens were seriously, chronically ill."

In the 1980 federal census, the questions were asked correctly. In fact, this was the first time that senior issues were addressed, based on the overall lifestyle, income, health status, outlook, and expectations of the people surveyed. The result was just the opposite. About 85 percent of the age sixty-five-plus respondents characterized their health as good to very good, with only 15 percent reporting serious problems or limitations.

You Should Assume That You Will Have Ailments. Not quite right. Your body is like a machine. If you keep the machine well tuned and lubricated, fueled and operated properly, it will run well with few or no problems for years and years. If the machine is not well cared for, its parts will break down, its efficiency and ability to perform reduced significantly.

There is a story told of a man, seventy-five, whose painful right knee was being examined by a physician. "Sam," said the doctor, "what can you expect? You're seventy-five and your body parts are sure to fall apart because of your age." "No, doc," replied the patient, now standing. "My left knee is the very same age as the right one, and it's okay—so the problem is in how you're looking at it, not my age."

Afflictions like heart problems and arthritis might be more prevalent in the mature years, but age is not the specific cause. It is the wear and tear of a lifestyle that does not take care of the body, and it is the accumulation of toxic influences over years (such as smoking) which produce the majority of heart, cancer, and other problems that affect many mature adults today.

As the body is a living organ, with an immune system that may be restored through lifestyle changes, nutrition, exercise and activity, many of the physical problems and debilities previously assumed to be inevitable can be halted and even reversed.

At Age Sixty-Five People Should Be Retired. Wrong—seriously wrong. There is, physiologically, no age at which anyone or everyone should be retired. The ability to work or be creative or productive is determined by the individual and his or her own mental and physical condition.

The use of age sixty-five for "mandated" retirement is a fluke—and a cruel mistake for most people.

In the 1870s Chancellor Otto von Bismarck of Germany wanted to move older people out of the work force, to appear benevolent, and to open more jobs for younger people. He decreed sixty-five as the age for retirement and a small government pension. Even being a fiscal conservative he did not face a financial crisis, since only a few people lived much beyond that age. When the American Social Security system was being created, the Administration and Congress simply adopted Bismarck's sixty-five year age as qualification, without any research, without any testing, without any examination of ages or lifestyles in the nation. From that point, the assumption in government and business has been "sixty-five and out."

Not until recent years have lawsuits successfully challenged that age for mandatory retirement, and legislative changes have been made. Today, with predictable longevity into ages eighty and ninety, there is all the more reason to question and challenge any assumption of absolute retirement at age sixty-five. It should be a decision individually based on financial, physical and personal desire and conditions and not on any other assumption or legislative mandate.

You do not have to retire from working if you don't want to do so. For many, working is a highly-desired and fulfilling part of life. Government and business still need to learn more about the high value of mature workers, particularly as the number of younger workers is diminishing rapidly. Today, more than ever before, the opportunity for continued working beyond age sixty-five is becoming one of personal choice.

Senior Citizens Are Lonely. Not quite. People who are lonely in earlier life and do nothing to correct the situation are those who are lonely in mature years. Also, those who are cranky, short-tempered or miserly in earlier years exhibit the same traits in maturity, unless they change their ways.

At any age those who just wait for the phone to ring are all the more depressed when no one calls. At any age many of those who do not control their lives productively find the void as that of loneliness. We may all miss other people, ones special to us, and that is natural. Loneliness, though, is something beyond that, and something we can correct with new relationships and activities. Loneliness is not something to be assumed in mature years. As your age changes, so do your friendships, family relationships and opportunities—and they may actually be changed for the better.

Your New Direction

If you are still working, you have the opportunity of assessing your present situation, particularly how it relates to your future retirement, at what age, at what lifestyle, at what activity and to what goals.

If you are already retired, you still have the opportunity of assessing your present situation—your lifestyle, goals, and deciding the direction in which you want to take your life. If you suffer present financial limitations, you can design a plan to remedy and remove them in order to fulfill your plans and goals.

No matter where you are in life, you can still design or redesign for your best, most creative, and fulfilling retirement years.

Your retirement might be determined to be complete freedom from any work; or, alternatively, it might be a redesign of your life to include some satisfying employment or business endeavor that attracts you. There are many people who want to continue to work and be financially productive.

In retirement you might want to continue living in your home, or you might want to move—to a smaller home, to a new city or retirement complex, or to a motorhome in order to travel the continent full time.

You might want to have more time for your present friends and acquaintances; or, you might feel yourself in a rut, with present relationships limiting, holding you back, and that you will want to create a new life with new friendships.

You might want to be closer to children and grandchildren; or you might want to put miles of distance between you, for your and their growth and independence.

You might want to dedicate your retirement to new discoveries, education, development of talents and skills; or you may want to continue and extend your present lifestyle.

You might want your new life to be full of active sports; or you may determine that other activities and hobbies are what you want.

You might want to double your planned income in retirement; or you might find that your current income and assets are quite sufficient.

You might want to change the world with the freedom of time in retirement years; or you might find a role as a volunteer in your neighborhood.

You might want . . . The possibilities and alternatives are endless because there is no single "right" plan in retirement. The best retirement program is whatever you design for yourself, taking into account your own needs and desires. Seek fulfillment for yourself.

Start with a clean sheet of paper, just as an artist faces a clean canvas, just as a writer starts with blank paper.

That's why we call it "creative retirement planning"—like the artist or writer, you must use your inner resources and talents to determine exactly what goes into the plan that will fulfill your desires, dreams, directions and goals.

As I travel around the country, speaking before various groups, I am often asked unthinking questions, like: "What do senior citizens eat for breakfast?" . . . "Do senior citizens have trouble chewing their food?" . . . "What do senior citizens do with their time?" Each question assumes that, on reaching maturity, we all become alike. "All of you with gray hair, jump into this mold," might be a line from a Grade B movie to be written by one of these questioners.

Of course, you eat for breakfast what you, individually, want to eat for breakfast; you chew what you want to chew (based on how you have taken care of your teeth); you do or not do with your time as you determine, again as an individual and without assumed conformity because of age.

The main concern for you, as you read this book and consider your path forward, is that the plan for the future is yours. It should not be shaped by a government. It should not be shaped by sons or daughters, who might put their own interests first—"When do I inherit the house?"—over your own desires. It should not be shaped even by the "experts," many of whom believe that their "best ten years" are already behind them.

The mission, if you choose to accept it—in the style of television's "Mission Impossible"—is to consider, define, refine and put into action your own creative, individual retirement plan.

Read the next chapter and discover some fascinating people who, in their own words, will share recommendations for your consideration—and serve, too, as "you can do it" role models and as proof of the freedom that we can all share in the retirement years.

SOME THOUGHTFUL PEOPLE TO MEET

Life as a journalist has given me many opportunities and insights, some of which deserve to be shared more than once. Some special people have provided me opportunities for learning, for thought, concepts, and examples of better living in retirement years.

Some of these people are famous; others have not attracted national attention. Each message is different, but each is given by a successful person who has put thinking and experience together with practice.

As vital input to your creative retirement planning, meet Jane Withers, Art Linkletter, Dr. Thomas C. Namey, Milton Feher, Don Ameche, and Woodie Hall.

The Actress and the Miracle of the Mind

Depending on your age you may remember her as the child star who played opposite Shirley Temple, or as the popular actress who grew into many young adult roles, or as Josephine the Plumber in the longest running series of commercials on television. Whatever your era, you know Jane Withers.

The purpose of our meeting was not to reminisce about her life in motion pictures or on television. Jane Withers wanted to talk about arthritis, stress, and especially the beneficial working of the mind. Our discussion focused on the time between her motion picture career and the first Josephine commercials. That was her time of greatest challenge.

At the age of twenty-seven Jane Withers was a severe arthritic, bound to a hospital bed where "it took five people just to turn me over." The symptoms flared badly when, as a young married woman with children, she was in a stressful conflict with her husband, a problem that eventually led to divorce. "Medicine did not have the treatment that it has today," she stated. "I had to resolve to do something myself, and that was to put my mind to it.

"I could see myself walking out of that hospital. I could see myself dancing again and running. And I never let that image out of my mind while in the hospital, and I have had to recall that image a number of times through my life."

Jane Withers walked out of that hospital in under nine months' time, and danced and ran freely again. At times of stress in later years the arthritis symptoms returned—but in each episode she put her mind and visions to work while she teamed with her medical doctor in effecting a full recovery.

The effect of mental attitude on physical well-being is just now being researched by medical specialists. Fred Kantrowitz, M.D., faculty member at the Harvard Medical School and respected rheumatologist, agrees with Jane Withers: "Stress can be a contributor to or catalyst of arthritis. There has been an increase in juvenile arthritis and it affects more the children of broken or single parent families. There is an increase in arthritis in women age 20 to 40, which appears to relate to the increase in divorces and the return of more married women to the work force," states the doctor.

How about the increase in arthritis in older women? Could it be triggered by traumas of retirement and the death of a spouse? "Yes, it is very possible," Dr. Kantrowitz affirmed. "We don't know yet what really causes arthritis, but stress appears to play a role based on our new research."

Jane Withers, in making her mind an ally in the battle with illness, alleviated her stress with very positive images, and she has defeated the painful and limiting symptoms of arthritis several times during her life. In her sixties, she is still going strong—lecturing to women's groups, volunteering for charitable causes, acting in television movies and specials, and touring nationally with her famed collection of dolls.

Jane Withers looks you straight in the eye: "Please tell your readers: 'You can beat arthritis—just put your mind on the right track, by gum.'"

The Art Linkletter Plan for Seniors

"Senior citizens have options for themselves, and that is my message to them in rallies, in speeches and interviews all across the United States."

Art Linkletter grabs my attention with this statement as we sit in the television station program office before we are to appear together on a morning talk show. The voice is strong and his eye contact drives his point home.

You remember Art Linkletter as the host of two of the longest running radio and television shows in history: "Art Linkletter's House Party," and "People Are Funny." What you might not know about Linkletter is that he is one of America's pioneering entrepreneurs. Today, at 76, he has lost none of the enthusiasm that made him one of the best known people in the entertainment business.

His new mission has been "developed after years of traveling and interviewing people throughout the nation. I need to communicate to senior citizens and to the rest of the population, too, that the stereotypes of aging have to go," Linkletter states emphatically. "We are not 'old' because society says we are to be 'old.' As senior adults we are what we want to be; what we create and accomplish for ourselves."

His theories and recommendations are presented in a book, his twentieth, but according to him one of his most important, titled *Old Age Is Not For Sissies*. "My recommendation is that mature adults take charge of their own lives, set their own direction . . . and get out of the rocking chairs."

Art Linkletter achieved fame by making people laugh, and he can still dominate an interview by lacing it with anecdotes from more than fifty years in broadcasting. When he talks now about mature adults, he's not playing "People Are Funny." He's talking straight from the shoulder and making sense. This just might be his campaign for the next fifteen or twenty years.

The Miracle Prescription

"If I could offer you a pill that would make you healthier, more limber, feeling better and living longer, what would you pay me for it?"

The speaker paced the stage as he made his comments, then pointed to the audience for his next dramatic statement:

"This pill is so great you need to take it only once each day. And this pill will work on people of all ages, all faiths, national origins and skin color.

"What is it worth? $100 a dose? $50 each time you take it? $25? Or, how about $10 or even $5 for a health treatment that will accomplish all of it—longer life, better health, a more limber body—and even a more agile mind?"

The members of the audience edged forward in their seats, in ready anticipation for the word of this wonder drug.

"Will you pay $5 for each dose?" the speaker shouted.

"Yes!" The reply was unanimous.

"Do you want all of the great benefits that my medicine will give you?"

Again, the answer was "yes," the response level rising.

The speaker paused, taking a moment to loosen his tie, and to study the audience. "Then you shall have the miracle medicine!

"But with one change." The apprehension, or anticipation of denial, was apparent.

"I am going to give you this wonderful prescription—for free. No charge. But remember its great value—you were ready to pay me $100 a dose. But it is yours, in this very moment to take every day, to treasure, to gain from in good health and long life."

He fumbled with the pockets of his coat and then his vest, and then stopped mid action. "The prescription is not a bottle in my pocket. I will give you this miracle prescription verbally, right here and now—so listen carefully.

"Take a walk—a brisk one for more than 40 minutes at least four to seven times each week.

"Cut out smoking and lower your intake of animal fats to under 20 percent of your calories.

"That is the simple prescription and it comes with a money-back guarantee."

The speaker is one of the most respected sports physicians in the United States, Thomas Curtis Namey, M.D., Director of Sports Medicine and Chief of Rheumatology at the University of Tennessee Medical Center at Knoxville. Built like some of the wrestlers and weight lifters he has trained, he paces in a style reminiscent of the former professional football coach John Madden, thrusting a hand forward in a boxer's jab in order to emphasize his main points.

If Dr. Namey had created an actual "magic pill" he could sell them by the millions because of his charisma and his rapport with audiences. But his message only tells people how to be healthy through lifestyle.

"Our bodies were not designed to be sick, even in older years," he tells us in an interview. "Ideally, we would run along actively and productively until that time comes to die. We will have lived life to the fullest, with dignity and pride, and without being a burden on anyone.

"Just by changing lifestyle we can bring our bodies back into shape, pump blood and oxygen better and more healthfully for our entire system and mind, limber up joints, and remove the negative, harmful influences and toxic substances that are killing us or making us ill."

Dr. Namey has also gained national recognition for his work in reversing the symptoms of arthritis, again in persons of most all ages.

His prescription for dealing with arthritis includes walking, exercising—even with light weights—all the muscles that support or assist the affected joints. He recommends range-of-motion exercises for the affected joints and, when possible, bicycling and particularly swimming.

"In swimming the water supports the body, removing weight from affected joints like knees. You can then do exercises in the water to strengthen muscles, to stretch for increasing the body's agility, to work on the fullest range-of-motion possible, and to maintain—and increase—coordination through the swimming motions."

For years Dr. Tom Namey has been teaching fitness as a key to positive health and a longer, happier life. It is only recently that the medical profession has adopted the concept.

"Fitness does not have to mean four hours a day of workout in an exercise gym. It does not have to mean 'no pain, no gain.' It does not mean having to compete with young hard-bodies, or feeling guilty if you do not become a mass of muscle.

"Fitness means aerobic exercise—even as simple as walking briskly—enough to work up a sweat—for more than 40 minutes each time.

"Fitness means getting toxic substances like tobacco smoke out of your system; and you can do that just by stopping smoking and starting your aerobic walking.

"Fitness means getting your body moving every day, and when your body is moving actively, you're giving your mind fresh air to think and work better, too.

"Fitness means cutting down on fats in your diet and, by plan, adding the things you need, like fruit and vegetables. Fitness means eating what you need to keep the body working best, and that generally means smaller quantities.

"This is the miracle prescription. It cannot be bottled or packaged by a pharmaceutical company. It cannot be performed for you by someone else. And I cannot sell it to you.

"You must sell the concept of the miracle prescription of fitness to yourself, and then fill that prescription every day—as if your best and the rest of your life depended on it. Because it does."

The Master of Movement

"How did you used to walk?" The teacher directs the question to his twelve students, each dressed in black leotards, each focused on the slender man who speaks with the soft, gentle, low voice.

The students respond quickly, hunching their backs, spreading their feet apart, one hand reaching out for support from an imaginary cane, and then inching forward, one painful step at a time.

They are not acting. This is actually the way they did walk—if they could walk at all. Two of the class members had been bedridden.

"How do you walk now?" the teacher asks, with a smile that grows with the expectation of what he is about to see.

Each of the students stands to a natural tallness, moves feet together, and strides forward in a tight, straight line. The stride becomes a joyful march to music as the pianist in the corner adds melody and a strong rhythm from a grand piano.

This scene is repeated every day in the Milton Feher Studio of Dance and Relaxation on West 58th Street in New York City. The setting is a once-grand apartment near Carnegie Hall, now and for more than forty years a studio for training dancers and actors, athletes, and, for the past 20 years, very special students like the people in this class.

The special students all have arthritis, the symptoms of which can be crippling. When many medical professionals were prescribing "rest" and "take it easy" to arthritic patients, Milton Feher was teaching activity, balance and posture, stretching—and dance.

Some have been coming to Milton Feher's classes for as long as twenty years; others for just a few months. All, though, are moving and stretching, exercising and dancing in class and in their own workouts at home.

These special students range in age from 65 to 97—ages when others assume that they will be limited or in pain, crippled or even housebound. But each student looks quite trim in leotards, and even the experienced eye would assume them to be from a decade to a score of years younger than they really are. Each now moves gracefully and actively both in and outside of the studio.

The concepts for the classes were developed by a severe arthritic— Milton Feher himself, an accomplished dancer and actor on the Broadway stage until his early thirties. From "giving his all" in performance, he developed arthritis in his knees, serious enough that physicians decreed that he would never dance—and possibly never even walk—again.

Rather than accept the medical opinion, he launched his own study of the human body, developed his own concepts of posture, balance, and movement. He worked on the ideas, first to correct his own condition, later to teach others.

Those concepts of posture, balance, relaxation, and exercise have worked in returning other arthritic patients to full mobility. He's accepted referrals from medical practitioners and physical therapists unable to produce their own solutions.

The "old lady walk" is fact for most special students who come to Milton Feher. And it is fact, too, that before long they are walking with poise and grace. His teaching involves balance: "The trunk of the body is directly over the feet, and the feet are close together, stepping forward in a straight line. Shoulders are directly over the trunk—not like the military 'attention,' where shoulders are thrust back.

"The trunk comes forward, with buttocks tucked in as you walk. There is no strain, no use of muscles to support body parts out of balance. In this way you can walk more surely and farther than ever before."

Students lie with their backs to the floor. "Press your entire body to the floor, including the small of the back. Turn your palms to the floor, and press, too. Feel your strength against the floor—and feel the support and strength of the floor in return."

Floor exercises concentrate on the tummy, for strength and to bring it in line for proper posture.

Relaxation is practiced, allowing tension and strain to disappear, and to enable the best posture when standing.

Then it is time to walk and to dance. The steps are reminiscent of Astaire

13

and Rogers. "Fred Astaire was graceful because half the time in his dance he was completely relaxed." Feher demonstrates an Astaire swing step, showing how proper balance allowed relaxation at least half of the time and little strain most of the time."If we can do this in walking, we remove the strain and the intensive work we traditionally demand of our bodies."

Milton Feher found that his relaxation techniques could help actors, both in stage presence and action, and particularly in their voices—and so he has taught many famed and near-famed thespians over the years. Athletes, too, have learned from Feher, and dancers have had better and longer careers because of his teaching of movement. And, Milton Feher could still emulate Fred Astaire, step for step, graceful and agile. Not bad, not bad at all, for a teacher at age seventy-six.

The Voice That Spans Generations

Don Ameche has achieved stardom in just about every medium known. In the grand days of radio broadcasting his voice was the signature for scores of programs; his banter with Charlie McCarthy made him the perfect host for the "Chase and Sanborn Hour," and you can still be brought to your knees in laughter by the wit of "The Bickersons," where he teamed with Frances Langford. He became a movie star with his acclaimed portrayal of Alexander Graham Bell.

And then came the surprise motion picture hit of 1985, *Cocoon*, where he joined with other mature actors in one of the most remarkable film concepts ever. The acting veterans presented a love story with the fascination of science fiction. And what a cast: Hume Cronyn and Jessica Tandy, Wilfred Brimley, Jack Guilford and Gwen Verdon.

This was followed by other hits: *Trading Places, Harry and the Hendersons, Things Change,* and *Cocoon II.*

Don Ameche, in his eighties, is in more demand than ever. And if you've seen the swimming pool scenes in *Cocoon*, you have evidence of his fine condition. "This is the one body I have and I do everything possible to keep it in the best of shape."

He described his simple regimen: fifteen to eighteen minutes of exercise and a six-mile walk each day, plus careful attention to his diet. The combination has worked for him for years. "If I keep myself fit, I can do anything," he said in the interview.

That voice is still deep and rich, his sincerity is strong, and his opportunities open wider every day. It's difficult to hold onto stardom and a challenge to remain in that firmament for more than fifty years—but I got the idea that Don Ameche was ready for even more new challenges.

And for His Third Career, Fun

When Woodie Hall retired from a career as an officer in the U.S. Army, he didn't want "just to do nothing." So he launched a second career as a salesman and then sales manager for a company that made foil stamping machines for airport gift shops and specialty stores. After twenty years at that career, achieving major increases in business for his company, he retired a second time, anticipating, at first, long days of sunshine and golf at his new home in Lake San Marcos, California.

But then Woodie grew restless. He wanted to get back into business. Over the years, he made many notes about all the stores he had called on. As he reviewed those notes, ideas started to flow.

His first ideas seemed silly, but they wouldn't go away. "Why not be silly if that's what makes people smile?" he reasoned, and so Woodie Hall launched himself into the most failure-ridden business in the world. He became an inventor.

He didn't invent serious things. One of the first was a game called "Don't Bug Me." It was based on what he heard people say as they were playing other games in frustration. The game was a hit. Then came oversize kick dice, "happy faces" in three-dimensional shapes, and trophies for the "World's Worst Golfer" and another for a "Hole in One (after seven strokes)."

Woodie determined that he would remain a small operation and that others would do the manufacturing, risk taking, and selling—and so he devised a royalty technique, where he could spend more time inventing and very little time in manufacturing or marketing.

His fertile mind produced over 150 viable products, each placed with a manufacturer on a royalty basis. Just one or two royalty items in a lifetime would please most inventors, but for Woodie Hall his average is about fifteen each year.

So many other would-be inventors wanted to seek his counsel and concepts that he wrote a book, *Your Ideas Can Be Worth A Fortune*. This is the one product that he self-markets, by mail, from his home office. And in his spare time, Woody makes personal appearances throughout the West, at business clubs and organizations, senior citizen groups, and inventor conferences.

In his late seventies, he's still inventing, sharing with others, and laughing, along with the purchasers of his products, all the way to the bank.

In Summary

Each of these interesting people presents a message through commitment and performance. Each denies limitations and teaches that we, at any age, may accomplish whatever we desire, may gain in health, and multiply wealth and opportunity.

For the personal profiles chosen for this chapter there were thousands more possible from this reporter's notebook. You will find others around you—active adults who have taken charge of their lives in mature years and set their own course and goals.

Maturity can be the time of opportunity and fulfillment, as is proven by every mature adult who looks with positive anticipation to the best of retirement years.

Choose your own direction. Be your own best role model for the best of life after fifty.

| CHAPTER 3 | # RETIREMENT— WHO, WHAT, WHEN, WHERE WHY—IF AT ALL |

Let's start using the word *retirement* in a positive way, as the time of change to a new direction.

In our concept, retirement means opportunity, where you are in control. Therefore, the retirement years can be anything you want them to be, where you write the game plan and the program to be fulfilled.

Earlier in life you were asked the question, "What do you want to be when you grow up?" Now you are grown, and the question is, "What do *I* want to be and do in this new time?"

Unlike younger generations, as you start this new adventure you have more going for you—probably more, too, than when you started working decades ago. As you approach retirement years, you might have some income projectable from Social Security and/or pensions, some savings, real estate, other assets. How you package those assets and relate them to the desired lifestyle of your retirement years will be the key to your creative planning.

When do you want to move into the retirement phase of your life? At fifty-five you should have at least thirty more years of productive life. At sixty-five, consider that you may have twenty or more years for this new phase and opportunity.

Retirement years take planning in order to make them what you want; financing in order to fund the plan and direction; the shedding of other concerns—call them 'tethers' to yesterday's constraints; and the application of discipline in making the retirement program work.

Most people—and counselors, too—make a serious mistake by basing prospects for retirement years only on what we have today. They base the future exclusively on a limited-income assumption, building a structure of constraints, disappointments, and reduction of expectations in the process. And others assume that retirement years will involve little work or productivity.

The first step in proper retirement planning is to throw away these out-of-date assumptions. Let's structure retirement years as living the way you want it, and then work backward from that image and produce a plan for getting there—like a road map to a defined destination. The concept called "success imaging" works well in business; properly applied, it can be the key to personal growth as well.

About Retirement Years

The exact timing for your retirement will depend to a great extent on your line of work. Some employers assume that you'll go off payroll after twenty or thirty years or at age sixty-five, while others might offer you an incentive to leave the company earlier, and still others might leave the opportunity open for you to remain as long as you choose.

The time for your change in work path should be in your sights as early as you can define it. If you have a ten-year lead time in which to fulfill each of the necessary steps to make the transition possible, all the better. But, for many, it can be done in three to five years. Still, for others already with the gold watch in hand, the plan needs be underway yesterday.

Let's start with the basics: How happy are you in your job or business? How motivated are you to make a change, setting off in a new direction? Your answers to the following questions will help define your goals.

• In your retirement-years lifestyle do you see yourself working in the same business, in a new career track, in your own venture, or some other vocation or avocation?

• Are you motivated to continue working for satisfaction and fulfill-ment?

• Are you motivated to work because you like the continued income?

• Are you motivated to continue working to some degree because of the social benefits?

• Do you want to work full time or part time?

There is nothing wrong in working in your retirement years. Surveys of American retirees—those not working at all—show that at least 40 percent wish they were still working. In addition, the latest surveys of pre-retirees show that a majority do not want traditional, enforced retirement at age sixty-five.

Let's begin drawing your retirement-years plan. Don't assume any limi-tations at this point, unless your dream for the next phase of your life is to be a famous concert pianist and you don't know a sharp from a flat.

18

Today's Posture List

Let's move on to a written assessment of what you like and don't like, so we have a basing point. Use the accompanying form, or, if you don't want to mark up the book, on large tablet paper draw lines to create three vertical columns. Over the first column write "Subject"; over the second, "What I Like About It"; and the third, "What I Don't Like or Need to Change About It."

Take our suggested subjects one at a time, so that you have lots of room for answers. As you consider each subject don't try to edit your response, just put down what comes to mind. Couples should make separate lists—and don't compare notes or try to help each other with what to write.

Present your responses tersely, quickly. Leave extra room so you can add more thoughts over the next few days or week. What you will find might surprise you, as you'll be able to see what you really don't want to do in the retirement phase of your life.

Ready? Let's start. Here are the subjects—take them one at a time and write what really comes to mind. There are no wrong answers, just your real answers.

The Subject List	What I Like About It	What I Don't Like About It
The idea of working		
Past 60		
Past 65		
Past 70		
Past 75		
Making money by Working		
Making Money by Investment		
Making Money by Operating Business		
My Present Career/Work		

The Subject List	What I Like About It	What I Don't Like About It
Working With Others		
Working on My Own		
Working Where I Am Now		
My Home Town		
My Neighborhood		
Free Time		
This House or Apartment		
Travel		
Hobbies		
Housework		
Gardening		
Helping Others		
Smoking		
Drinking		
Grandchildren		
Fitness/Sports		
Others/Add your own		

There are probably more subjects, where you have feelings about "like" and "don't like." Add them to your list.

Again, write the answers from your own point of view and not with anyone else in mind.

When you have completed the list, read it over before you go to sleep and as soon as you wake up for two or three days, adding as many thoughts as you want in each session.

When you're satisfied that the list is complete, read it again. If you're a couple, read the lists together, first identifying the things you really do not like. Underline them, and make another list of them as "things to avoid in our retirement-years program."

Then underline those things you feel good about, and put them on a list of nice, rewarding things to be included in your retirement-years plan.

From this combination you have the initial concepts that will serve as the basis for your retirement-years program. This process might take several days, but will prove to be worth the time and effort.

Listing Your Desires

Now it is time to look at what you really want in your next twenty or thirty years. Make a new list, modeled after the form on the next page. The first column is "Subject;" the second, "What I Envision;" and the third, "What I Can Do Without."

Deal with one item at a time, leaving lots of space between subjects, so that you can add more information. You'll want to write these answers as graphically as you can.

Allow yourself to think about each subject and then to see yourself doing it or having it. If it feels comfortable and enjoyable, put a check mark in the first column without further thought—knowing that you'll be back to amend or elaborate on it later. If your feelings are negative, put a check mark in the second column. Here you will see what present possessions, problems, situations, or conditions are not pleasing to you. It is easier than you think to free yourself from present constraints or pressures by not including them in your new lifestyle.

Don't hold back because "I'm too old to change" or "I can't afford it." One housebound lady to whom I gave this exercise was lonely and unhappy. Her friends and acquaintances all talked to her and about her as "poor Ellie in the wheelchair." She wanted that image gone, too, and she wanted to change her life. What happened? Ellie realized that she wanted to talk with people, wanted to get off welfare, and wanted a reason to get up every morning. The answer to her problem came rather easily: she could establish a telephone wake-up service in her home, where she would rise early and greet forty to sixty people by phone, rousing them brightly each day. At last count she was netting $1500 per month for part-time work, talking to people actively, and was off welfare. Her new friends dropped in to visit with the brightest lady in the neighborhood. She even volunteered as the telephone chairlady for a local service organization and was recognized for her efforts.

Just as Ellie found what she really wanted in her retirement years, you can too—at whatever level you choose. But you've got to make the first move.

So, take this step next for the development of your vision for your next twenty or thirty years. After this, we discuss the many elements from which you can draw in making it happen to your retirement-years program.

My Retirement Years List

Subject	What I Envision	What I Can Do Without
Present Job		
New Job		
City		
Neighborhood		
Income		
Home/Apartment		
Health		
Car/Transportation		
Associates		
Business Venture		
Hobbies		
Sports/Golf/Tennis		
Travel		
Family		

Subject	What I Envision	What I Can Do Without
Family Proximity		
Crime		
Television		
Culture		
Cards/Games		
Social Club		
Present Workplace/Staff		
Investments		
Garden		
Housework		
New Challenge		
Education		
Volunteering		
Liquor		
Smoking		
Grandchildren		
Weather		
(Add your own)		

From this list you will start to identify where you want to be and what you want to do in your next phase of life. Again, scan first the list of subjects/items that you can live without. If there are physical assets to which you are no longer attached, or situations that have been costing you money, identify them so you can cash out the assets and cut your costs on the negative items.

Again, study this list at least three nights before you go to bed, then again immediately as you awaken in the morning; feel free to add more notes and comments. Underline those items in both columns that are the highest in importance to you for your own lifestyle. Transfer these items to another sheet, again in the column format.

It is from this kind of personal information that you can start to define where you want to be and with whom, what you want to do, and how you will be rewarded for your life of accomplishment to date. It is then that you can start to shape your image of that future, so that, with the information on the following pages, you may draw the road maps that will lead you inot the future.

In addition, by identifying those items or subjects that you don't like or want to get rid of in your life, you might be able to remove some or all of the stress in your life, thus eliminating a deterrent to your very best of health and living.

This is also an appropriate time to do this kind of thinking and vision playing. Most of us have been unhappy, frustrated or limited in the jobs we have held at some time in our careers. When teaching journalism at San Diego State University, I took part in career counseling seminars for the entire student body. I did not come from academia but from the real world of business. In one session I said to the students: "Your career planning now is vital, because *half* of the people working today are unhappy or limited in their jobs. Therefore you must know all the more what you want and the direction you should take." The placement counselor for the university stood up deliberately and walked to the lectern. He puffed thoughtfully on his pipe, then spoke to the students slowly, profoundly: "Students, I want you to know that Professor Hansen is wrong, seriously wrong when he says that *half* of the working people are unhappy or limited in their jobs." He paused. "The fact is that nearly *two-thirds* of working people are unhappy. Students, remember that, and learn from what Professor Hansen has told you about the real world. Think about it before you head in any direction."

Getting to the Draft Plan

You have catalyzed your thinking and should now be able to start defining your desired directions, the available opportunities, and more about your retirement years.

Again, make three columns on the paper. The first is "Subject"; the second is "What I Want;" the third is "What I Need to Know/Research." You will probably make many copies of this draft, as you refine your thinking and directions.

Note that we have not talked at all about money to make it happen—that can only be determined by what you want your lifestyle to be. If you really want a cottage in coastal Mexico, earning money singing in the local clubs, your cash needs might be quite small. If you're a single man wanting to live full time aboard cruise ships plying the seven seas of the world, you may be able to do that without a large retirement income, also. If you want to be a jet setter shuttling between Europe, your Paris apartment, Swiss chalet, Malibu beach home and that lovely grass shack in Tahiti, you better have the Brink's truck backed up to Fort Knox.

We need to know where we want to go and do before we know how much it is going to cost for the ticket. On that premise, let's venture forth, as you start to identify what you really want in your retirement years. Work with the form on the next page, shape it to your own needs, and get ready for the best years of your life.

- -

The Draft Retirement-Years Plan of _____

Date:_____   **Version Number:**_____

Subject:	What I Want	What I Need to Know/Research
Living Quarters		
City/State		
Job/Status		
Job/Type		
Job/Full/Part-time		
Business Venture		
Project to Develop		
Marital Status		
Family		

Subject:	What I Want	What I Need to Know/Research
Health		
Auto/Transportation		
Friendships		
Travel		
Recreation		
Hobbies		
Activities		
Education		
Service Projects		
Financial Affairs Management		
My Biggest Goal		
My Second Biggest Goal		
(add your own subjects)		

Signed and Agreed as a Direction for planning:

Signed: _____ Date:_____

Signed: _____ Date:_____

From this self-evaluation a picture will develop, and with it a program so that prices and budgets can be established—for both income and outgo.

Reconsider the draft plan as you read through this book, as you'll find answers to many of your questions presented in the many chapters. You'll want to add to your plan as you discover new ideas and explanations that will support exactly what you want to do.

You have started the ball rolling for your retirement-years adventure. Read on for the information you need in order to make it happen.

<table>
<tr><td>CHAPTER
4</td><td># HEALTH AND YOUR RETIREMENT YEARS</td></tr>
</table>

There is nothing more important than your concept and attitude toward health—how you plan to be healthy—in your retirement years. If you have good health, goal setting and financial planning are possible. Without good health, there are limitations on what you can do, and medical and long-term nursing costs may create a serious financial drain.

For years we have heard that long life is primarily a result of wondrous advances in medical technology. That is only partly true. In fact, more people are living longer because they are living healthier lives.

Almost forty years ago a health "prophet" named Jack LaLanne taught that what you eat today would be an integral part of your body in just forty-eight hours. He didn't have much scientific proof of the statement then, when he was doing a daily exercise program on KGO-Television in San Francisco. But he knew he was right. I remember his presentation before an advertising club luncheon. The assembled professionals were expecting a television personality to talk about his daily show, but Jack was not a typical celebrity. He jarred the audience to attention when he slammed a thirty-pound chunk of animal fat on the lectern and shouted, "This is what you are carrying around your waistlines today and every day! Imagine having to carry this in your arms, up the stairs, as you try to stand after sitting in your chair, or having to walk around the block!

"This fat is not good for you, around your middle or in your body as food. Please, for your own good, cut it out or cut it down. Get back to nature with fresh fruit and vegetables; and get outside by running or walking, and get into exercise!"

Many in the audience turned away, finished off their bountiful desserts, ready to resume their drinking and talking following his speech. "When will it end?" they stated visibly with eyes drawn to the ceiling.

But today's research shows that Jack LaLanne was right; and the world would have gained if people had listened to his message. The real proof of the LaLanne message is a fact of life and death. Jack LaLanne has remained vibrant and healthy, teaching and performing feats of strength and endurance into his seventies. I was acquainted with many of the advertising people in that particular meeting. Of the 300 or so who came to see but did not listen to Jack LaLanne, most are dead or dying today from heart disease, cancer, and other debilitating diseases.

Jack LaLanne is still teaching the world. The legacy of many or most of those advertising professionals is now forgotten.

For years government and the medical industry have focused on remedial treatments, assuming that the human body inevitably gets sick. The solution to any condition would generally be found with a scalpel or a prescription form—for that is what doctors were taught to do. As a result North Americans became the most-operated-on and most overprescribed people in the world. It has been a medical solution, making acute repairs to the body, rather than a health solution, one of positive and preventive steps to maintain the best of health.

The medical solution has been to prescribe sedatives for mature adults, "to help you sleep," without considering the addictive nature of the drugs, the complications and negative side effects. A better prescription would have been for exercise and activity to produce a reason for natural sleep.

The medical solution has produced "drug" stores where you can buy a pill or potion—prescribed or over-the-counter—for most any real or imagined ailment.

The medical solution has prescribed invasive surgery, more than half of which is unnecessary, and all of which presents risk to the patient. Most radical mastectomies, hysterectomies and Cesarean births are not needed or medically warranted, according to recent research. Most cataract surgery is unnecessary. Even most coronary bypass surgery has been challenged by scientific evidence.

"You can do more for your health than your doctor can," state James F. Fries, M.D. and Donald M. Vickery, M.D., in their bestselling book, *Take Care of Yourself*. "These ideas seem foreign in a society that is heavily dependent upon experts of every kind and seemingly addicted to ever more complex gadgetry and medications."

The Surgeon General of the United States issued a 1981 report, *Health Promotion and Disease Prevention*, which stated, "You, the individual, can do more for your own health and well being than any doctor, any hospital, any drugs, any exotic medical devices."

This means each of us can be healthy if we work and concentrate on being healthy. Being healthy is what the health model—or health solution—is all about. Surgery, pills and exotic technical intervention are steps in the medical model—repairing diseases, injuries and physical problems.

We don't deliberately walk into automobile traffic, for the predictable result would be injury and possible death. But, until recently, medical model practice has not taught us how to avoid disease and physical problems by using a positive health program. Smoking, overeating and poor diet, lack of exercise and activity, overuse of alcohol, overuse or misuse of drugs are all predictable ways to be catastrophically ill—but most medical practitioners do not teach their patients how and why to be healthy by avoiding these proven steps to physical peril.

Do we need to assume illness in mature years? No. Are illnesses a part of the aging process? No. Can an individual use positive and preventive health programming to slow, stop or even reverse present medical problems? In most cases, yes.

"If we all had good health habits, what would happen?" ask Doctors Fries and Vickery. "Lung cancer and emphysema would almost completely disappear, death due to all cancers as a group would decrease by approximately two-thirds, and cirrhosis of the liver would be a rare disease. Peptic ulcers and gastritis would decrease greatly, massive upper gastrointestinal (GI) bleeding from the esophagus, stomach, or duodenum would become unusual, inflammation of the pancreas would be rare. High blood pressure would be infrequent, and there would be many fewer strokes and heart attacks. Hardening of the arteries would occur less frequently, decreased perhaps by more than one-half. We could eliminate half of the hospital beds in the country. The cost of medical care would decrease, the price paid for the expensive bad habits would be saved, and the consumer would have more money for both needs and desires. The number of sick days would be decreased by over one-half, and the national productivity would rise. What an array of opportunities!"

The medical model was called humane because it corrected the terrible things that happened to people, and it assumed that most every one of us was destined to illness. The health model is an individual program concentrating on preventing illness—in the same way that we don't walk directly into auto traffic—so that the terrible things won't happen to us.

Your Health Is Your Responsibility

As you now plan for retirement, you must look upon your health as a major and positive asset.

In this chapter we look at health and how you may assess it, identifying any present problems, conditions, or concerns. We also offer the thoughts and recommendations of various experts on how you can start correcting those conditions. This is not intended to teach you to start practicing medicine. It is a plan on how you may get involved in your own health-maintenance program—how, in consultation with your doctor and other health professionals, you may take care of yourself and avoid many of the dangers to your health that exist in today's world.

There are four parts to positive health: nutrition, fitness, lifestyle, and remedial medicine. Each needs to be coordinated in order to achieve the very best health and the most active of living at any age.

Here are briefings on the overall subject areas—each developed from research and interviews with experts. You'll find charting techniques at the end of this chapter, so that you might set—in writing—your own health resolutions and plan. And, if we have done our job correctly, you will want to do added reading in special areas of interest, as outlined in the bibliography in the back of this book.

Nutrition

Give your body the right food so it has the nutrients to sustain its working functions and to maintain its effective immune system. Reduce or eliminate the foods which harm your body and its best functioning now and in the future. These are two simple statements with healthful promise.

The human body is a miracle in its own function. It is an incredible combination of cells that somehow stay in the same shape and perform the same functions even though they are constantly changing, being replaced, regenerated, and destroyed each day, each hour, each minute. In the normal, healthy body there is order to the interaction of the cells, until we throw them into an imbalance in one way or another.

Into our bodies each day we introduce new elements—food and other substances—that are absorbed by and become part of our molecular structure, that affect or are affected by that structure.

In the vast choice of foods for our meals, some will be beneficial, some neutral, some actually harmful. For example, if your dinner last night included fresh broccoli, your system would have extracted from the broccoli beneficial amounts of vitamins A and C and selenium—all vital in the functioning of the immune system—and fiber, which helps maintain intestinal health. But if you also had a large choice steak, your system would have extracted both good and bad elements. The protein may be a gain, but the saturated fat content can create or accelerate problems in the immune and cardiovascular systems. It is a question of degree: a small steak periodically may prove beneficial, where a large steak or hamburger every day may increase low density blood cholesterol (LDL) and release more free radicals to harm the immune system over time.

Free radicals are extra oxygen molecules which upset the normal molecular balance, allowing a weakening of the immune system. New research ties free radicals to a wide variety of maladies, including arthritis, some types of cancer, and even cataracts. The free radical concept may provide, for the very first time, an understanding of how and why disease happens and, more importantly, an opportunity through health measures to keep the body in balance, and to make possible the reversal of the process of a body's deterioration.

Your body's immune system is one of your most valuable assets. It can be far more effective than most drugs in dealing with many problems and it has no negative side effects. Drugs, on the other hand, are powerful chemicals introduced into the body as "intervention" to achieve a specific purpose. And as chemicals, they often do their job by altering some of the body's molecular structure and function. As it corrects one problem, a drug may create an imbalance or problem in another part of the body. "There is no drug that does not have a multitude of effects on the body," states Dr. Robert Arnot in *The Complete Manual of Fitness and Well Being*. "Tranquilizers act on areas of the brain responsible for arousal. Thus it is logical that they make you feel drowsy, lethargic and weak. They may also affect your concentration and your memory, making you slightly absentminded. Large doses, taken over a long period, can lead to slurring of the speech and double vision, especially in the elderly. All drugs that affect the mind produce dependence."

Nutritional Concepts and Goals

In order to function the body needs the right kind of food—food with vitamins, minerals, fiber and other elements it needs to assimilate in order to function. The body needs far less food than most of us eat traditionally; moreover the body needs far less saturated fat and far more fiber, far less red meat and far more fresh fruit and vegetables.

The body actually does not benefit from most "crash" or fad diets. In fact, many of these regimens can actually be injurious to health in the long run and of no long-term effect in reducing weight. The body, in most cases, just needs better quality food (and less of it) and proper exercise.

There is a terrible word in the English language: Diet. To many, "diet" conjures up a mandated, restrictive menu from which we must not deviate. As penance for our overweight sins we may not eat more than a piece of whole wheat toast, for example, with a grapefruit half and two spoons of oatmeal for breakfast. For lunch, in this imagery, a few pieces of lettuce, an obscure vegetable, and four strawberries for dessert.

You have heard the *"can't have"* approach of other diets. And you might have experienced them: "I love _____ but the diet says I *can't* have that at all." However, based on new scientific studies, today's nutritionists are building eating concepts from individual desires and lifestyles. Just as your retirement plan should be individual, so should your healthful diet plan. Eating is one of the sensual pleasures of life, and in effective nutritional programs there is reasonable room to accommodate some favorites as well

32

as the healthful foods that benefit the body.

There are some basic facts you should know. Calories are still important, since they represent both the volume and the fat content of food. Most men can do well consuming about 2000 calories per day. Those with physically demanding jobs or who engage in rigorous exercise activity will need more—up to 3000. Those who want to lose weight can do with less—1700 to 2000, depending on body weight. Most women can do with a bit less and consume as low as 1500 to 1600 calories to lose weight. The correct number of calories will vary according to your age, body size and build, and amount of daily exercise and activity.

Calories are the fuel the body burns for its operations. If you take in more calories than you need, the body will store them as fat—added weight. On the other hand, if you were to reduce your calorie intake severely in order to lose weight, the body will draw the calories from lean mass—the muscle you need to maintain strength, posture and ability to function. Any weight-loss program that seriously reduces caloric intake should, therefore, be combined with active exercise.

Most packaged foods are labeled with the number of calories and the percentage of recommended dietary allowances (RDA) of vitamins, minerals and other nutritional elements in each serving as established by the U.S. Food and Drug Administration. You will also find details on the fat content and cholesterol volume. A new and important consideration in the nutrition community is the type of calories we consume. Research studies by the National Cancer Institute and the American Heart Association, for instance, recommend that no more than 30 percent of the average person's calorie intake should be from animal sources.

Cholesterol is another important factor in today's nutritional recommendations. Most authorities urge the very limited use of red meats, a significant increase in fish and other seafoods, the addition of fresh fruit and vegetables, and the substitution of polyunsaturated and monounsaturated fats for saturated fats. They recommend the removal from your diet, or a cutback in your consumption of fatty meats, rich ice cream, most cheeses (all but low fat), mayonnaise, and prepared salad dressings.

Despite the current hysteria on the subject, cholesterol is not all bad. It is a necessary part of the human body function and is produced *naturally* by the liver. Science defines cholesterol as being of two types: LDL (low-density lipoprotein) and HDL (high density lipoprotein). In today's vernacular, LDL is considered the "bad" cholesterol, as it may affix itself as lesions in the arterial walls, building up as plaque and narrowing the blood passages. HDL is the "good" cholesterol, necessary for good health and for washing away some of the "bad" cholesterol.

Everyone should have a cholesterol reading or test performed medically to measure the body's combined count at any one time. A reading of 200 is considered "safe"—particularly if at least one-third is comprised of HDL. A zero count is not the ideal—unless you want to produce a rash of new and added problems for yourself.

When the cholesterol count rises to 220, 280, or more, there is reason for concern. This is because the higher the cholesterol count, the more possibility there is for the LDL buildup in the arteries, slowing down and eventually stopping the flow of blood and oxygen—as a heart attack.

Your cholesterol count may swing from day to day or week to week, depending on diet, activity, and other factors. A high count does not necessarily mean you're an immediate candidate for a heart attack— because the buildup of cholesterol in the arteries is a long process. A high count, therefore, is a warning. If you have followed the same diet and lifestyle for a number of years, it's almost surely a time for a change.

As you reduce your cholesterol count to under 200, you should not assume that your problem has gone away—for it, too, is a long process. Once you've lowered your cholesterol count, you should continue your diet and exercise commitment for the rest of your life. As long as you follow good health practice, the body itself should be able to clear those arterial walls. On this, do seek your physician's opinion, in the event there is significant buildup which should be treated with pharmaceutical intervention.

Myron Winick, M.D., tells it very simply in his remarkable reference book, *The Columbia Encyclopedia of Nutrition*. "Evidence has become irrefutable that the right diet can lower certain people's risk for developing some of the most serious diseases afflicting our society. Heart disease, cancer, osteoporosis, high blood pressure, obesity, anemia, and many other diseases are related to the food we eat.

"In addition to preventing disease, there is some evidence that the quality of our lives can be affected by our diets. Our performance at work or school, our ability to participate in athletics, even the time it takes to fall asleep at night may depend to some extent on the food we eat and on the time we eat it." Dr. Winick spoke softly but with authority when we met for an oatmeal, fruit, and juice breakfast at the U.N. Plaza Hotel in New York City. He is the director of the Institute of Human Nutrition at the Columbia University College of Physicians and Surgeons in New York, and is recognized as one of the leading experts in the field. Dr. Winick has published hundreds of articles and over twenty books on nutritional subjects.

The good doctor has some words of caution for those who would run out and pay hundreds or thousands of dollars for one of the endless weight-reduction schemes and nutritional supplements touted as being the miracle cures for everything from baldness to heart disease.

"Proper nutrition starts and ends with each one of us, and we are each in charge of ourselves. What we put in the body is what it will be or how

34

it will work."

A summary of recommendations from other specialists interviewed include:

When to Eat. Experts differ on whether heavier meals should be earlier or later in the day. "Depends on the individual's body clock" is the most common recommendation. The earlier you have dinner the better, however, so that you can still move around for a few hours, to aid digestion, before going to bed. This also works better if you're prone to heartburn.

How Much to Eat. It's an inescapable fact: Most of us eat far more than we need. The excess calories remain as fat. My favorite Aunt Agnes had a framed needlework panel: "We must eat to live; not live to eat." In her wisdom she addressed eating with common sense; and, within that goal, she prepared the most elegant and tasty of meals including those from her Danish heritage.

Experts suggest presenting variety on a plate, but with smaller portions. If you're hungry between meals, a snack of fruit can work wonders, as well as being refreshing and filling.

What Foods to Eat. Start your meal planning with your vegetables and other foods that we used to consider only side dishes. Instead of a big steak, a baked potato, and a garnish of broccoli, consider presenting half a potato dressed up with a generous portion of broccoli and serving a smaller steak. That is, if you really want to have a steak. Try shifting to seafood, even to four servings a week. Fish often seems expensive these days, but remember that only a small quantity provides excellent nutritional value. For price savings, buy fish in season or from local anglers who catch more than they can eat. Broil the fish, going easy on the butter. Chicken without the skin is another tasty and low-fat main dish.

Reduce your intake of sodium—the average adult in North America consumes five to ten times what is necessary for living, even without trying. The Surgeon General's Report on Nutrition and Health cites a relationship between a high sodium intake and the occurrence of high blood pressure and stroke. Salt contains about 40 percent sodium by weight and is used widely in the preservation, processing, and preparation of foods. When cooking, use herbs and spices instead of salt; and don't bring the salt shaker to the table at all. Buy a copy of a nutrition reference chart book, such as the *At-A-Glance Nutrition Counter*, by Patricia Hausman, to learn the best foods low in sodium and high in beneficial nutrients.

Increase your consumption of complex carbohydrates and fiber. Shift to low fat or skim milk, low fat cheeses and other dairy products.

Vegetables such as beans, peas, brussels sprouts, and broccoli are fine sources of protein, without the heavy fat content that comes with many animal protein foods.

Nutritionist Scott Pritchard of Spokane, Washington, recommended to

35

a senior citizen conference: "Cut out the butter and margarine. It's more fun to put on some strawberry or raspberry preserves—and far better, in comparison, for you. Skip the regular mayonnaise for your sandwich. Get some 'designer' mustard, and I'll bet you'll enjoy the sandwich all the more. Skip also store-bought salad dressings. You can make better ones yourself for less, and without the incredible fat content of the bottled kind. Try plain lemon for a change. Or a home made Italian dressing with olive oil.

"Try ground turkey instead of the fat-laden ground beef. You'll find it quite tasty and far better for you.

"When you have chicken or turkey, trim away all of the skin and you'll remove more than half the fat content.

"Take care to prepare a meal for more appeal, and you'll enjoy it more while eating better and less in quantity. That's the positive side of a diet."

Yes or No to a Diet

Eating can still be dining. There is no "penalty box" for dieters, limiting them to stuff they normally would not eat. It's just a matter of being sensible. By maintaining a caloric limit, reducing animal flesh to less than 10 to 20 percent of your calorie intake, by eating six different fruits and vegetables each day, and by creating new "adventures" in salad dressings, for example, eating may remain as one of your sensual pleasures each day.

This is a "yes" concept to proper nutrition. You might take this concept to a registered dietitian—check the yellow pages of your telephone directory, or ask your physician for a recommendation—and start eating your way to your best of health. Potato chips might be out of your regimen, but popcorn will be in—and that's not a bad tradeoff for better health.

Your Physical Fitness

You have probably seen the ads with muscular people sweating and straining, grimacing, even moaning as they act out that foolish slogan: "No pain means no gain." Forget that image of exercise as torture. Just as healthful eating can be a pleasure, so can sensible exercise

Exercise for fitness means just a few simple things—aerobic exercise for the heart and lungs, stretching exercises for mobility of the joints, and perhaps muscle holding exercises for strength and/or range of motion.

As sports physician Dr. Tom Namey teaches it: "Take a walk. There is more aerobic benefit in a brisk forty minute walk than in any other exercise." He also highly recommends swimming and bicycling. Not one of these is a "no pain/no gain" procedure.

"Aerobic exercise should be performed at least four times each week—or every other day. There might also be some stretching exercises to keep the body limber, and these may be found on videotapes, in classes at the YMCA or YWCA, in adult schools, or in your own sessions based on a book," Dr. Namey reports.

"You should not judge yourself against the young hard-bodies running along the track or lifting hundreds of pounds in a bench press. They are exercising for their own reasons—right or wrong; you are exercising as you need for healthy, active living."

Aerobic exercise as practiced by some entertainment personalities may not be for you. Many of their exercises are high-impact aerobics—that is, your feet hit the floor hard, and that can be injurious to bones and joints.

Exercise walking is the number one sports activity for mature adults, with about five million persons over the age of fifty-five involved in the activity, according to the National Association of Sporting Goods Dealers.

Where do you walk? College, high school, or public tracks; the shopping mall before the stores open; through safe parks or lanes where you don't have a lot of starting and stopping. President Harry S. Truman took a brisk walk every morning that he could, as part of his own health plan. He lived well to age 88. For aerobic benefit, it is important for the walk to be brisk and continuous. A first-time walker might start out with a goal of a few blocks—say, one-quarter mile—increasing time and distance each day until a forty- to sixty-minute walk is a regular habit. The continuous and brisk pace, combined with the length of time and distance, provides the healthy aerobic benefit, while the movement is beneficial for bones, joints and muscles.

"Takes too much time," one audience member told me in a workshop. "Takes too much work," another said in a session. My reply in each case asked if they had seen the television commercial for the auto transmission treatment, where the payoff line is "pay me now or pay me much more later." The hours spent today just might be the key to preventing years in a debilitated condition in a nursing home later. That is simple fact.

"The body needs the exercise, and you can even get tired naturally," we were told by an enlightened physician. "The walk brings fresh air into the lungs and increases their capacity; brings oxygen into the system, bettering the blood, even muscles, heart and brain, and keeps the body parts moving."

"I'd rather wear out than rust out," was the sign posted in a midwest senior center. And it makes sense.

Stretching and other light exercise, perhaps ten to fifteen minutes a day, can be accomplished in the living room, in front of a television set, indoors or out of doors. You need not join a gymnasium. You need not suit up to go through the agony of "no pain or no gain." To keep yourself in good health for active mature years, you need spend less than one hour each day.

37

Exercise Is for Everyone

What do you do for exercise when you have some physical limitations such as arthritis?

"People with arthritis need range-of-motion exercises to keep the affected joints as loose and active as possible, and then simple strength exercises for the muscles near the affected joint." The speaker is Teri Aagaard, M.D., an emergency medicine specialist in Salt Lake City, who also travels the nation teaching senior citizens and medical practitioners the importance of range-of-motion exercises. "Don't give up on the affected joints and do nothing," she urges. Her eyes reflect intensity as she delivers her message.

Range-of-motion exercises are those which continue to stretch affected joints, firmly but gently, to maintain maximum flexibility and range of movement. Arthritis patients who do nothing but favor the affected joint, find that their ability to move becomes all the more restricted.

"Range-of-motion exercises need not be painful. In fact, if there is pain, you should back off. But, remember, if you do nothing and the joint is not used, it will not bounce back into movement on its own. You have to help it," states Dr. Aagaard.

Light weights or isometric exercises can be used to strengthen the leg muscles, as an example, above and below an affected knee. Exercises in water are particularly effective: "The water removes the body weight from the legs and provides isometric effects to the leg movement," according to Dr. Aagaard.

Where can one get such exercise instruction? "Your physician, medical association, a medical college, and/or physical therapy association should be able to give you a choice of two or three referrals." Interview them all. Or, ask your doctor for both a recommendation and a prescription.

Readers have written my syndicated newspaper column, stating that their physicians said, basically, "Forget it, you're getting older—give up trying to keep the knee working." My reply has been made several times in hundreds of newspapers across the continent: "Fire the doctor and get one who wants you to be in your best of health and activity."

Unless rigor mortis has started to set in, you can probably exercise to some degree. There are even video programs that demonstrate stretching and exercises to be done in bed or in a chair or wheelchair.

The reason for this type of exercise is the same as it is for all other exercise—to keep all of the body's good parts and joints moving, to gain the maximum amount of aerobic benefit for the cardiovascular system, and to strengthen the muscles that must be used to support the affected joints or disabled parts of the body.

Combining Nutrition and Exercise

One of the most innovative programs ever conducted by an insurance company is also one of the most successful in the nation, not only in reducing people's medical expenses, but also in helping to better their health.

The insurance company is Blue Shield of California, which engaged Dr. James F. Fries of Stanford University and Harry Harrington, a health and fitness consultant from San Francisco, to develop the concept they called Senior Healthtrac. Beginning in 1987, policyholders over the age of sixty-five were invited to participate in the first preventive/positive health care program developed and operated by an insurance company. Extensive educational materials were published with nutritional guidelines, exercise programs, and recommended lifestyle changes. Almost 30,000 adults participated in the first year of the program. At the end of that year, a progress review and report showed that:

• **Vital age at the end of the first year** was an average of seventy—six years younger than the participant's average chronological age, and down from more than seventy-six at the start of the program. (Vital age is a compilation of the factors used by an insurance company to assess risks for a policyholder.) After a year's participation in the positive health program, the risk factors actually went down. This is just the opposite of conventional wisdom and stereotypic thinking, which claim that after age seventy "it is all downhill."

• **Reduction in risk factors was 5 percent overall**; by quitting smoking, 10 percent; by reduction in saturated fat intake, 20 percent; and number of days reported as "sick" in the year was reduced, 14 percent.

• **Extended life,** as indicated by the company's actuaries, who determined that most members of this group had a reduced risk of illness and death than when they entered the program.

• **Reduced premiums,** as Blue Shield of California *cut* the rates charged senior citizen policyholders by up to 4 percent in January 1989, at the very same time that many other insurance companies were increasing rates by as much or more.

Blue Shield of California is now licensing its Senior Healthtrac program to other Blue Shield and Blue Cross companies across the nation. The results show that positive health makes sense for healthier and longer living—and for reducing insurance premiums.

Weighting in Line

The progress report on how well you are eating and how regularly you are exercising is readily obtainable from an instrument available in most homes—the bathroom scale. It is essential for good health that your weight be at the proper level for your height and bone structure.

Excess weight adds serious stress on the heart, increases the probability of hypertension—high blood pressure—and is a major factor in adult-onset diabetes and all of its serious complications. According to one expert, "obesity kills through its complications."

Many retirees in the past have added weight, patted their tummies, and pronounced themselves satisfied with the "good life" of leisure. But reduced activity without reduced calories can produce added weight. "Once you are 10 pounds over your ideal weight, each additional pound costs you a month of your life," according to Stanford University's Dr. James Fries. "Fat people are hospitalized more frequently than people with normal weight; they have more gall bladder problems, more surgical complications, more cases of breast cancer, more high blood pressure, and more strokes."

Every expert I have interviewed has identified proper nutrition, sensible eating, and exercise and activity as vital in keeping personal weight in check. Consuming fewer calories while continuing to burn them through exercise and activity is the key to maintaining ideal body weight.

Making It Happen

Your plan for retirement should identify your healthiest lifestyle as a matter of practice. Use the charts at the end of this chapter as a planning base. By starting with health and exercise as your foundation, all things are possible as you look to your financial and other concerns and directions and as you go forward to the best time of your life—the retirement years.

Lifestyle for Your Healthy Retirement Years

This is your tomorrow.

I like that line, having first written it as a theme for television personality Dick Stewart at KPIX Television in San Francisco some thirty years ago. Our program was the KPIX Dance Party, and our mission, in addition to airing the live ninety-minute program six days a week, was to take an important message to high school students.

This is your tomorrow. We toured the high schools, and Dick delivered the message, telling the students that what they did with their lives and education today would shape what they could be or would be in their future.

How true it was—and is.

This is your tomorrow. The message fits today as you consider how to tailor your lifestyle so as to achieve and maintain sound health in both the present and in the many years to come. Consider these factors:

The Case Against Smoking

"Tell your readers that if they quit smoking they will live up to fifteen years longer than those who do smoke.

"Tell your readers that if they think AIDS is a serious killer, give them the facts that tobacco kills one million persons a year worldwide, 350,000 in the United States alone each year . . . that the tobacco kill rate is more in two weeks than that of AIDS for the entire year.

"Tell your readers that one in four Americans will die earlier, suffer more, and pay more than others in medical bills specifically because of cigarettes.

"But, tell your readers that the day they quit smoking is the day their bodies can get back on the track to health."

The speaker is John Richards, M.D., of the faculty of the Medical College of Georgia, and a family physician in private practice in Martinez, Georgia. He is also president of the gutsy organization of 5000 volunteers and over 100 local chapters of DOC—Doctors Ought to Care.

Dr. Richards and members of DOC have mounted a major campaign to get other medical practitioners to urge patients to quit smoking.

In a presentation to newspaper and magazine editors, Dr. Richards spoke intensely in a style that offered only a hint of the southern drawl that would richly flavor his personal conversation. "Smokers have sixteen percent carbon monoxide instead of the life supporting oxygen in their hemoglobin. When they stop smoking there is an immediate return possible for the oxygen.

"Nicotine stimulates blood pressure—which can be very harmful—a stimulation that disappears and is corrected when the person stops smoking.

"And unless the person already has emphysema or lung cancer, after stopping smoking for one year, the chances of getting lung cancer are reduced significantly; after ten years of not smoking the chances of dying from a tobacco-induced lung condition are no greater than for someone who has never smoked.

"One-third of all hospital admissions and one-quarter of all deaths are attributed directly to the human damage caused by tobacco. Those who smoke even have twenty-five percent more automobile accidents than do non-smokers."

If Dr. Richards and his volunteer organization are successful, they will probably hurt their own pocketbooks, because projections show that the need for remedial and acute medical care would be reduced by at least one-third if everyone in the nation stopped smoking. But the members of DOC press forward, teaching their own patients, speaking wherever possible, testifying before committees of Congress, and writing respected research papers and articles. They fund their own effort voluntarily and have no paid organizational staff.

"The tobacco industry is unhappy with us," Dr. Richards states in an interview. "Each day they are losing one thousand of their best customers to death; and another thousand who quit."

"Will people gain weight if they quit smoking?"

"No. Research proves that one-third will lose weight, one-third will gain, and one-third will stay the same."

"Will people become more nervous or jittery if they quit smoking?"

"No," states Dr. Richards. "The jitters are actually caused by the nicotine withdrawal. When someone quits smoking and the nicotine withdrawal has passed, it should not return again."

There is no question that the first step to health in mature years is to cut out smoking today, no matter what your age.

The commitment might even be formalized as a contract with the living—your spouse, friends, and relatives—a sworn agreement that you will stop smoking today, so as to enjoy life all the more with them for years to come. You will find a draft contract at the end of this chapter.

In 1989 the U.S. Surgeon General reported that tobacco was an addictive drug, that smoking was a habit as difficult to kick as taking heroin. Some people can quit smoking successfully all by themselves. Most can't. About 80 percent of smokers surveyed in 1988 by the Centers for Disease Control wanted to quit, but only about 11 percent sought help. If you'd like to quit smoking, look into all the aids and programs offered by both local and national organizations, such as the American Cancer Society and the American Heart Association (you'll find their addresses in the "write for" section at the back of this book, along with other helpful resources). Ask your doctor, too.

The secret in quitting is having a vital reason to do so. Don't be complacent. Do you really want to have a lingering illness in your retirement years? Do you want to die before your time? Are you really so weak that you depend on burning tobacco to get you through the day? Think about it, and quit. Your gain will be a healthier, happier, more satisfying life for years to come.

Controlling Alcohol Consumption

For some retirees, a significant increase in drinking adds both a heavy dose of calories and a sedated, sedentary lifestyle. Such is the stuff from which many problems are created. A glass of wine before or with dinner might be a good way to enhance a meal, perhaps even replacing an assumed need for a sleeping pill. And, for many, a little alcohol periodically is just fine, depending on one's own metabolism. Some research studies even show beneficial results from moderate alcohol consumption.

There is also a dark side to this situation. Studies by automobile manufacturers and utility companies have shown that their "line" workers, people who had labored steadily at the same job for many years, often turned to heavy drinking on retirement, incurring more illness and earlier death. The workers looked on retirement mainly as an escape from the tedium of work, and not as the start of new, positive, active time of life. These surveys have been misused by some "experts" to claim that all retirees become alcohol-dependent—an assumption that is absolutely false.

There is no real reason why anyone should have more alcohol problems in retirement. Some people might experience changes in metabolism that may affect the absorption rate of alcohol—as in any other food, beverage, or medication consumed. And, if so, there will be a change in how the alcohol works in the system and the results it produces. Knowing this, you can adjust to the change without too much difficulty.

Heavy use of alcohol will probably increase the risk of thiamin and folacin deficiency, both vital for the proper functioning of the human immune system. A weakened immune system opens the door—without defense—to other diseases and conditions. Thus, there is reason in the best of retirement living to keep alcohol consumption at a moderate level—for the physiological as well as overall lifestyle needs. If you have questions, get a recommendation from your physician.

Chasing the Stress

Stress has become a pop media buzzword in recent years, as various "experts" have proclaimed all kinds of drastic effects of this condition and what it is claimed to do to human beings. The "condition" came to popular notice when aircraft controllers wanted raises, reduced working hours, and earlier retirement because of the "stress" of the jobs. When the public and politicians started listening, everyone else stood in line to claim how stressful were their own jobs, lives, or conditions.

Stress is a normal condition for human beings and, indeed, for all members of the animal kingdom. Each of us experiences a degree of stress anytime we face a challenge—a physical injury, a mental or emotional difficulty, a personal tragedy. Life without stress would probably lead to complete lethargy, itself a very negative and injurious state. Therefore, stress is not "all bad." Like cholesterol in the bloodstream, there will always be some stress in our lives.

Some people thrive on stress. For others, any form of stress is painful, and as such deepens the draining effect of the condition.

The body has a built-in stress-reaction system, one that normally works quite well. First to react are the nervous and hormonal systems, which meet and then mediate the stressful situation or event. The second stage of the response mechanism is one of resistance, draining some human reserves in order to build a defense against the stress. And the third stage, according to experts, is the recovery process, where the system puts itself back in balance. If the stress condition continues at high intensity, the body reserves can be drained; rather than recovering, the system exhausts itself and collapses.

The stress reactive system works throughout the day, quite naturally. To deaden its ability through tranquilizers or other sedations weakens its ability to perform, interrupting the natural performance of one of the body's best protective mechanisms. This system is a miracle in the human body's makeup. It must be maintained with proper nutrition and with positive exercise to restore balance.

The most emotionally stressful times in life have been reported in a study by the Metropolitan Life Insurance Company. In order of ranking, from most to least frequently cited, are the following:

Death of a spouse
Divorce
Marital separation
Being jailed
Death of a close family member
Personal injury or illness
Marriage
Losing a job
Retirement
The change in health of a family member
Pregnancy
Sexual problems
Addition of a new family member
Change in business status
Change in financial status
Death of close friend.

Sociologists identify two significant stages of human "trauma," events which produce significant stress as well as major changes in life patterns. Retirement is defined as the first trauma, and death of a spouse the second. Today's mature adult can, as part of retirement planning, know and understand these events, removing or reducing the traumatic effect.

Dr. Fred Kantrowitz, introduced earlier in this book, identifies stress as a possible catalyst in the occurrence of arthritis symptoms. This would explain the increase in arthritis in older women, accelerating at the time of retirement and then the death of a husband. Though not clinically cited at this time, enlightened new research is looking to this correlation.

We can reduce the impact of stressful times by better planning, by more nutritious eating, and by more effective exercise, rather than by reaching for yet another pill bottle to intervene in the symptoms without ever fixing the cause or aiding the body's own effective system to deal with the situation.

Stress is a fact of life. But its effects won't be that bad if your internal system is prepared to deal with it in the normal course of events. In fact, if you were to live completely without stress, you'd probably be inert of body, unthinking of mind, and unchallenged in opportunity.

As you face both the changes and opportunities in retirement years, know that what you do with your overall lifestyle will help determine how you will react when you come to times of strife or stress.

Remedial Medicine

Medical science has provided remarkable remedial solutions for just about every form of disease or illness. Unfortunately, most modern medical research has been conducted to develop cures or treatments in the forms of prescriptions, surgery and technology.

Precious little research has been devoted to finding ways of preventing illness, of building and maintaining the body's immune system, of using proper nutrition and exercise to keep the body functioning properly, as it was designed to do.

Twenty-eight journalists who write on health matters recently met in Williamsburg, Virginia, to hear of the latest research gains in the field of nutrition. The experts who addressed us came from medical and educational institutions, industry and research centers, government and government-funded agencies.

"Why," we asked, "are we just now seeing research on the positive vitamin influence and role in the immune system?

"Why," we asked, "is there little or no correlation of studies of nutrition and exercise?

"Why," we asked, "are there only three or four nutritional studies on older adults, when it appears that nutrition information is critically lacking, and the role appears so vital?"

The most frequent answers were: "It is just being funded now" and, more often, "We have not been able to find funding for that type of research."

There has always been money for research on miracle cures, magic pills, and expensive new technology, but very little for research how to keep people healthy.

We have been operating on a "medical model"—designed to improve methods of medical intervention—rather than a "health model"—the development of concepts and programs to keep people healthy. Of course, there is more money to be made in the operation of a medical model—selling prescriptions, filling hospital beds for surgery and other procedures, and in scores of other remedial methods, fixing you up after you're already sick.

The real test of this philosophy came with the establishment of Medicare in the United States in 1965. At that time persons age sixty-five and older were paying an average of $490 per year in medical costs, and the program was supposed to "relieve this serious financial burden" and fund 80 percent of those costs.

Before the legislation was enacted, a number of changes were made in the coverage. Lobbying forces led by the American Medical Association were effective in having all preventive care removed from the coverage. Also removed were holistic, chiropractic, optometric treatments, and any annual health screening or checkup programs.

What this left was an acute care program that rewarded doctors and hospitals for performing surgery and repairing people—and omitting all steps that would keep people healthy. Over twenty years later the price tag would be known: federal expenditures through Medicare had exploded, and the taxpayers were footing the bill.

The original legislative intent was to fund 50 percent of all senior citizen medical bills through a very simple program. After all the lobbying and politicking, the program was redesigned to cover 80 percent but only of specified treatments and procedures. Because of the program's complexity, a massive and costly bureaucracy was created. The average annual senior citizen medical bill had escalated over time from $490 to over $2000 per year, and instead of covering 50 percent as originally intended, or 80 percent as legislated, Medicare actually covered about 38 percent!

Expansions of the program enacted in 1988, under the guise of "catastrophic care," only increased the coverage for physician services and hospital acute care, and did not provide coverage for what is widely recognized as "catastrophic care": that is, nursing home coverage. Also, the legislation did not add coverage of medical treatment in any areas or services not already covered.

But what of preventive care?

The one-time Secretary of the Interior, Walter J. Hickel, had the right idea when he was Governor of Alaska. He went to Washington with a program to develop the "health model" concept in the forty-ninth state, as a laboratory for testing and proof for later adaptation by the nation. "Just

46

give us the same money as you are presently funding," he advocated in 1967. The program funds he sought included all the federal money flowing into and through the many health programs in Alaska. "Let us, in our concern for our people, redesign our programs to a 'health model.' We will still be able to treat those already sick, but we will dedicate new efforts to keeping the balance of the population healthier."

The concept made great sense, but the authorities and special interests in Washington would hear nothing of it. "It will be a great day," he stated many times, "when we remove the signs calling them 'drug stores,' and instead call them 'health stores.'"

Remedial medicine today reaches for a prescription pad in two out of every three medical visits, according to Steven Fox, O.D., director of Wellspring Gerontological Services in suburban Chicago, Illinois.

"The problem is that only four percent of the physicians have ever taken any geriatric courses to understand the older body and system. Most have had only one course in medical pharmacy, and less than one percent have taken any continuing medical education courses in geriatrics or pharmacology," he states emphatically. His position is supported by many medical doctors and specialists.

"If doctors don't understand pharmacy then they are unaware of the damage they are actually doing when adding one prescription on top of another; and patients are not told of the potential human damage to their systems by overmedication, mismedication and conflicting medication.

"One quarter of all hospital emergency room admissions for senior citizens are for mismedication—and this does not have to be.

"In a recognized study of prescriptions, Dr. Knight Steel reported that thirty-five percent were improper and twenty-five percent of those were actually life-threatening.

"We compound that when we do not explain the drugs, why they are being administered, how and why they work, to the patient. Therefore, half of them are never used or the patient stops using after awhile, and the other half can cause damage to the patient," charged Dr. Fox.

"What can we do?" we asked him.

"Build a relationship with a primary care physician and work with him or her to stay healthy, and, when necessary, to treat existing conditions or problems."

We'll add one more professional commentary before moving on to recommendations.

C. Everett Koop, M.D., is either the first or second most recognized and respected name in America, depending on which survey you read. At age sixty-five he left his own practice in pediatric surgery, teaching and directing hospital pediatric services, to become the Surgeon General of the United States. In a position that was normally considered obscure or hidden, he took a leading and, at times, controversial role in the formulation and implementation of health policy in the United States.

"We know today that disease is not a part of aging, and from thirty years of longitudinal studies in Baltimore, that there is, indeed, disease-free aging. In the older body most all natural functions continue, but even if there is a decline in the system output it is still enough to support the body in a disease-free condition.

"To assume that aches, pains and diseases are all a part of aging is bad medicine, plain and simple," he stated to a group of writers in the health and senior citizen fields.

"Each of us ages individually and differently. There is no norm or conformation that says that all persons over sixty five will have any specific disease or condition.

"Even the mind continues in fine shape. In Washington State, batteries of intelligence and achievement tests were given to the same participants over a twenty-year period, and eighty percent showed no real change in mental performance."

The former Surgeon General believes that physicians, generally, are overdiagnosing conditions and then prescribing or recommending acute care procedures based on those findings.

About Prescriptions and Over-the-Counter Medications

"The role of the pharmacist has had to change," says Robert C. Johnson, Pharm.D., executive vice president of the California Pharmacists Association in Sacramento. "For years it was traditional for the pharmacist to remain behind the glass in the pharmacy and compound or fill the prescriptions presented to us.

"But with the massive number of often-conflicting prescriptions given to patients, our profession is now directing pharmacists to get involved. We are now talking with individual patients, explaining medications to them, logging all of their medications into our computers so we can identify conflicts in drugs and interactive problems. We will analyze prescriptions and dosages now, and even call the physician to question the applicability or instructions."

The neighborhood pharmacist should be an important member of each person's health team, advocates Dr. Johnson, and he carries that message actively in both public appearances and in presentations to the medical profession. "If you have questions about your prescription, know you can talk to your pharmacist. Most patients are not instructed well on medications, and we believe it is vital," he states. "Therefore pharmacists want to do more, not less, in communicating and serving professionally."

With pharmacist involvement or intervention, might there be a reduction in the actual number of prescriptions to be filled? "We hope there will be a reduction," he states, "and for the remaining, appropriate prescriptions we hope, too, for the correct usage by the patient."

What are the impediments to the full role of the pharmacist? Mail order prescription fulfillment is one. And cost-squeezing by insurance companies to force mail ordering of prescriptions.

Are generic drugs as good as the brand-name prescriptions? In many cases, yes, states Dr. Johnson, if the formulation is identical for that specific drug. There should be a concern for those generic lines that have been subject to recalls for imperfect batches, and this is the type of question that may be asked of the pharmacist.

For enlightenment on prescriptions that you might be taking or that your doctor is recommending you take, make a trip to the library or bookstore for a copy of a book on the subject like *Complete Guide to Prescription and Non-Prescription Drugs* by H. Winter Griffith, M.D. We have found this one particularly understandable for the layperson.

When you have read through the book you'll understand the reasons to proceed carefully in taking prescription drugs, and why pharmacist Robert Johnson describes aspirin and acetaminophen—both widely advertised under their brand names—as "two of the most dangerous drugs in the world." If you ever have a headache and reach for an over-the-counter-pill, you should learn about the side effects of these two common drugs that you probably have in your medicine chest today.

There is of course a need for remedial drugs—but there is also a need for careful use, for exact compliance with the professional instructions, and for your own involvement in asking "why" when you are told to take these drugs.

Pharmacists recommend that when given a prescription you ask the doctor:

- What is the condition that the medication is designed to help?

- What is the drug, and how does it work?

- What are the alternatives to the drug?

- What should you be doing in your lifestyle, nutrition, and/or exercise to better the condition in conjunction with or instead of the drug?

- What are the specific instructions on use, and for how long?

- What are the possible and predictable side effects—and does the risk of side effects outweigh the possible benefits of the prescription? Are there any possible permanent side effects or damages to the body that might result from the use of the drug?

• What experience has the doctor had in working with this drug? Has he or she worked with it in testing or experience, or has the knowledge mainly been gathered from pharmaceutical representatives ("detail persons"), product literature or free samples?

• Has the doctor considered your existing medication(s) and the conflicts or cross-purposes when prescribing this medication?

Your questions just might cause the doctor to stop and think. Your questions just might protect you from being yet another person overprescribed, overmedicated, and in danger of serious side and conflicting effects. If you don't get satisfactory answers, consider another doctor; and/or take your questions for candid analysis by your neighborhood professional pharmacist.

The magic potions will then be a part of your life only as you really need them. And your body will be more able to work for you in health.

About That Recommendation for Surgery

Most elective surgery in the United States is unnecessary—whether it be a mastectomy, hysterectomy, and even coronary bypass surgery. Recent studies have shown that there are viable and less radical, less intrusive methods of dealing with many conditions previously assumed as acute and to be addressed with the scalpel.

There is no question about surgery in the case of serious accident, in a time of emergency. But if the surgery is elective, there should be a question. Operations are not totally safe. In fact, it is estimated that one third of all surgeries have complications caused by the surgical procedure itself; in addition, there are dangers from the post-operative period.

If your doctor recommends surgery now or in your retirement years, ask a series of questions about the procedure:

• What is the condition I have, and why is my body not working as it should?

• What is the procedure you are recommending, and why or how will it offer correction (or relief or proper functioning)?

• What imbalance will it cause in my system? Are you removing a functioning part of the body that normally is supposed to do some interactive work in the system, and how will that function be supplied in the future?

• What are the alternatives to surgery—in pharmaceuticals, in lifestyle change, in nutrition and diet—and the prognosis for each?

• What is the possibility that added/later surgery will be needed?

• What will my life be like if I choose to undergo the surgery, as opposed to life if I do not elect to have the surgery?

• What are the odds on errors or complications from the surgical procedure? What is the record on this? What is the doctor's own track record with this recommended procedure?

• What are my risks with the surgery and without the surgery—in detail?

In considering any surgical recommendation you must see another doctor for a second opinion. It is normal procedure for you to ask the recommending doctor to send your file to another doctor of your choosing, so that you can have another diagnosis done. In this meeting, you just might find a different diagnosis or recommended therapy. Ask the same series of questions if you do receive a recommendation for the procedure. The second opinion is not an affront to your doctor, and you should not be concerned about offending him or her.

This is not a recommendation against surgery or other procedures. It is a recommendation that you know the why and how of the procedure because it is your body and it should be your decision.

A Summary on Health

As we started this chapter we conclude it with the thought and commendation that your best retirement programming should start with a plan for health. When you assure your best health, all of the other accomplishments are possible.

In your retirement plan you should become an active, vital member of your health team, partners with your physician, your pharmacist, and perhaps a nutritionist. Be the quarterback and take a positive role in developing and maintaining an effective health plan.

Make your decisions and record them on the Retirement Health Worksheets following. Put your plan into action now so that your best of health will be the key to your best years in retirement.

- -

RETIREMENT HEALTH WORKSHEET

Name: _____   Date: _____

Today, I assess my health as: ___ excellent; ___ good; ___ average;
___ poor; ___ failing.

I identify my health concerns today to include:

_____

_____

I identify the following as my steps to better health daily:

Smoking: ____ Stop; ____ Never Start; ____ Other: _____
(see the "Nonsmoking Contract," following)

Weight: Present weight: _____   Ideal Weight: _____

Goal Weight one year from now: _____

Alcohol: ____ Reduce to: _____
____ Stop (type) _____
____ Other _____

Exercise: Present Level: _____
New Level: Walking: _____; Aerobic: _____
Gym: _____; Home Exercises: _____
Swimming: _____
Other: _____

Activities/Sports: Identify present/future activity:
____ Bowling; ____ Golf; ____ Tennis; ____ Softball;
____ Jogging/Running; ____ Track/Field; ____ Dance;
____ Other: _____

Diet: My present diet/eating-pattern: ____ is too rich;
____ has too many calories; ____ has too much fat;
____ is poor nutritionally; ____ is unpredictable;
____ is unplanned; ____ Other: _____

In my new diet I will:

_____ include at least 6 servings of fresh/steamed fruits/vegetables each day;

reduce meat to _____ time(s) each week;

increase fish to _____ time(s) each week;

_____ include fiber in my diet daily;

_____ plan to supply the RDA of vitamins and minerals;

_____ see a Registered Dietitian to develop a positive eating plan;

Other: _____

Doctor: _____ I will ask my doctor for an analysis of my positive health and how to maintain it; and to identify, too, any present/perceived medical condition that will need correcting, and how it can be assisted by lifestyle changes.

_____ I will ask my doctor to reconsider all my prescriptions as to their absolute necessity, to examine all side effects and complications, and to discuss alternatives with me.

_____ I will ask my doctor to explain, in depth, any recommended surgical or other procedure, including all risks and alternatives.

_____ I will ask another doctor for a second (or even third) opinion before any surgical or other acute procedure.

_____ I will ask my doctor about his/her training in positive/preventive health care, geriatric medicine, and pharmacy.

_____ I will resolve with my doctor my present concerns about: _____

_____

Pharmacy: _____ I will discuss whatever prescriptions I have with my local pharmacist.

_____ I will shift whatever prescriptions I have to one pharmacy, so that the pharmacist can readily be of counsel and evaluation for me.

_____ I will ask my pharmacist about my present concerns over the following

prescriptions and/or over-the-counter medications: _____

_____

Life: I plan to live a very healthy, active and productive life for at least the next _____ years.

And: _____

_____

_____

This is my plan and agreement with myself to achieve the very best of health now and in future years.

Signed: _____

Date: _____

Copies: Present a photocopy to your spouse, kinfolk, or a friend, so that he/she/they can be of positive support to you in this great effort. Take a draft copy to your doctor, nutritionist, exercise/fitness consultant, et al, for their suggested input/counsel.

‒ ‒

My Smoke Free Contract with You
    I want the rest of our years together to be the healthiest and happiest ever, and I want to be all that I can be to you and for you.
    Therefore, effective today, I have contracted with myself to stop smoking or using tobacco in any form, to allow my body to recover from past smoking, and to go forward without this toxic damage.
    It is with my love and care for you that I sign and pledge to honor this contract, a symbol of my gift of better health and better living now and in the future.

Presented

To: _____

By: _____

Date: _____

Note: This is a guide for a "smoke-free contract for the best of health" which you might draw up for yourself, with copies to be prepared for your spouse, friends, relatives, or others. It is a stated commitment, where each recipient can be notified of your commitment, and can be supportive of that commitment.

‒ ‒

PRESCRIPTION STUDY SHEET

List here all medications—prescriptions and over-the-counter—that you are taking or have been taking. Then, take this list to your doctor and/or pharmacist for evaluation. Also, do some of your own research in medication reference books, such as *Complete Guide to Prescription and Non-Prescription Drugs* by H. Winter Griffith, M.D. Write in the side effects and conflicts as you learn of or read about them, so as to understand what these drugs might be doing to your body and mind.

Prescription Name (generic and brand)

Prepared as: ___ pills; ____ liquid; ___ other: _____

Size/Dose: _____ mg; _____ ounces; _____ other: _____

Take: _____ times daily; _____ other: _____

54

Prescribed for: (condition)_____

How long taking this medication: _____

How long the doctor estimates you need take it: _____

What side effects are you feeling that you have not felt before (i.e., pain, dizziness, blurred

vision, heart racing, etc.): _____

_____

This is one of _____ (how many) prescriptions and/or over-the-counter medications taken

regularly (do a similar sheet for each). List them here also: _____

_____

Research on side effects: The following are what I have learned to be the possible side effects

of this drug: _____

Possible effects of interaction with other drugs I am taking: _____

_____

Possible effects of interaction with other substances (food, etc.) _____

_____

Warnings and precautions on this drug: _____

_____

Actions to take if overdosed: _____

Possible effects if I quit or miss using the drug: _____

_____

Note: You may do the primary research, if you desire, or complete the top half of the information and take the page or several pages to your doctor and/or pharmacist. Make sure you complete a form for each over-the-counter drug you take daily or frequently (aspirin, heartburn medication, cold medicine, etc.). Do not get into the practice of self-medicating. Collect the information for professional evaluation. In this way, you will know exactly what substances you are putting into your body and the possible positive—and negative—effects of those substances.

- -

If it is to be, it is up to me.
—Anonymous

| CHAPTER | WHERE WILL |
| 5 | YOU LIVE IN RETIREMENT? |

Your home—where it is, what it provides, and how it is ideal for your mature lifestyle—is an important consideration in your mature years planning. If you're like most Americans, your home is also your largest asset.

If you own your present home, it might serve well if you want the same amount of space and in the same location. If it is too large, or not located where you want to be geographically, it may prove to a be a very important asset in your mature years lifestyle program.

In the United States, a mature adult—age fifty-five plus —may sell his or her personal home and have a one-time capital gains exclusion of $125,000. The home must have been owned for at least five years, and have served as the owner's personal residence for at least three of the most recent years.

Examples: If the sale price of the home today is $180,000, having been bought for $40,000 originally, and with $15,000 in capital improvement costs, there would be no capital gain whatsoever—and therefore the net gain from the property sale would be tax free.

Another example might show the same $180,000 present day sale value, reduced in gain—or profit—by the original purchase price of $40,000 and a $55,000 purchase of a condominium. The cash gain will not be federally taxable if you qualify by age and residency for the one-time exclusion.

Many mature Americans have refinanced themselves in this way, buying or renting a desirable smaller home and investing the balance. If $100,000 were invested, even conservatively, it could provide $6,000 to $8,000 in added income each year, without ever touching the principal.

In considering where you will live, consider the disposition of your present home as one of the most important decisions to be made. It is possible that a home large enough to raise children in is too large and, thus expensive to maintain. Perhaps, your lifestyle choice is for more travel, so you'll desire a simpler home arrangement.

Is it your ideal to live in the Sunbelt or closer to the ocean? In a rural area or a mountain hideaway? We'll discuss the variety of opportunities later in this chapter.

Or, as you consider your lifestyle choice, your present home might be just fine. But as we started the mature years planning process with clean sheets of paper, we do similarly here, with no assumptions on what you have to do, based on the past or present.

We have found some mature adults who regretted holding onto their traditional homes. "We thought of it as bedrock, and so when we retired we just vegetated and grew frustrated about what we were not doing. We found that, by hanging onto the home, we were also hanging on to all of the things, people, events, problems and memories of the past that we had wanted to change."

Another typical statement from older adults: "We kept the big house not for us but to have space for children and grandchildren. They would visit just once or twice a year for a week, so during the balance of the year we just looked at the emptiness. If we had it to do over again, we'd move where we wanted to be, spend more time traveling and learning, and have more time and opportunity to visit with family and friends."

Others tell us of retaining the family home and expanding its use to encompass more activities and interests. Spare bedrooms become dens, centers for hobbies or offices for consulting, for a business, or for community activities.

With a larger home, some mature adults invite their parent or parents to live with them.

Some mature adults are "just more comfortable" in their traditional home, without having to readjust. Others find it difficult to make the desired changes in their lifestyles and to go on to new accomplishments in their retirement years until they move. Your consideration and decision to stay or move are serious deliberations as part of your overall planning for retirement years.

Here are briefings as thought-starters for your deliberations:

Here or There

Your choice of city or location should be one of your first considerations. Are you really happy in your present city and neighborhood? Do family and friends provide reason to stay right where you are? Or have they moved, and do you desire now to move closer to them?

About 5 percent of mature adults move to another city—such as to the Sunbelt areas—soon after retirement. At least another 10 percent choose to move to new residences within the same geographic area. Many experts believe that those figures will increase as mature adults do more lifestyle planning. Here are half a dozen questions mature adults should answer before rejecting the idea of moving to a new environment.

• Do you have concerns about your present location in regard to problems that have arisen—crime, economic, social, environmental—or do you predict that these and other problems will be more serious in the future?

• Is your area booming—or sure to boom—in demand so that you could "make a fortune" from the appreciated value of your present home?

• Are you "property rich and cash poor," where the sale of the home may be used to provide significant cash for investment and for interest income?

• Is the cost of living in your area escalating to where it is a concern?

• Is your present home the right residential base for your lifestyle, or should you be looking for something different—now or at some point in the future?

• Do you have any health concerns that should be considered as reason to move or not to move?

Write down your thoughts on each of these questions, to share, to think about, to amend, and then to use as a basis for resolution.

Make a two-column chart on tablet paper again. On the left side write down all the reasons and thoughts that come to your mind that are positive about retaining your present residence. On the right side write down all thoughts that are negative about your present residence, along with any reasons for moving to another home, to another area, or even to another country. A couple should each make a list separately, then share what they have written after completion.

Don't be inhibited about the process! Allow your ideas to flow, adding to your list over a week's time, without doing any editing. Then clear your mind of the thoughts and feelings regarding the home and your direction forward. After a day or two, return to your list and identify the most important points in each column. Share and discuss your ideas. Then copy the list, putting the priority items at the top.

You may be surprised at the result of this expression of your real feelings.

Your thinking will be crystallized, so that whatever you decide, you will now at least know why. If your resolution is to retain your present home, you may have identified necessary or desired changes to improve your current lifestyle. If your resolution is to move to a new home, you will have defined your desires in many areas—the better for targeting your search for the right property.

What might be some of your questions and concerns about your home in mature years? Here are some suggestions:

The Physical Things to Think About

If your present home is older—twenty, thirty years or more—plan for upgrades that will make it both safer and less costly to maintain:

Lighting: Is there sufficient exterior lighting for safety when walking and to deter thieves? Also, consider increasing the level of lighting available indoors, in the event you have any diminishing eyesight (this may start as early as age thirty). Finally, will your present electrical system— wires, fuses, and fixtures—handle the added load? If not, what adjustments need be made, and at what cost?

Weather Protection: Are all your windows and doors weather stripped to prevent the entry of cold or hot air from the outside, and to protect the ideal temperature inside? Are there other leaks in the house—such as the weather protection padding in the roof, attic or walls? Heating and air conditioning costs may run as much as 30 percent higher just because of ineffective home insulation.

Have you blanket-wrapped your water heater(s), to retain the heat more effectively? Are there rooms you could or should close off, so that you won't have to heat or cool them?

What are the costs of such upgrades? How will you budget for them? If such costs are significant, will you decide to avoid them by selling the home?

Plumbing and Heating: How old are the pipes and pumps, the ducts and furnace? Do you have questions about their efficiency? Are there needed repairs that had been deferred earlier? What costs do you anticipate?

In making any plumbing changes, consider installing water-saver spouts in showers and baths and water-saving devices in toilets; check and correct all faucet leaks, too, indoors and out. And, consider installing single-lever controls for hot and cold water. The latter recommendation is advanced by a University of Florida and federal government study, which produced the concept of "A-Factor" housing. The concept identified about forty recommendations for mature adult housing, both for new construction and remodeling for older homes. "Even a child can operate levers better than knobs, and it becomes far easier for an older adult with arthritis or other limitation," states Michael F. Pfaff, aging and adult services project manager for the Florida Department of Health and Rehabilitative Services in Tallahassee.

The A-Factor Home concept recommends nonslip floors in bathrooms, kitchens, and exterior walkways, covered and well-lit entrances, lights in closets, and raising electric outlets to at least twenty-four inches above the floor. Testing of the concepts with mature adults in Florida, even at higher costs in a new home purchase or for retrofitting existing homes, brought overwhelmingly positive responses, according to Pfaff.

Security: Is your present home secure against burglary or other criminal intrusion? There have been technological advances in electronic security systems that are both affordable and effective. As a bonus, you may earn a reduction in your insurance premiums by installing new, improved security devices.

Do you participate in a Neighborhood Watch program so as to deter intruders in your area? Law enforcement statistics show a reduction in crime wherever residents participate actively in a Neighborhood Watch program. When was the last time you had the locks recored and the keys changed? It is a good idea to do this periodically, particularly if anyone else has had access to your keys.

Safety: Have you equipped your home with fire extinguishers, and do you check regularly to insure that they are fully charged? If you have a newer, programmable telephone, have you set a predialing for 911 or other emergency numbers in the case of fire or other need?

Do you have smoke alarms placed effectively around your home, and are they checked regularly—by "appointment" on your calendar—to assure their effectiveness?

Maintenance and Repair: Are there any other improvements that should be made around the house? Check the paint (indoors and out), the stairs and fences, the walkways and windows, the landscaping and watering system, and all the other parts and areas of a home that need to be properly maintained. In this checkup, pay particular attention to the roof for necessary patching or replacement, and the drains which run from it to the ground.

About This List: I suggest the above not to provide you with an overflow of slips in the "job jar," but to help you realistically identify the steps and costs that must be planned and budgeted whether you are retaining your present home or purchasing another home where there is work to be done.

If you sell the home, how much of the above do you have to do? Would your upgrades be limited to the cosmetic appearance of the home, to enhance the sale? What are the costs and benefits of the ways you choose to go?

Moving Down the Street, Across the Nation, or to Another Nation

Moving your home is a decision to be made only after extensive research. If you choose to move, consider all alternatives, including staying right in your own town or city, where you know the area already.

There are many mature adults who have a genuine need and desire to move to a new area. If you are in this group, be sure to consider and compare several different areas. Start by writing the chambers of commerce and convention and visitors bureaus for information. Go to the library and check the information in almanacs and books on the regions considered. Take out a trial subscription to the newspapers in each of the areas in which you're interested.

By reading the newspapers you'll learn about social and economic conditions in the respective areas. Are there problems reported similar to those you're seeking to get away from in your present home area? How about cultural activities, spectator sports, entertainment and other events and attractions that may be part of your desired lifestyle? Prepare a file folder for each of the areas under consideration; clip pertinent articles and pricing; and make notes about your observations.

Study the classified ads, too, to get an idea on home and condominium availability and prices. Consider rental units, too. Study the supermarket and general retail ads to compare prices for what you buy—there will be regional differences that may range from slight to significant.

Following this research process, consider the areas in view of your desires for your retirement lifestyle—as determined in your chart-making, evaluations, and resolutions. Then, hit the road to visit each of those areas still under consideration.

If you can take the time, rent an apartment or house for a month in each of the areas, just to see how it all feels—the area, the people, the rhythm, the activity—and how it "fits" for you. If you want to work, use this opportunity to explore the possibilities—even if your actual or planned move is several years in the future. If you want to establish a business, chat with bankers and entrepreneurs alike, to gauge their attitudes about doing business in the area. If you're so inclined, check the golf, tennis or other sports facilities in the area. Many clubs have trial memberships. How does the area fit your needs and desires? Remember, you are setting the direction for the best years of your life, so personal research and comparisons are vital.

If considering a move to a retirement complex, rent a unit there for a week or two to give it a good test before buying. Sun City and Leisure World developments—and many others—have such rental units available for you to "try the area on for size and fit." Some developments offer the rental opportunities at low rates as an inducement for your trial visit.

When doing this in-person research, consider first if your new home will provide the amenities and lifestyle that you have defined in your mature years lifestyle plan, in addition to other benefits it might offer. Never lose sight of what you want—and don't want—as defined by your chartmaking, evaluation and thinking. This will remove the possibility of your just being "sold" into a new residential area. and don't sign any contract "on the spot." Any major purchase should be made only after research and careful, unpressured consideration.

But Where Do You Move?

Where? Here are some background thoughts:

The City: You will be close to all kinds of cultural events and other activities, continuing education, participant and many spectator sports, airports, libraries and other community services, in a city. On the other hand, in many cities there are pollution, crime and social problems. But, if needed, you might find better and more readily available medical care and social services.

Property costs might be higher, or lower, depending on the social and economic trends in that city. Low prices may mean that a neighborhood or property is in serious decline. You'll need a qualified real estate expert as consultant to your selection. Property and other taxes tend to run higher in cities than in rural areas, in order to support a higher level of community services. Emergency service response times are often quicker in a city than in other types of residential areas. Cable television service will probably be more available and predictable than in many suburban and most rural areas.

In the city you might be able to scuttle one or both of the cars, at some point—if mass transit is good—and trade for a motorhome for extended travel adventures.

You'll probably think of more ideas to add on the subject of cities, pertinent to your special interests. Many mature adults have started a trend in moving from large homes in the suburbs to smaller, easier-to-maintain apartments or condominiums in the city.

Suburban: The bedroom communities of the fifties, those towns that used to be considered the "suburbs," are in many cases now quite sophisticated in what they offer. Their residents became the lure for the development of shopping centers, health facilities, schools, colleges and more. In most suburban areas you will need at least one car, for you'll have to drive most everywhere to get what you want or need.

Property tax rates might be comparatively high, too, as the communities are still paying for topnotch schools and increasing local services. Depending on the suburban location you might be reasonably close to city features, attractions and entertainment—or you might be caught in a driving nightmare on crowded freeways.

Rural: If you want a more self-generative life, there is probably no more ideal setting than in a rural community. That's the contention of Lee Fisher, a retired banker in Seattle who serves as a consultant for rural communities in Washington state that want to attract new, mature adult residents.

It's a fact of life in many smaller rural communities that most younger people seek their economic opportunities elsewhere, at the same time as a much slower birthrate is not replacing them in the population. Fisher has polled community leaders and residents in scores of smaller communities, asking what they like about their towns, what services are offered, and how they would welcome mature adults from other parts of the nation. The response has been astonishingly positive, and promotion campaigns have been developed.

In the South Dr. Mark Fagan of Jacksonville State University has developed similar programs for communities in Alabama, and is consulting nearby state governments on their own appeal to mature adults.

Whether in Washington, Alabama, or another state in the contiguous forty-eight, Fisher identifies the advantages to include: a community where you can get to know people; property prices that are, in most cases, much lower than in the suburbs or the city; cost of living as much as 40 percent lower than in the more developed areas; community and activities that welcome new residents who want to get involved; and much less pervasive crime and social problems.

Of course, medical and health facilities, banking and financial services, and cultural, sports, and entertainment programs are not at the level available in most cities. "But big cities are not for everyone," Fisher states, "and we present this concept for those mature adults who might want to share more and not have to race against the world where they are."

The rural concept has applications and opportunities in most areas of the country. Real estate agents in rural areas, generally, have a fine grasp on what their communities do and do not offer. In a driving tour to discover rural communities, allow lots of time to visit with the real estate agent, a local banker, a local supermarket or grocery store, and the chamber of commerce, if they have one.

In Colorado, for instance, the town of Durango boasts of clean air and very affordable homes for purchase or rent. In the southwest corner of the state, the boomtown of a century ago is today home to approximately 13,000 people. It has a four-year college (with many cultural events), resident theatre, a fine health and medical center, and a very low crime rate. One local policeman told me: "We're very serious about keeping order here. Our main business is tourism, and we want it to be safe so that they will come back again and tell their friends to visit here."

Durango is 6,500 feet above sea level, and but for the whistle of the narrow gauge steam train that huffs its way to the former mining town of Silverton each day in summer, you can hear the quiet. The airport is tucked behind a hill so there is no noise pollution from the jets.

Residents fly-cast for abundant trout in the Animas River, which runs right through the heart of town, or hike or ski at Purgatory or Telluride, less than thirty minutes away. Unlike the Sunbelt, though, Durango does have four seasons, with snow in winter, and a temperate summer.

As an alternative, think about Guntersville in north central Alabama. This town on the Tennessee River dates back to the early 1800s and was the embarkation point in the 1830s for the Westward trek of Indian tribes exiled from this area. Then known as Gunter's Landing, the community was a shipping port for locally grown agricultural products and supplies up and down the Tennessee River. Then 50 years ago the Tennessee Valley Authority completed the Guntersville Dam and a 69,000 acre reservoir was created.

Today's population is approximately 6,000, with a growing number of mature adults as new residents. They move here for the fishing (Bass, Crappie, Bream), sailing and boating on the reservoir, fishing and cruising on the river, touring the surrounding foothills of the Appalachian Mountains and to other historic, colorful and adventurous parts of the southern United States.

A quality two bedroom home in town prices at around $60,000, and higher if you want to live on the shoreline. Guntersville has operated its Residents Retiree Board since 1985, specifically to encourage mature adults to move there, and to draw the new residents into the mainstream of life and activity.

Guntersville's present and future opens to the great out of doors, and the people enjoying it most are the mature adults who chose this area for their best retirement living.

You will find rural communities throughout the continent, and if this becomes your ideal, your exploration itself can be an adventure, a discovery of your very own.

Retirement Places Rated is a Rand-McNally publication that evaluates many smaller communities, selected because of quality of life, safety, cost of living, and other features and opportunities. Other similar publications are available at your bookseller or library.

What are the drawbacks of a rural area? If you want to take jets around the country, your air tickets might cost more, and you might have a longer trip to the airport. If you need specialized medical care, you might have a distance to travel. And there won't be the variety of retail establishments to be found in and around urban centers.

64

Going Over the Border

Have you ever considered moving to another country? Early in this book I referred to the difference in cost-of-living, using as one (hopefully humorous) example, moving to the coast of Mexico and playing in a Mariachi band. That's not a recommendation, but there are tens of thousands of North Americans who have chosen Mexico as the setting for their preferred lifestyle. Unless you move to a high-population or in-demand tourist destination, Mexico might be that right change of pace for mature adult living. We hear regularly of mature adults who live very well on $500 to $600 per month with the services of a full time maid included.

There are colonies of Americans in Mexico City and Guadalajara, for instance, with at least one local newspaper catering to their interests by publishing its news in English. Many Mexican universities have low tuition and welcome American and Canadian nationals as students for degree programs or special curricula.

Many European countries welcome North American retirees, but they have regulations regarding your financial ability and health. Some prohibit your working in competition with their citizens. Some will allow you to buy property; some do not. The value of the dollar determines your buying power as resident of that country and it may vary depending on international conditions. In Portugal and Spain your retirement income might afford very pleasant accommodations and lifestyle; while those same dollars will buy far less in Switzerland or France.

Many foreign countries have senior citizen discount and benefit programs for those age sixty-five-plus, recognizing the benefit of your years while not challenging your nationality.

There are opportunities in other countries, too, which would welcome you. In many, your retirement dollars will go much further than at home.

But what of the drawbacks? There are many:

- In a foreign country you are an alien, subject to laws and cultures that you might not understand. You do not have the protection of your home country.

- Your Social Security benefits can be paid to you in a foreign country, but government benefits, such as Medicare, do not cross the border, and you cannot file claim for reimbursement of medical costs if living in another nation.

- You may have to convert your currency into that of the foreign country, and that currency may fluctuate in value, even drastically. (The Mexican peso has fallen in value more than 10,000 percent between 1974 and 1989. And, as mentioned the value of the dollar fluctuates.)

• You may not be able to hold full title or, indeed, any title to real property. (Such is the case on coastal Mexico.)

• You may not be allowed to do any work or to own a business, or if you did, the income return might be very small.

• You may have to travel back to your home country once or twice each year in order to maintain guest status in your adopted country. This will come at some cost.

• Medical and health facilities may be inferior to those at home.

• You may be at a distinct disadvantage if you do not speak the language well.

If, despite the possible disadvantages, the idea still has appeal, you will want to head again to your bookseller and library, to secure all of the reference books and materials you can get your hands on. Study the history and culture of the country in which you are interested, along with its economy and social conditions. If there are any English language newspapers in the chosen areas, subscribe to them, to do the same kind of research that you would do when considering cities or areas in the United States or Canada. Study the language. (I do my foreign language "learn up" with audio cassettes and handbooks from the publisher of this book, Barron's, before I travel to any country with a foreign language. You'll find them at bookstores and travel specialty stores.)

Write to the U.S. State Department in Washington, D.C., to secure briefing materials on the countries of your interest. Contact the embassy or consular office of the countries you are considering, asking them for all of the information available. Ask for their recommendations, too. Establish a personal contact—by letter and telephone—with a representative in that office, so you can get ready answers to your questions, speedy and more effective processing of any necessary paperwork, or even a visa endorsement on your passport.

Travel more than once to any areas in which you're interested, again to see what "fits." Can you handle being the easily identified "outsider?" Can you make the proper financial arrangements to allow the desired cash flow to you in that foreign country, leaving some funds and the collection of any notes, contracts, or retirement benefits to a financial institution in your home country?

Does a foreign country make the best of sense to you? For some, it will—

for the escape, the adventure, the new exploration, and for perhaps the higher quality of living at possibly much lower cost.

About the Type of Residence

Unlike the rose, a home is not always a house. And, in mature or retirement living, the variety increases in dimensions and opportunities.

The most traditional types of housing are the single-family home, condominium, or rental apartment. These come in an endless array of shapes and sizes, but we should readily understand each other in using the terms. You will find all three types in city or suburban areas and in most rural areas. The quality and selection will vary by area, by price range, and more.

In addition to these basic housing types there are other opportunities, such as residential communities, retirement residences, life-care complexes, and, if need be, nursing homes.

Let's explore the choices and types:

Single-Family Residences:

The most typical type of residence in the nation is the single-family home, with most of them owned outright by mature adults. In this type of residence you own the land, its improvements and its structures, and are responsible and liable for everything thereon. That means you pay the mortgage, maintenance, insurance, and all other costs of operating the property for residential living.

You are Lord and Lady of the Manse for all its assets, and banker/provider, too, for all its needs.

Single-family homes are detached (with some land on all sides of the house); semidetached (sharing one wall with your neighbor), or attached (being in a row of houses, as in a townhouse development).

In some of the newer planned residential developments, lawns and walks are considered community property, and you pay a fee to the homeowners' or community association to fund maintenance of the common areas.

For your home you may choose a traditional neighborhood, a retirement community, or planned residential community. Each offers some variety and, therefore, varying costs of maintaining your property.

About the Condominium

In the condominium you own your unit—individual house or apartment—and an association of all homeowners in the complex or defined property owns and provides the maintenance for all common areas, such as lawns and walks, lobbies and hallways, even furnace and cooling units, along with other services. A board of directors runs the association, often hiring a property manager or firm to oversee the buildings and grounds. If well run, the association should be able to provide the services at a fraction of the cost you would pay for individual contracting. If the individual owners are lax and the association is poorly run, or if there are unforeseen problems (perhaps caused by faulty construction), the monthly cost to homeowners might escalate to a figure much higher than one would expect.

The condo association may also provide and coordinate recreation facilities and programs, and even security and fire services, depending on the size and scope of the development. You may have a condominium development with just two homes or with thousands of units.

The gains in condo ownership are, generally, in more carefree residency for you. The drawbacks may include political problems within the homeowner's association, financial problems—or even bankruptcy—for the organization, or maintenance and service standards below that which you desire. The condo association is run by its member/owners. If they're a good group, the development can survive most any problems. If they're not, if the normal human emotions of selfishness, jealousy, and greed are allowed to hold sway, the association will founder.

The Rental Apartment

Once the starting point for young singles and married couples, apartments make sense for many mature people today—for a variety of reasons. In a rental apartment you make monthly payments for the use of someone else's property, usually on a lease basis. Your obligation is to live up to the terms of the lease, and the owner—or landlord—must provide the contracted property, maintenance, and services.

Other than a first-and-last month rent payment and a security deposit, you have no investment in the property. You don't have property taxes—or the income tax deductions from them, if applicable.

Whether mature years apartment living makes sense for you depends on your desired lifestyle. An apartment is generally smaller than a house, so your present seven-foot sofa may not fit, and in some buildings there will be a prohibition against pets or water beds. Many mature adults want the flexibility of apartment living, to be able to move across the street or across the nation, if desired, and this is possible, of course, at lease renewal time.

The drawbacks include an uncertainty about lease rates in the future—in the case of inflation or housing shortages (forcing rental rates upward), a landlord conversion of the units to condominiums, or even an owner decision to scrap the development in order to build something else for the "highest and best use of the land."

Renting an apartment is an inexpensive, less binding way to "try out" a new residential area. This allows you to learn the community and its opportunities, to shop for the right home purchase, and to have time to affirm or change your decision. (Remember, if you sell your home at a net profit of more than $125,000, you have a two-year grace period to look for and purchase a new home in order to avoid paying federal income taxes on your capital gains.)

In selecting an apartment you will want to check for general safety, asking, too, about the other tenants in the complex. Do you want to live primarily with other mature adults, or do you desire mixed ages? Do you want a complex with recreation and social facilities and programs? Walk the property at two or three different times of day and night so as to ascertain if there is offending music or other concern.

As a mature adult you're a desired tenant by quality apartment complexes—for it is well accepted that you will pay your rent on time, will take better care of the property, and create far less problems or conflicts than will younger tenants.

Is renting an apartment the right step for you for a limited time or even permanently? Think about it as part of your overall lifestyle plan for mature years.

Retirement Communities

Del Webb started it all with his Sun City developments—entire towns built just for mature adults, with "active living" included in the design and operation. A new idea some twenty-five years ago, there are now scores of similar developments throughout the North American continent.

For some mature adults the concept is a dream come true:

• A planned community with residential units for purchase, where all maintenance and common areas are tended by someone else.

• Within the development or nearby are medical facilities, where some services and treatments might be provided on an insurance-type basis for residents.

• Recreation facilities and programs are all included, perhaps with golf courses, tennis and other game courts, bowling lanes, recreation centers, swimming pools, and more.

• Social programs and entertainment events span the day and many interests.

• A representative governing body of residents works with the devel-

69

oper/operator in order to insure that the legitimate concerns and desires of the residents are carried out.

Could anything be more carefree? You buy your home or unit, thus are a homeowner, and fund the monthly maintenance and membership fees—and then just concentrate on socializing, sports, and other activities. For many mature adults this is ideal. For many others, it is not—because it might not provide creative satisfaction or accomplishment. Fortunately, if you buy in, you can generally resell the unit if you desire to move later.

The drawbacks of residential communities? There are rigid codes, covenants, and restrictions (CC&Rs) and a homeowners association or management organization that determines—for the good of all—what you can and cannot do with your property. The communities, therefore, may seem like something out of an Army manual: dressed right and covered down, with everything properly stored in the right locker or bin. The management might tell you how much you may, must, or cannot decorate your house for the holidays. Concepts for CC&Rs for retirement residential communities had been introduced as early as the early 1950s by Henry Doelger for his Westlake development in San Francisco.

And, do you want to live only with other mature adults? The generally accepted minimum age for residency is forty-five, with many developments requiring the householder to be at least fifty-five.

Perhaps your desired lifestyle has a retirement community as an ideal. Perhaps not, when you think about it. It's a matter of individual inclination and desire.

Retirement Residences

There are many types of retirement residences, a specific building or a complex of buildings for older adults, offering condominiums or apartments or rooms for rent. Generally, the move-in age is at least sixty-five and, for some developments, seventy-five or older.

Retirement residences usually offer social programs and facilities, and are three-to-one the choice of widowed or single women in later years. The complexes offer an effective transition for persons in the second trauma stage—after the death of a spouse. (The first trauma, according to sociologists and gerontologists, is the retirement process.)

Many retirement residences will offer dining room service for two or three meals each day as part of the program. Residents, on move-in, must be ambulatory on their own, as these residences are not licensed as nursing homes. However, some developments also have a nursing home on the same or adjacent property, in the case of need. Many will offer transportation services and other personal assistance as requested.

The drawbacks: Are you ready for an institutionalized setting, where meals are planned and you're expected to take part in the structured programs and activities? This is a setting of the least pressure, where you will be cared for. Rental rates are set according to the facilities, the size and location of your unit, your meals, and more.

The retirement residence concept is epitomized in Sun City Gardens, in Sun City, California. In 1980 I was engaged to turn this development from a deep loss to a successful and profitable operation. We identified the advantages as "carefree living," "activity without having to create it for yourself," and a "desired lifestyle."

The resulting headlines told the story of ideal retirement residence living: "Let George Do Your Cooking" (with a photo of the chef, replete with tall white hat and skillet in hand) and "Let Mary Make Your Bed" (with a photo of the housekeeper changing a pillow case).

Other themes that advertising counsel Gary Beals and I considered for the ads: "Let Janie Take You To The Movies" (with the social director posed with the passenger van) and "Let Jorge Tend The Garden" (showing the head groundskeeper presenting fresh-picked flowers to a resident).

The concept worked as part of the overall marketing concept, and based on the promise of carefree living and service, Sun City Gardens filled to a waiting list in a few short months. Those who moved in were looking for just that promise and fulfillment for their desired retirement lifestyle.

Mobile Homes

By definition, mobile homes must be fitted with wheels so they can be moved—but most of them have been moved on trailers and then set on concrete foundations. This home type allows in-factory construction, rather than the more expensive conventional on-site building.

The concept of houses on wheels became very popular before and during World War II, when the units were metallic and the residents were nomads from economically depressed states who moved to jobs in defense production. Units were parked close together or helter-skelter in clusters called trailer parks. You'll still find trailer parks around the nation—but don't confuse them with mobile home parks.

Mobile homes are complete homes, twelve or twenty-four feet wide by sixty feet long. With more than 1,400 square feet of living space, the larger units include two or three bedrooms, perhaps two small baths, living and dining rooms, kitchen, closet space, and more.

Many mobile home parks have been developed exclusively for mature adults, and offer the concrete pads for the units, plumbing and electric tie-ins, streets and landscaping, recreational centers with laundries, and social and activity programs.

The cost of mobile homes is generally less (sometimes far less) than comparable units of conventional construction, but the park sites may be limited. In some states, the park owners control the sale of the units as well as the rental of the pads. Mature adults represent the highest percentage of mobile home park residents, and in some areas they have also become owners, grouping together to buy out the parks to operate them on a condominium basis.

The drawback of mobile home park living is determined by the area, location, and facilities at any particular park. In areas where there is more demand than available space, the landlord has the upper hand and may increase rents and other charges significantly. And, if your home is on a foundation, cost may be a major deterrent to moving if you later change your mind.

With more parks and availability, though, mobile home living may be the ideal solution for mature adults having a limited amount of money for a home purchase or desiring to have more money for investment and interest income to supplement retirement income.

Hit the Open Road

What if your home was on wheels, so that you could go where you wanted whenever it struck your fancy? Do you want to be a vagabond? A remarkable number of mature adults are opting for this lifestyle, purchasing a motor home—a home on wheels—and moving about the country at will.

Those who want such flexibility can live in the Sunbelt during winter months and in northern states for summer. Their home is wherever the open road takes them, as they park for a day, a week, or months in camper parks at very reasonable prices.

A motor home is a traveling residence built on a truck or bus chassis, and may include most of the comforts of home, though in much tighter space. A married couple living in a motor home must not only share a wanderlust, but they must also get along with each other very well.

Entire caravans of motor homes cross the country for prearranged campouts or to enjoy the best of seasons. The units are eighteen to forty or more feet in length, and range in price from $30,000 to as much as $200,000—depending on the size, furnishings, power, and "bells and whistles" included as options.

Attending regional camper and motor home shows and shopping every dealer within reasonable distance will give you an idea of the type, size, and variety of units available. Prior to buying any unit, rent it and others several times. Try them for satisfaction, to test your patience with each other, and to see if being a vagabond satisfies your sense of adventure.

If you choose the open road for your new home, you'll need to establish some permanent place to receive your mail, and perhaps a bank to receive your retirement and other checks. But, if you don't need any more than these elementary "roots" in any particular place, this type of lifestyle may be one for your consideration.

About Nursing Homes

I report on this type of housing not because you will necessarily ever be a resident of a nursing home, but to identify some helpful provisions you might make in case there is need in the future or in case you, like many of your contemporaries, are in charge of making arrangements for an elderly parent who is no longer able to take care of himself or herself.

Nursing homes are not a preferred or even predicted form of retirement housing, unless you have an chronic illness or other medical condition that mandates a need for nursing care. As reported elsewhere, less than 5 percent of mature adults are institutionalized in any way, and the predictability of being in a nursing home does not increase appreciably until after age eighty-five. That percentage will probably be reduced in the future, as more home health or personal-maintenance services become available.

For most senior citizens nursing homes are not "the end of the line," but only temporary care stages for recuperation before returning home. Statistics show that one-quarter of those age sixty-five and older will spend some time in a nursing home. According to the *Statistical Handbook on Aging America*, 36 percent of nursing home admissions are discharged in under one year, most of those in less than three months; 15 percent stay three to five years, and 16 percent will remain for five or more years.

If you are concerned about needing nursing home care at some point you can insure for that possibility, as the cost averages $2,000 per month. In mid-1989 there were more than 70 companies offering long term care insurance policies, 29 of these meeting all criteria for acceptance by the National Association of Insurance Commissioners. Possible coverage varies widely, funding as little as $30 to $40 per day, to $100 per day or more. Limits vary, too, from coverage as short at one year to as much as a lifetime benefit. Some policies have inflation protection, with benefit levels increased at the nationally-recognized inflation rate each year. The costs for these policies also vary widely, therefore, depending on coverage and limits, and the date when first insured. A policy purchased at age fifty or fifty-five will have an annual premium far less than that for someone buying the coverage at age sixty, sixty-five, or seventy.

If you have concern about long term care, you'd best insure for it, as the federal and state government programs either do not cover this type of hospitalization, or have severe restrictions in how you may secure such funding.

73

There are three levels of care available to residents of nursing homes throughout the United States.

- **Skilled Nursing:** Medically operated facilities where other than acute care services may be offered. You may need a skilled nursing facility for recuperation following hospitalization. This type of care comprises less than one percent of nursing home care, and some of it may be funded by Medicare. In order for the federal/state program, Medicaid, to fund your care, you must meet certain low income or poverty qualifications.

- **Intermediate Care** has some medical attention available where routine nursing and assistance services are provided. About 5 percent of long term care is in this level of service. There is no coverage whatsoever by Medicare for intermediate care, as of mid-1989. Funding by Medicaid is subject to the same poverty/low income qualifications, and it provides a payment rate far below the market rate for the same bed. Therefore, intermediate care facility operators will limit the number of Medicaid patients they will accept, if any.

- **Custodial Care** provides residential and supportive services for those who are unable to provide such for themselves, and this comprises more that 94 percent of long term care use and costs. There is no coverage by Medicare, and limited funding is by Medicaid for those who qualify by welfare standards.

Nursing home care can be an expensive proposition, from $20,000 to $35,000 per year, in addition to any medication, or costs for special treatment or services.

The possible need for nursing home care should be a consideration in your overall budgeting. You might create a cash reserve—although it's difficult to estimate how much, or how little you might need—or consider buying nursing home insurance to cover the possible eventuality. The earlier in years such insurance is purchased, the lower the premium level will be throughout the policy. If you have a health concern, insuring now might be a prudent step.

Because my column has received so many questions on the subject, I provide the briefing above. Nursing homes provide a needed service, but they are not a preferred residential assumption or choice for most mature adults. Please read Chapter Four again, to learn how you might use positive health care to avoid the possibility or predictability of nursing home care in the future.

Property Rich and Cash Poor?

Not everyone has a stash of cash to use for unanticipated or major expenses. Even businesses with massive property and inventory assets have to run to the bank to borrow when they have cash needs. Your situation might be similar, with a major asset in your home but little in cash to meet your timely needs.

Although we deal with your overall financial plan in Chapter Seven, it is pertinent here to consider the asset you have in your home—even if you want to continue living in it. You might be "property rich and cash poor." That is a common state of affairs, and nothing to be ashamed of; it is just a fact that you can deal with.

There are ways to have cash from your house and live in it, too. Try these:

Sale/Leaseback: How about selling your home to investors and then leasing it back—for a few years, until you want to move, or for the rest of your life? This is a viable way to turn the property into cash that can be handled by a commercial real estate broker or real estate investment firm.

The buyer either establishes a new mortgage through a financial institution or directly with you. If a new mortgage, your bank account or other financial instrument receives the funds from the sale and you agree to lease the property back for a period of time or for life. The interest on the money, less the lease payment, should still provide positive cash for you every month, augmenting your other retirement income sources. In a contract directly with you, the buyer would make a downpayment to you, and then make monthly payments large enough so that you have surplus cash over and above the amount of the agreed lease. In both cases, your principal should be sound and untouched, with the interest earnings large enough to provide you with a good monthly cash flow.

In either concept you will need the services of the best real estate attorney and accountant you can find as counsel. But the concept is viable for many people, when it is properly contracted.

Does the concept work? The former baby-sitter for our family was a lovely lady in her mid-70s who had a very limited Social Security benefit and a tiny pension from her late husband's employer. In order to keep life and limb together she worked forty to sixty hours each week as a baby-sitter. She was very good at it but talked at long length about her intense desire to travel. When we operated a travel club, she was one of our first and very best tour escorts—but she had to decline most assignments, because she needed to earn her living.

She owned a cottage she and her husband had bought in the 1930s for a few thousand dollars, and its value had increased to more than $160,000. We spent long hours talking about the sale and leaseback concept, and she went to mutual friends in the real estate business. An investment group was found, which bought the house at the market price, paid her a down payment and then funded regular monthly payments to her. In under two years she exercised the option that she would move out and they could resell the property. And she moved to a luxury apartment complex.

From the time of the sale/leaseback she traveled, sometimes as a tour escort; many times she just funded the trip to travel as a passenger.

She was no longer cash poor and property rich. Her interest earnings paid for most of her travel. The last time I saw her she gave a big smile when I asked if she was going to visit us later in the day. "Can't," she responded. "I am off on a short trip this noon because I feel the urge to do so; and then Monday I am off to Hawaii for two weeks."

Gladys Thayer visited my family after some of those trips and regaled us with stories of her adventures all over the world. She had worked for more than sixty years, and she was finally experiencing her dreams. When she died, almost eighty, her estate was well funded and met every distribution she directed in her will.

One Alert: There is one specific caution, and it comes from Ken Eikenberry, Washington State Attorney General. Beware of some scam artists who approach you about selling your home, asking you first to sign a note allowing them to gain financing for repairs to the property before it can be bought or sold on your behalf. Eikenberry's staff has investigated the scam and prosecuted some perpetrators because the "simple note" actually subordinates the owner's interest to that of the con man. The charlatan then uses the note to secure a "home improvement" loan on a first or second trust deed, and then disappears with the cash. The victims find themselves with creditor claims on their property, which can ultimately lead to its loss.

Know with whom you are dealing; have the best legal and accounting counsel possible; and have it all checked by your banker.

Reverse Annuity Mortgages represent a concept that is gaining more acceptance around the nation. The program involves a mortgage that provides a payment each month to the mature adult. The process continues for life or until a move by the mature adult, at which time the house is sold to repay the mortgage balance. Excess income may be directed to the home owners or their heirs. Of course, the longer the monthly payments continue, the less equity the mature adult resident-owner would retain.

The major concern in this type of financing is that the mortgages are often established at a discounted rate, and the new mortgage holder— investor group, financial institution, or government agency—recovers its costs at the full value of the mortgage, plus any appreciation and all interest charges. As this form of financing becomes more popular, perhaps the discount rates will become smaller and payments to the mature adult seller larger because of competition.

The Alternative is to market the home at the highest price possible, buying or renting a smaller, less expensive residence. The net gain, if invested well, will provide added income from the interest earnings alone.

If you are property rich and cash poor, discuss these possibilities with a competent real estate attorney and an accountant. They should be of counsel, both in constructing the right approach for you and in making sure the contract, buyers, and payments meet your need.

Where Will You Live in Retirement?

We started this chapter with that question. Now it is time to bring the subject of housing to focus, for answers, for identifying your own desires and direction. You should have started some chart-making.

Now, consider the following "resolution" chart, where you may synthesize your thinking into the formulation of a new direction for your life:

- -

RESIDENTIAL DECISION CHART OF:

Name(s) _____

Date: _____ 19 _____

As part of our mature lifestyle plan we will:

Present Residence: Retain or Sell, and When

If sold, what will be net income? And how applied/invested?

Move: Elsewhere locally; or to _____

Desired type of new residence:

Areas/types that I/we will explore:

If home retained, detail the changes, upgrades, other:

My/our real ideals for our residence in mature living is: (write this out simply, and to the point, so that you can actually "see" it happening.)

Here is what added information, research or counsel I/we need in order to effect the desired program/plan:

I/We will start this program/change on the following date:

My/our other ideas, hopes and plans include:

Signed:_____ Date _____

— —

WHAT WILL BE YOUR CAREER?

As children we were asked: "What are you going to be when you grow up?" Few of us became firemen or doctors, nurses or baseball stars, as we seemed to idealize then. In fact, our career paths were developed later, with many resolved by chance, some by need or opportunity, and only a small percentage by reasoned direction and plan.

There were wars and recessions, families to house, feed, and raise, job shortages, and many other problems to solve. Each of these situations gave us the opportunity to gain strength in facing facts and doing what had to be done. For many of us, the challenges limited our options—as to what career path we would or could take.

We were taught to hold onto jobs for security. To this, the companies, organizations, and governments for which we worked added inducements for us to stay on the job: health and life insurance, pensions, profit-sharing, salary reviews, added vacation time for longevity, and other perks of seniority. But the style of many businesses has changed, with mergers and mega-mergers, restructuring and redirection. As a result, many of the incentives to stay have been reversed, into inducements for mature employees to leave jobs early, even in their early fifties.

Technology has forced some changes, in many cases eliminating jobs. In addition, the nature of North American business is shifting from industrial production to service and high-tech operation. Small businesses have grown in number and unions have become smaller, changing the employer-employee relationship. Imported products have replaced those made domestically in many homes and offices. Many of today's jobs and businesses did not exist twenty years ago. From the financial markets on Wall Street to the retail stores on Main Street, there is everywhere evidence that the much-heralded Global Economy has finally arrived.

Today's workers—including professionals and laborers, entrepreneurs and technicians—are affected by these transitions, either as victims of corporate or government decisions or as opportunists who see a chance to make their lives better. Change is the order of the day.

Buggy whip makers of the past made transitions to new fields, or went out of business. Career military people have made and are making transitions to the private sector, some earlier than expected. Family farms have gone under while other agribusiness has soared. Mines petered out and miners either moved to new lodes or forged new trades or careers. Bookkeepers who worked with calculators, pens, and pencils have made transitions to computers, mainframes, modems, disks, and printouts.

A law of physics states that anything not going forward actually goes backward. Change is all around us. For better or worse, change is a fact of life for each of us.

Moving from an established, probably comfortable life to a position of uncertainty has never been easy. Even thinking about change can be scary. But whether you elect to continue doing as you are now, or opt for a different path, there will be changes ahead. How we prepare for those changes is the stuff of this book. We explain the points to consider . . . you remain in control of your life. Change can be channeled as you determine and desire it.

As you look forward in mature years, do you want to be doing the same thing as today? Or do you want to leave the work to others when it comes time to "retire?" Do you want to change directions now or later?

The Future in Time

In thirty years there are 10,957 days. More than 10,000 mornings to wake up in bright anticipation of fulfillment for that day. If you haven't awakened the past 10,000 days with such anticipation, do you want to have just more of the same in your future?

At the turn of the century, 10,000 days was a lifetime for many people. Today you may anticipate the span to be only about one third of your lifetime, if you keep yourself healthy, active, and productive.

Ken Dychtwald, Ph.D., consultant and author of *Age Wave*, predicts that future life spans for most people will involve several phases of working and resting—sabbaticals, if you will, of one, two, or more years. In such lives, there will be time for raising children and taking extended holidays, career changing, and revitalization.

But the life spans we are talking about are right now, not decades or generations in the future. We are talking about now for you and me, as we count fifty, fifty-five, sixty or sixty-five birthdays.

Is it time to consider a new life span of thirty—or even, twenty—years, with a new career direction?

I want to tell you a personal experience. In my early career as a writer, producer and director in radio and television, I was the happiest, most satisfied professional anywhere. But then my own ambitions for managerial status and income got in the way. I became an executive, working for a series of companies, campaigns, and organizations that proved to be quite successful. From there I sought independence, launching my own ventures and forging new concepts in publishing and broadcasting, campaigns and politics. Again, I was fortunate enough to meet with success, but there was also a significant problem. Instead of working and producing and creating, I was, instead, managing people, balancing budgets, manipulating contracts, wrangling with lawyers, negotiating with vendors, paying bills and collecting money. Because running businesses is not what I do best, my days stretched from four in the morning to late at night, in order for me to accomplish what others more talented could do in less time. Business and the creative side of journalism were on a collision course, and one suffered when my attentions were turned to the other. In trying to do both, I was always behind the power curve, working ever longer to "come over the top."

Dr. Laurence J. Peter and Raymond Hull, in their remarkable book, *The Peter Principle*, stated that "everyone rises to his or her own level of incompetence." And they were right in my case.

Finally, at age fifty-four, I said: "This is insanity." So, even though I was partner in several successful ventures, I fired myself. Canned. Shut off the paychecks. Stepped out of those duties that gave me stress, strain and nightmares, and handed the reins to others, professionals whose life desires, experience and abilities were in the field of business management. The ventures are now running much better, and my own career redirection as a writer, speaker and consultant is vibrant and flourishing. I am fifty pounds lighter and exercise actively; blood pressure is down to 120 over 76; blood cholesterol level is nicely below 200. Somehow the "press of time" never allowed such dedication earlier. I even have time to cook breakfast for the family each morning.

By trying to do the things that I did not do best and did not enjoy, I robbed myself and my family of a lot of time and happiness. Perhaps my ego would not allow me, earlier, to admit that I was in the wrong job. I cannot go back and change history, and I wouldn't want to! But I know that I am happy with these changes to a new direction, a new career for now and the next thirty years.

Each of us faces the time and opportunity of transition. Will we choose the direction for ourselves, or will we blow in the wind to the direction of others? As we look at what we really want for our next twenty or thirty years, do we continue in the same direction or set off to new goals and satisfaction? Author Joe Karbo said: "Most people work too hard to make a living and never have time to make any money."

In my own case I have been working in the fields of writing, speaking and consulting for years, but was always frustrated in being unable to launch them as my full-time career. I was holding on too tightly to the problems of what I didn't like to do, feeling a responsibility to do them, pouring all the more effort in trying to get to the top of the mountain, so that I could finally make the shift to what I really wanted to do, to what I really could do best.

I finally listened to what I had been writing and lecturing to others: "Let go and take the new direction." When you step over a threshold to put something behind you, you also open a door to a new direction. When you close that door of yesterday the new opportunity is yours.

As noted elsewhere in this book, surveys indicate that the majority of people are unhappy in their jobs or careers, so it is very possible that you are not satisfied with what you are doing or have been doing. Perhaps your career direction has been one demanded by necessity, economic times, or other. The circumstances that were don't even matter now. What you do about your own direction does and will matter.

The choice of path is yours.

Here Are Questions to Answer

Imagine this typical scene. You're at a social event where you hear two questions being asked whenever people meet:

"What is your name?"

"What do you do?"

These are two critical questions we have to answer every time we meet someone. Your name. And, what is it that you do?

Close your eyes for a moment and create that scene as if it were ten years ago. You're standing in front of a stranger. Answer the questions: "What is your name?" and "What do you do?" Did you feel a tinge, wanting to say something like: "I paint houses—but if times hadn't been so tight I really wanted to be an astronomer (or pilot, politician, lawyer, artist or other)." Or, "I'm a supermarket manager—but I really wanted to be a representative for a major food manufacturer."

Create in mind other social situations, also eight or ten years ago, and answer the questions three or four more times. How do you feel about your answers? Is there any anxiety in your answers, or is there a pride and fulfillment swelling with each response?

Then create in mind new social scenes today. With your eyes closed, imagine new people you meet—asking the same questions of you:

"What is your name?"

And, "What do you do?"

How do you feel about your answers?

Now, open your eyes and write down what you feel about your answers to "What do you do?" Are you satisfied with them? Is there an "I would like

82

to . . . " explanation attached to your answer?

This little exercise in self-evaluation is not presented to incite you to switch careers—far from it. Instead, it is important to think about this now, to assure yourself that you are getting what you want and expect from your career or job. And it is important, at this time, to consider what you want to "be" and what you want to "do" in the next 4,000, 8,000 or 11,000 days.

If you want to launch a new career, there are many important questions to answer: how can I gain what I need from my present career and income? What training or education do I need to make the most of my new career or direction? What period of time will I dedicate to the testing, planning, and training necessary to effect that new career direction? When will I make the change?

In Chapter Two you met Woodie Hall, who retired from the military and then planned retirement again after a career as a salesman and sales manager. He never failed to ask himself the key question—"What do I really want to do?"—throughout his careers. For five years he devoted all his spare time to getting ready for his transition to a career as a full-time inventor. He created a den/workshop and put his mind to work, "feeling" his satisfaction while creating. It is significant to note that, even though he was an experienced salesman, he chose to have others do the actual marketing of his creations. The results: today there are more than 150 of his curious, humorous, silly, cute, and imaginative inventions being marketed. He is busier and happier than ever before.

What do you want to be in your next ten, twenty or thirty years? You have an inventory of twenty-four hour days. What you do with them is up to you.

The Path to a Career Change

Changing a career takes some planning to research the field, to refine your direction, to gain any necessary training, to build your transition program and path, to create your resume of experience and credentials, and then to make it happen. This transition period may be as short as one week or as long as five years, depending on what you want to do and how you choose to do it.

• How do you feel about your present position or situation? Is it a nagging problem, one with income limitations, or one you don't enjoy, that doesn't yield satisfaction and rewards?

• What are your vested interests in your job? Are there financial or other reasons you must remain for another six months or two years? If longer, is the ultimate reward worth the wait? How predictable is the reward—such as a pension or other incentive?

• How stable is your present employer or employment? If there is a takeover or restructuring of the company, will you be vulnerable? If so, you need to start planning for your own best interest and protection.

Here are thoughts to consider and recommendations that may work for you in an action plan—even if your ultimate resolution is to make no career change at all.

Timing for Your Consideration

It is never too early to evaluate your career path. I recommend that adults, at all ages, ask themselves the question, seriously, four times each year: "What am I going to be when I grow up?" Put it on your calendar or date book for the first Saturday morning of January, April, July, and October. If your answer supports what you are doing now, you may be elated. If the answer is otherwise, you should ask yourself follow-up questions: Why do I feel impelled to do something else? What do I need to change in my present position in order to feel better about it? What are my specific frustrations or drives relative to wanting to do something different? Your answers should be candid and not be couched in concern for security, protected against uncertainty, or held back for fear of honest expression.

On the other hand, if you determine to remain where you are, are there any changes needed to make your career more satisfying or acceptable? What is your timing for resolving or correcting those concerns? If the problems prove persistent, what are your other options?

Make notes so that you capture your real thoughts at the very time you answer the questions. Read those notes again a day and a week later. Then draw your conclusion—either that you really do like what you are doing, or you will identify the need for a change. If the latter, make notes on how your present situation impacts or affects your life. That process alone knocked me for a loop, but then became the threshold point for my own decision. Scary? You bet! Impossible? No way! . . . unless you aspire to something for which you are totally unfit or untrained.

Are There Jobs and New Careers for Mature Adults?

Yes, there are.

The age-old assumption of debility and inability in mature adults is a sham in its presumption.

Your professional relocation, when shifting from a present employer or to a new career, may take longer than it does for a younger person. There are more jobs at the lower levels, for the younger workers, than there are for more experienced people.

Your job quest might take four months or as long as one year. Your success will be based on your realistic determination of your desired field or career change, and how well you identify your potential target employers or business potential.

About Timing

If your employer makes an announcement tomorrow morning that the company has been sold and 20 percent of the staff will be cut under the new ownership, you don't have the luxury of time. That is, unless you were already considering, and planning for, that possibility.

Start thinking now about what you would do in the event of an "unthinkable" cutback or change possible in the future. This preparation will remove the worry and reduce the personal and professional trauma when and if a change does happen. You will already be in charge of your direction, and not the hapless victim of someone else's decision.

Start your thinking and planning now if your "what do you do" and "what do you want to do" answers identify the need or desire for a change.

When will you be ready for a change? How long will your research take on the job prospects and career change? How long will any training or retraining take? How long will it take to identify and set aside the financial resources to handle the change? (If the decision is made by others, you won't have much time at all, so it is best to be ready now or soon.)

Set a target date on the calendar, and schedule—on a back-timed basis—the time necessary to effect that change. Some of these steps may be accomplished simultaneously—training is possible at the same time as field research and funding set-aside. Set a mind image of your accomplished transition on or before that date, and write down your impressions on a three-by-five card so you may carry the thoughts with you. Reread the statement four to six times each day, starting now—so your plan and goal will be ever in mind and working positively.

Your timing path might be accomplished in one month, one year, or as many as five years. It all depends on your own need, direction, tolerance, and patience in defining and achieving the program.

Your Financial Underpinning

If you are considering a change of job or a more comprehensive change in career direction plan for a six-month transition period. You may have to be out of work, so it's a good idea to set aside funds now so that you will be able to pay your bills and expenses when the time comes for a change. Thus, you allow yourself some independence in waiting for the right position, instead of having to take "a job" in order to pay the light bill.

Calculate in that set-aside, too, any added travel costs or other expenses involved in the quest for professional relocation. You may reduce your expected costs if you eliminate daily commuting or other current costs of getting to or holding onto your job. Plan, though, that you will be going to see people, and not just at home, waiting for the telephone to ring.

If you don't have someone at home, readily available to answer the phone when you're out, buy an answering machine to do the job. Get one that has a remote ability where you may phone the machine while away from home. I, for one, find the machines irritating, but it is better to have one than to miss callbacks.

Your funding should provide for quality resume production and copies of any endorsement letters or samples. Buy, too, quality envelopes and writing paper for sending queries and followup letters. Consider having a batch of letterhead envelopes and paper printed (paper that matches that of your resume). Your impression will be much better as your presentation comes in the door to prospective mentors or employers.

Do up a budget sheet to provide for the above and arrange to set the funds aside specifically for this purpose. Track your actual expenses and payments on the ledger so that you know where you are at all times. This practice is supportive psychologically to your effort while allowing the freedom of choice for you.

Launching Your Program

Let's say you have made your decision to change positions or to launch a new career. Where do you start?

Your decision results in a plan, written in chapters. Start with the assumption that you have already made the successful transition, and then think backward to discover how you got there. That might sound silly or impossible at first, but it works!

Assuming the new position or career, following are some of the methods you probably used in getting there.

A Resume and Materials

You will want and need a resume showing your qualifications for the position you seek. There are suggestions and examples in Chapter Eight.

Prepare the resume in a quality way. Use an electric typewriter or word processor, eliminating any errors and strike-overs. Use upper and lower case, as this book type is prepared—not all capital letters.

Print the resume on good paper stock (a twenty or twenty-four pound rag, linen or laid finish) in a tinted color (such as light grey, tan, or off-white). Secure some business size (number ten) envelopes and extra blank sheets of the same stock.

If you have supporting information, such as two or three letters commending you and the quality of your work, have these printed or photocopied onto white paper. Send them along with the resume, or present them at the interview. Make copies of any documents that are vital to establish your credibility—licenses, certifications, etc. Never present originals, and never ask an interviewer to copy them for you.

Carry at least six to ten extra resume copies with you at all times—for special opportunities to present them. Why? We'll give you the reasons as we go forward in this chapter.

Finding Mentors

The best people to tell you about your desired field are the people at the top of that business or profession. When we ask them questions they are able to provide truthful and effective answers, and they may make recommendations about possible openings, and possibly assist you in making contacts.

Few top professionals will turn you down when you make a request in this manner:

(Name), you are one of the best and most recognized professionals in my desired professional field. I am anxious to put my career (new career) on the right track and to do it I ask for just fifteen minutes of your time— at a date and time convenient to you—where I may introduce myself and ask a few questions. Will you grant that counsel to me?

Most responses will lead to an appointment. You will send your resume in advance, with a cover letter that thanks him/her for the first responsiveness, presents the resume, and confirms the appointment date and time. Of course, you will close the letter with a thank you for this special opportunity.

On the day prior to the interview, phone to confirm the agreed time. And, on the day of the interview, arrive ten minutes ahead of the appointment, prepared to meet early or later.

In the interview, you will:

• establish that the person has received the letter and resume package, asking if he/she has any questions based on it.

• ask for comments on which of your identified abilities and experience "fit" best in the position you are seeking.

- ask for recommendations of any added training or experience you should attain as part of your professional relocation program.

- ask for any recommendations on where you should start your quest for the right position—and then ask for the best way of contacting each of the people or firms recommended.

If the interviewer makes specific recommendations, it is because you have built a human bridge and he or she will help you open some doors. It is possible that the interviewer will pick up the telephone to establish an introduction for you. When that happens, you have a "mentor" . . . someone who really knows the field, is respected in it, and who might lend some of that credibility to you as you talk to others.

Before you enter the interview, have your questions written down, with lots of room on the paper between them for notes that you will make. Think through the questions in advance, even rehearse them to sound natural, so that you are able to accomplish the entire meeting in the requested fifteen minutes. Plan, though, to allow for a longer period of time if it is offered.

If the interviewer offers to introduce you to others, you will have resumes on hand for presentation.

Arranging this interview is possible through a secretary, adjusting the opening call and request accordingly. If the secretary or assistant has helped in arranging the interview, make sure to say "thanks" as you leave the office.

Most professionals in business remember the times in their lives when they, too, were out of work or seeking change—how hard it was when no one helped; and how much better and supportive it was when people did assist. So, most often, even the busiest of executives or professionals will take time to be of help, if the approach and request makes sense.

Note that you have not asked a mentor for a job. If that person has a job open, he or she will mention it in the interview. Your mission is to reach, in person, the top professionals in your chosen field. Do not start only with personnel managers; they receive job descriptions and fill them by order. It is the head of the company who knows where the jobs will be.

Do you need one mentor or three, five or ten? It depends on how you build your program. The more top people who know of your ability, the more referrals they can make for you. Most of the best positions are never advertised in the classified section of the newspaper. The best way to have an insider advantage is to have a mentor "inside."

Letters and More

Your successful campaign is not built by flooding the mail with resumes, with the expectation that the recipients will phone you if they have something that might fit in with your experience and desires.

Your letters and resumes, instead, should be targeted to the person of highest authority in the company, facility, or department, and should be personalized. Advance phone calls will provide this information, including the correct spelling and title, and the best telephone number for your telephone call follow-through.

Phone to secure the interview. And send a thank you letter following that interview, even if that interviewer offers little.

Your letter will present your candidacy, refer to the resume, and ask for an interview at the earliest convenience.

When you look good on paper—from letter to resume and support materials—you will be ahead of most people looking for positions. And when you look back from your achievement of having made the best professional move, you'll find an important factor was how good you looked on paper.

Training for the Right Spot

What kind of training do you need? Is it in your specialized field? Or, are you in middle management where a move to top management would be possible if you knew more accounting, personnel relations, public relations, business law or computer applications and management? When you look at where you want to be, each of the educational or training needs may be identified, with assist from your mentors and from your own experience and evaluation, too.

If you need training for your professional move, plan for it now. For that training, consider:

• Specialized schools and programs. There may be retraining funds available through your state department of employment.

• Colleges and universities, where there may be specialized classes or workshops in the specific subjects or areas you need.

• Adult or trade schools operated by your local school district. Many of these offer cost-free programs for mature adults, and cooperate in retaining programs endorsed by federal or state agencies.

• Your local Area Agency on Aging, for information on retraining programs available from federal and state agencies and programs.

Professional reference books are available as are subscriptions to magazines and journals in the field. Learn about these published sources from your mentors and your librarian. Reading will give you a better knowledge base in the field, provide indications of trends, and may even have professional job leads and listings. Two hours each evening with these valuable sources is far more beneficial than watching television reruns.

But What If You Don't Want a Job?

What do you do if you are not looking to be hired somewhere, but instead want to establish your own practice or business? You do everything recommended above. Seek out mentors, but just not someone who would be an eventual competitor. Your resume is also necessary.

That process takes the very same planning steps, but adds necessary factors of selling the clients needed for income, performing the service predictably, and operating profitably.

Your Partner in This Decision

If married, you have an important partner in this decision, as it must be resolved jointly. The reason I recommend individual entries onto the charts and tablets is to draw out what you personally feel and desire. It is then that the thoughts and notes may be shared.

Too often we don't compare thoughts in any organized or disciplined way. It's like having a pet peeve and never telling the person who is causing it so that he or she can make adjustments.

You might find that you're really blissful about the past 10,000 days, and expect more of the same in the future. Or, just as productively, you might find reason to question and change for the better.

About Your Career Change

Take some deep breaths and answer this question:

"Would you be better personally, in health, with your family, professionally, financially and/or in prospects if you were to change your job or career?"

Refer to your notes from the earlier sections of this chapter. When you let your hair down, what are you telling yourself? Do you want your next 10,000 days to be like the 10,000 just passed? Do you want, instead, just to plan your retirement from working or business? And, if so, what will you do with your inventory of 24-hour days in your coming life span?

Are you on the right track? Or should you be on another? We have presented much grist for the mill of consideration, and have posed many questions as sparkplugs to fire up the engine of decision.

It is your life and your decision. What is best for you for the very best of days and years to come?

A Decision Chart

Here's a chart to focus your thoughts and decisions regarding your career path forward.

— —

CAREER DECISION CHART OF:

Name: _____

I have evaluated my past and present career. Here are my most important, capsule comments on it:

In Answer to "What Do You Do?" I can answer today:
Position   But wish I was/or/would like to be more right

I, therefore, want to: ___ change jobs to: _____

                            ___ change careers to: _____

                            ___ stay where I am: _____

                            ___ stay, with following changes: _____

                            _____

The timing for my action will be: (Date)_____

My action plan will involve: (write in details)

        ___ Career/Job Description:

        ___ Mentor Development/Follow through:

        ___ Financial Set-Aside Budget/Plan:

        ___ Materials/Resume:

        ___ Training/Define/Accomplish:

        ___ Financial Goal Forward:

___ Targeting of Prospects/Program:

___ Endorsement/Participation by Spouse:

___ Program Resolution:

___ (other)

___ (other)

___ Accomplishment/Celebration Event

I presently make/bank: $ _____ per year

In one year I will make/bank: $ _____ per year

In five years I will make/bank: $ _____ per year

In my direction forward I want to rid myself of the following things/people/events/conditions that I do not like:

In my direction forward I want more of what I do like, including:

I/we agree with the statements above, and set this as my/our plan forward:

Signed: _____ **Date:** _____

Signed: _____ **Date:** _____

— —

YOUR PERSONAL FINANCIAL PLAN

Y̶ou can retire whenever you can fund your life and lifestyle for all your coming years. How much money you'll need will be determined by your individual life expectations and lifestyle choice, weighed against your assets and income planning. In this chapter we present practical financial concepts for retirement, as a basis for assessing your own ability and determining your own plan.

Your retirement income will probably come from several sources—the average retiree has three to five sources. It may be a combination of Social Security, pension, Individual Retirement or Keogh Accounts, savings, investments, and earned income. Ideally, your retirement income sources will provide the necessary cashflow on a predictable and continuous basis, contain inflation protection, and yet not diminish the value of assets providing the regular income. Accomplish this by plan and you may live to any age, knowing that your retirement income will always be available.

Here is the simple formula:

External income + income from assets + other planned income + inflation hedge = annual/monthly income.

When the three income factors produce an annual or monthly income level equal to or more than your retirement living needs, you can afford to retire.

Here are the details for your consideration and charting.

Annual/Monthly Expenses to be Funded

Make a list of your expected monthly expenses necessary for your lifestyle in retirement. Include housing and its pertinent costs, food and entertaining, automotive expenses, clothing, health and health insurance, personal care costs, hobbies, travel and recreation, taxes, and other. Use budget figures based on today's dollars and costs, as our planning chart adds an inflation factor for each year forward.

Your actual retirement expenses will probably be 15 to 25 percent less than your working years budget needs—the national average is 20 percent less. Your budget will reflect your desired retirement lifestyle, a shift in financing health care, increased expenditures for special interests, and reduced expenses for business related needs. Project your costs monthly and annually for at least 10 years.

To calculate your expected costs of living in retirement, consider:

Your Home: If renting or planning to rent, enter this monthly cost and then detail the costs of tenants and homeowners insurance, utilities, furniture and other expenses. In projecting for 5 and 10 years in the future, you may elect to sell your own home and rent, and your future budgeting should anticipate this shift.

If you own your home and intend to continue living in it, include the cost of your mortgage payment (if any). In addition, allocate funds on a regular basis for repairs and maintenance. If you do not take good care of your property, it will deteriorate over time, and you will be left with an asset of diminishing value.

Food and Entertainment: Estimate your costs for food and beverage at home and away. Include in this figure household supplies, personal care products and other items purchased in the supermarket—this makes it easy to check your actual expenses against the budget. Allow some leeway for increased social times and entertaining.

Automotive: Budget for your car or cars, including any purchase payments, insurance, service, fuel and allied costs. You may not need all the vehicles you have; or you may want to substitute a motor home for one of the cars. Allow for increased personal travel, while in all probability you will reduce or remove business or work usage.

Clothing: You'll want to look good for your retirement activity, so allow for clothing purchases at some monthly average. People with positive self-images take pride in their appearance. Looking good is part of feeling good. By shopping sales and off-season close-outs, you can dress well on an affordable budget.

Health and Health Insurance: Plan for both health care costs and for the purchase of health insurance. At age sixty-five you'll probably qualify for Medicare, but the program only covers about 38 percent of actual medical costs. There will be need for either a Medicare Supplement policy or an overall HMO or health insurance program to replace Medicare. It is possible—or even probable—that there will be reasons to opt out of Medicare in future years, if you have the ability to fund an overall and more beneficial program. A Medigap insurance policy will cost $400 to $800 per person per year, based on 1989/1990 estimates. A replacement health care policy would run $1,800 to $2,400 per person, based on the same estimates.

Long term care is a concern of many people considering retirement. We report elsewhere in this book that most mature adults will never use long term—nursing home—care, but if needed, present day costs average $2,000 per person per month. Medicare does not cover 99.5 percent of long term care—at the intermediate and custodial levels. Government funding through Medicaid (MediCal in California) is available only for those qualifying at poverty levels. Though the subject has been much discussed in Congress and the national media, do not anticipate any major government funding for possible long term care needs. In your budget planning, therefore, consider the purchase of long term care insurance—averaging $800 to $1500 annually if you start at age 55; or as much as $5,000 to $6,000 per year if you wait until age 70 to purchase the coverage. If you don't purchase long term care insurance, you will then have to pay for nursing home care, if needed at all, from cash or asset reserves. In this area you will save significantly by keeping yourself active and healthy.

If there are health insurance provisions in your present retirement program, secure the participation cost for inclusion in your budget.

Hobbies/Activities/Recreation: Do budget a monthly allowance for hobbies and other planned activities you want in your retirement lifestyle. You will have time for bowling and tennis, movies and theatre, concerts and spectator sports—you name it—so give yourself a budget for such recreation. Increase this figure by half to allow for unplanned opportunities and added interests.

Travel: Unless you are planning reclusive living, anticipate that you will be traveling more for one- and three-day junkets, as well as longer trips, tours, and cruises. Anticipate travel budgeting at least one or two years in advance—as recommended in the chapter on travel—for the lowest prices for major trips. For this budget compile an annual figure, estimating both longer and shorter trips, and then divide that figure by 12 to get a monthly average.

Contributions and Gifts: Budget for contributions to charities, churches, community organizations or other interests, if you desire to do so. Planned gifts to others should also be included in this category.

Taxes: You will still need to pay income and other taxes on earnings and investment income. If you have taxable income of more than $25,000, at least one-half of your Social Security benefits will also be subject to income tax. Discuss your income planning with a professional accountant or independent financial planner, to explore the best ways of reducing your tax liability.

Inflation: This will be an added item at the end of the budget, where we may assume a 7 percent inflation factor, added to the total of all of the items. This figure may be projected now and then adjusted each year as the true inflation rate is known.

On this basis your expense budget may be projected by month and for the next five to ten years. Make adjustments for anticipated changes—such as a planned move to another city, sale of the home, a trip around the world, or other.

After you enter all of the figures, review and work with them until you believe they are practical and predictable. At that point you are ready for the next step—figuring out your income.

Your Retirement Income

You will need a variety of income sources in retirement. Social Security will be only one of them. An employee pension might be another, an Individual Retirement Plan (IRA) or Keogh Plan, yet another.

For the purposes of this budgeting program we'll define *external income* as that which comes to you on a predictable basis from another source— including Social Security, a pension, disability, or similar program. *Asset-based income* is earned income which comes from an asset-base you have created—including interest from savings and investments, IRA/Keogh, income-producing real estate, contracts and royalties, business, and similar. *Earned income* is that from continued working or professional services. And, the fourth category, *assets*, includes stocks, bonds, cash in the bank, real estate, or other property that you own. Ideally, once this asset base is created you can rely on it to produce income from interest or residuals without reducing the value of your estate. At some point you may have to sell assets, if your budget is not maintained or your expenses escalate significantly, such as for extraordinary health costs or other emergency need.

The combination of *external income*, *asset-based income*, and *earned income* should be at least equal to your retirement expense budget. The actual income from each area may vary by year as you project your budget into the coming years.

External Income

Through your working or business years you have earned at least part of your retirement income. Here is how and why:

Social Security: You have probably paid into the Social Security system throughout your working years, and should qualify for benefits if you have earned at least a very minimum income level in covered employment for a specified number of quarters. (Certain types of employees—mostly workers for governments and non-profit organizations—have been exempt from Social Security coverage; they have been covered by separate pension funds, such as The Railroad Retirement Board.) In 1990 you'll earn four quarters of qualification if you earn at least $2,000 through work covered by the Social Security program. In earlier years the earned income qualification level was as low as $50 in covered income per three-month quarter. To qualify for Social Security benefits at age 62 you would need recognition for at least 38 quarters by 1990, or 40 quarters if qualifying in 1991 or later years.

Benefit levels are calculated on the basis of your earnings, with an average replacement level of 42 percent—the actual benefit payment as a percentage of recent and qualifying earnings. Replacement levels actually range from 60 percent for a worker who has earned minimum wages, to 26 percent for someone earning at the maximum level. Therefore, your benefit level may range from a low of a few hundred dollars to as much as $1,200 per month (the latter for a retired worker and spouse, with 1987 covered earnings of $35,000 or more). In 1989, the average monthly cash benefit paid to a retired worker at age sixty-five or older was $546 per month.

Social Security will alternatively pay survivors benefits, or combine survivors benefits with the survivor's own Social Security benefits if a spouse should die. You may receive a statement illustrating these possible benefits, also, from the Social Security Administration.

Obtain a current analysis of your earnings and projected benefits, by requesting form SSA-7004 from the Consumer Information Center, Department 55/SSA, Pueblo, Colorado 81009. Or, phone toll-free to 1-800-937-2000 to request the form. The service is cost-free, and if you're age fifty or older I recommend you request the form and an update every two or three years. It is a sure way to know that Social Security has credited your past earnings—and if not, you may challenge them now, rather than when applying for benefits.

You may receive your full Social Security benefits at age 65; or you may apply at age 62 and receive approximately 80 percent of your full benefit level; at age 70 you receive approximately 120 percent of your full benefit. Social Security benefits are also indexed to inflation and are increased annually. Most recent increases have been 4 to 4.2 percent. If you retire before you qualify for Social Security, you will need to have other replacement income for budgeting purposes.

Under present federal law your Social Security benefits will be penalized if you continue to work between ages 65 and 70, losing $1 for each $3 earned over approximately $9,000 annually. Income from investments or pension funds is not counted as earned and is not subject to the penalty. You may anticipate some beneficial changes in this penalty situation by the time you reach the qualifying ages, if you are presently in your fifties. At age seventy and older there is no earnings penalty levied on Social Security payments.

Social Security benefits are considered secure for present recipients and those to start receiving benefits before the year 2010. Present government fiscal policy does present potential problems for new applicants after the year 2020. If you are age fifty or better, I advise you to be concerned about Congressional and Administration action on Social Security. Read everything you can on the subject, so you are able to act for your own protection.

Social Security was created as a supplement to retirement—and that is what the program represents today—as only one of your several retirement income sources.

Pension: If you have a pension plan, request a statement of anticipated benefit level at the time you will retire. If already retired, you have this figure and can enter the benefit level into your income budget. Ask if the rate is indexed to inflation and if there are any qualification ages. Learn, too, if there is any jeopardy to your pension benefits in the event of a corporate failure or merger. Most pension programs are backed by the federal Pension Benefit Guaranty Corporation, but assure yourself that these funds will be predictable for your retirement income program. Government and military pension levels should be checked also, if you qualify, for planning purposes.

Disability: Your disability benefits through Social Security may also be checked on that same SSA-7004 form filing. If you have a qualifying disability you may file at any age, and then switch to the higher Social Security benefits at 62 or 65. You may have additional disability benefits available through your employer and/or your personal insurance coverage. This is important information to have in the event of an illness or accident prior to qualifying for Social Security retirement benefits. Disability benefits from the Veterans Administration may also be continued into retirement years, and should be budgeted in the income chart.

Other external income: List any programmed inheritance or fee income.

Asset-based Income

Starting with the assumption that you will have some assets that can or should produce earnings income, we next budget these as a separate category. For the purposes of this section do not consider the value of your assets, unless you intend to sell them to produce usable cash from the principal.

Savings: Your bank accounts should produce earnings income to be scheduled into your budget—for, ideally, you should draw the interest without touching the principal. You will need some of your savings in accounts where you may access cash for any immediate need; but know that your traditional passbook accounts at the bank or savings and loan earn interest at a rate lower to far lower than that of inflation. The more you save in this type of account, the less you'll be able to cope with any inflation in costs. Re-examine your present savings and move all possible funds to higher earning—but safe and secure—investments or instruments. Moving $100,000 from a savings account earning 5 percent to a CD or other insured investment instrument yielding 8 percent will add $3,000 to your annual income.

Investments: For the most predictable income in retirement, your investments should be planned conservatively and for quality. This is not the time to take a flyer on gold mine stock or lotteries for options on oil well discoveries. Professional counsel can recommend your best direction in stocks and bonds, mutual funds, money market funds, and certificates of deposit. Some of these investments may be held in instruments convertible to cash easily in need or emergency. Subscribe to and read fine magazines and newsletters such as *Money, The United Retirement Bulletin,* and *The Retirement Letter.*

As a mature adult you'll be the target of every telemarketing and get-rich-quick schemer—but you don't have to listen or consider them at all. When receiving telephone calls offering "sure ways to make big money," such as investing in coins, gold and other metals, gold mines, I recommend you to say "no" quickly and hang up the telephone. You are most likely the target of a fraudulent scheme.

IRA/Keogh: There are stipulations on when and how much you will be able to draw from these accounts. Know that you cannot draw from them early, without a significant penalty. Learn the details and restrictions so that you may program your withdrawals by plan for your retirement income program.

Income-producing Real Estate: One of the most recommended investment possibilities, and one which tends to provide income and appreciation at a pace at or above the rate of inflation, is rental real estate. There is a financial exposure if occupancy rates fall and the rents do not provide for the mortgage payments, maintenance, and insurance—and that must be weighed as part of your overall investment and earnings concern.

Contracts and Royalties: Property and business sales where you have predictable, periodic payments should also be scheduled as income at the specific times they are due or expected. any royalty income from ideas or copyrights, income from personal loans, or similar cash-flow should also be entered.

Other Income: Any other income that may be projected as receivable from asset-based sources should also be scheduled when pertinent.

Earned Income

If you want to work in your retirement years, detail this in your earned income schedule. Be realistic in defining your goal. Be explicit in expressing how you will earn this income—as an employee, in your own business, as a consultant or representative—and whether you will work full-time or part-time

Read the chapters on making money and saving money, and on careers in retirement, before projecting your earned income in retirement. If you can meet your budget, there is nothing wrong in not working at all. If you want to continue working for your own satisfaction as well as income, you may do just that. It's your decision.

Assets in Retirement

List everything you own that has a real value: your home, real estate, automobiles, furniture and appliances, jewelry, cameras, workshop and tools, collections, and other physical assets. On another chart, list all investments you own that can or may produce income. You will have listed all or most of these in the asset-based income section, but they are listed here because they have capital value.

Scan the first list to evaluate those that you really want to keep. You will probably find more than enough to sell off, just because you really don't want or need the items further. Proceeds may then be invested to produce added, predictable income. Retained assets may then be identified as having value to you. If you still owe on your home mortgage or other property purchase, the sale proceeds from other assets may be used to retire these obligations.

Consider your investments, evaluating them for safety, security, predictability, and rate of income return to you. In implementing your financial retirement program you will need know that you can count on the cash-flow from your investment programs and properties. Contract the services of a professional accountant to analyze your investment intentions and program, so that he or she may advise you about the rates of return, tax implications, and directions for your most effective financial planning.

Balancing Expenses and Income

You will probably be surprised about your financial ability in retirement, as you have many assets, sources, earnings, and benefits which will combine to make your desired lifestyle possible. There are worksheets presented later in this chapter to facilitate your planning and decisions.

You are in control of your retirement planning. You determine your desired budget level, and then add up your several financial income and asset sources. If you can produce enough income without ever having to use or sell off income-based assets, you should be able to project your retirement finances for all the years you want in the future. Know that, when necessary, you may also plan to capitalize assets into cash to fund your retirement program.

About Inflation

Inflation is a fact of life and must be projected into the future. The rate is not known, but you will want to read actively on the subject in the *Wall Street Journal*, the financial section of your daily newspaper, *Money* magazine, and other quality journals. There are so many variables, including interest rates, stock market prices, employment/unemployment figures, the cost of government borrowing, government policies and programs, international relations, and the price of potatoes at the supermarket, that it is impossible to predict where price levels will be in the future. You will want to be as immune to inflation as possible—with income rising consistently with the rate of inflation, and with your expense areas planned to avoid inflation wherever practical. See the resources section at the back of the book for further information on inflation.

About Early Retirement Offers

When there are economic pressures, employers may seek to release the most senior of workers earlier than traditional retirement ages. Generally, the older workers have higher pay scales, and companies may create special "early retirement" inducements to reduce staff and overhead. The earlier you start your retirement planning, the better your chances will be for being able to accept an advantageous early retirement offer. (But don't make any changes without analyzing the offer and its consequences carefully.)

How Much to Save for Retirement?

There is no magic figure to recommend to you for retirement savings, but if you're like most people you should double the percentage you are saving now. A 1989 survey by Merrill Lynch showed that of persons age 50-plus, 12 percent saved nothing, 22 percent saved 1 to 9 percent, 32 percent saved 10 to 19 percent, and 18 percent saved 20 percent or more of their income for retirement. *Money* magazine in 1989 reported that of pre-retirees who had savings and investments for their retirement funding, 53 percent held savings accounts at a bank or savings and loan (the least inflation-proof saving/income method), 40 percent had Individual Retirement Accounts (IRAs), 27 percent held stocks, 25 percent invested in bonds, 25 percent held certificates of deposit (CDs), 24 percent owned mutual funds, 24 percent had money market funds, and 17 percent purchased annuities.

About Trusts

There are ways to protect your assets and income, and assure their transfer to heirs in the most effective and most tax-free method, by the use of a trust. These legal instruments are available in many types, vary by state, and are designed for differing purposes. If you are concerned about transferring everything possible to your survivors in the case of death, this is a subject you should take to an attorney specializing in trusts and estate planning. Ask your family lawyer for a recommendation, but do not assume this to be a routine matter to be handled by most any attorney, nor a process to be accomplished in any do-it-yourself fashion.

About Your Will

With all of the information collected for your retirement financial planning, you will also have most everything you need to have your will drawn or updated. I can stress nothing more strongly than the importance of your will. More than half of all persons who die in this country die intestate—meaning without a will. This means that the state court system takes control of your assets and determines any distribution. This involves a legal process that can be costly to your estate, reducing the actual distribution to heirs. State law also recognizes relatives on a specific schedule, so that brothers and sisters, who might not need money, may get shares of an estate before or instead of grandchildren.

It may cost $300 to $500 to have an effective will prepared, but in doing so you will control the distribution of your estate to the people and/or charities you determine. The time and cost invested today may save years of legal problems and costs later.

When preparing to meet with an attorney, have your entire list of assets, and notes on your preferred distribution of the estate in the event of death. Read up on the subject of wills and trusts in advance, such as in one of the fine publications of Nolo Press in Berkeley, California. (You'll find their address in the "write for" section at the back of this book.)

About Government Programs

Politicians have claimed for years that federal and state governments "take care" of older adults. The statement is mostly untrue, and you should not have high expectations about munificent programs and services being available at little or no cost. There are national programs operated by the federal government and local programs run by state and municipal agencies on aging, including weekday lunches, housing assistance, information and referral services, and social and transportation services. There are some very effective programs for very frail elderly. Most all are means-tested, meaning that participants must prove that they have low income and limited assets in order to qualify. The Department of Housing and Urban Development (HUD) does administer some low-income housing programs and rental subsidy programs. But the federal lunch programs, for example, serve less than one percent of persons over age 65; and other federal and state programs serve similar percentages. Less than 10 percent of America's senior citizens are served by federal or state aging programs, other than Social Security. If you are of lower-income, you may contact your local Area Agency or Council on Aging for information on their services and programs. You'll find them listed in the white pages of the local telephone directory.

Some Financial Hints

Here are added suggestions for your retirement financial planning:

Credit Cards: Pay off any balances due on credit cards on a priority basis. Interest rates of 12 to 20 percent on outstanding balances are expensive far beyond the rate of inflation or your investment earnings. Clear your credit card balances each month to remove finance charges. If your credit card is one where you are charged interest from the date of purchase, pay it off and cancel it. A regular credit or charge card which allows 30 days for your payment without interest is far better for you, even if there is a small annual fee.

Time Shares and Similar Real Estate: Time-share vacations and residential properties are probably a very poor investment in your retirement financial planning. Resale values for most have been poor, and your investment will not produce income for retirement planning purposes.

About Insurance: Examine your present life and disability insurance policies for any cash values you might want to convert to other investment. Some life insurance companies now allow policyholders to convert part of their paid-up insurance value to a prepaid long term care insurance policy. You might find an advantage, too, in borrowing against your paid-up life insurance to invest the funds in higher-yielding investments for monthly income.

Cost of Living: Your cost of living will be determined by your own retirement planning. Know that your costs may be reduced, even significantly, by moving to other parts of the country where the cost of living might be lower, or to areas where the lifestyle features you want are more abundant and, therefore, more competitively priced. Your retirement income goal is to have enough money to support your desired lifestyle—but there are ways to pay less for that desired lifestyle. Keep an open mind when considering the possibilities.

Your Financial Plan in Retirement

Now tackle the following worksheets, collecting your desired lifestyle costs and expected income information, as a vital step in your financial planning for retirement. Read through this entire book before trying to finalize a financial plan, because each chapter introduces added suggestions, concepts and possibilities for your consideration.

This concept of financial planning grants that you have created some positive retirement income sources, and that you will do more in making your retirement possible. Unlike many others we do not provide mandates in any category, because how you provide for your retirement is a personal decision and commitment. Other approaches which provide "musts" and "have to's" put their concept over your own interest and priority, and most probably accuse you as wrong if you don't have or do specifically what they recommend.

Identify your resources as pertinent in the chart, and you will be able to determine quickly your financial ability to retire, what your lifestyle in retirement will be, and when you may make it a reality. You probably will not have to reduce your expectations or lifestyle; and you are probably closer to making it happen than you previously thought possible.

Instructions for completing the financial planning charts:

Complete one of these charts for each of the next ten years. I suggest buying a pad of 13-column bookkeeper's ledger paper at your stationer. Enter budget figures for each month, noting any changes in any of the entries by underlining, if you anticipate any variance in the figures.

You will probably make many drafts before you resolve a final budget, so don't try to finalize it in a first attempt. Enter rough figures on completion of this chapter then amend the figures based on new ideas and new resolutions based on your own charts and worksheets at the end of other chapters.

- -

FINANCIAL PLANNING FOR RETIREMENT

The Plan for: _____

Date: _____ Draft Number: _____

RETIREMENT EXPENSE BUDGET

Month   Year _____

Category	Jan.	Feb.	Mar.	Apr.	May	June	July	Aug.	Sept.	Oct.	Nov.	Dec.	Total
Home													
Rent/Mortgage													
Insurance													
Utilities													
Maintenance													
Furniture													
Garden													
Other													
Other													
Other													
Property Taxes													
Home Subtotal													

RETIREMENT EXPENSE BUDGET

Month _____   Year _____

Category	Jan.	Feb.	Mar.	Apr.	May	June	July	Aug.	Sept.	Oct.	Nov.	Dec.	Total
Food/Entertainment													
Supermarket													
Dining Out													
Entertaining													
Personal Care													
Other													
Other													
F/E Subtotal													
Clothing and Personal													
Clothing													
Other Personal													
Other													
Clothing Subtotal													

RETIREMENT EXPENSE BUDGET

Year _____

Category	Jan.	Feb.	Mar.	Apr.	May	June	July	Aug.	Sept.	Oct.	Nov.	Dec.	Total
Automotive													
Car Payment													
Car Payment													
Insurance													
Insurance													
Fuel/Supplies													
Service													
Travel Expense/Auto													
Other													
Other													
Auto Subtotal													

Month

RETIREMENT EXPENSE BUDGET

Month _____   Year _____

Category	Jan.	Feb.	Mar.	Apr.	May	June	July	Aug.	Sept.	Oct.	Nov.	Dec.	Total
Health Care													
Health Insurance													
Health Insurance													
LTC Insurance													
LTC Insurance													
Medical/General													
Medical/General													
Other Medical													
Other Medical													
Medications													
Other													
Other													
Health Care Subtotal													

RETIREMENT EXPENSE BUDGET

Month   **Year** _____

Category	Jan.	Feb.	Mar.	Apr.	May	June	July	Aug.	Sept.	Oct.	Nov.	Dec.	Total
Recreation													
Hobbies													
Activities													
Activities													
Special Events													
Sports													
Other Recreation													
Other													
Other													
Recreation Subtotal													

RETIREMENT EXPENSE BUDGET

Month   **Year** ___

Category	Jan.	Feb.	Mar.	Apr.	May	June	July	Aug.	Sept.	Oct.	Nov.	Dec.	Total
Travel													
Short Trips													
Long Trips													
Trips													
Trips													
Travel/Miscellaneous													
Travel Subtotal													

RETIREMENT EXPENSE BUDGET

Year _____

Category	Month												Total
	Jan.	Feb.	Mar.	Apr.	May	June	July	Aug.	Sept.	Oct.	Nov.	Dec.	
Contributions & Gifts													
Organization													
Organization													
Organization													
Organization													
Gift to													
Gift to													
Other													
Other													
Special													
Gifts Subtotal													

RETIREMENT EXPENSE BUDGET

Month _____ **Year** _____

Category	Jan.	Feb.	Mar.	Apr.	May	June	July	Aug.	Sept.	Oct.	Nov.	Dec.	Total
Taxes													
Federal													
State													
Social Security													
Local Taxes													
Business													
Other Taxes													
Other Taxes													
Taxes Subtotal													

TOTAL _____

INFLATION HEDGE %: _____

TOTAL OF ALL DESIRED LIFESTYLE EXPENSES: _____

RETIREMENT INCOME BUDGET

INCOME PLAN

Month

Year ____

Type of Income	Jan.	Feb.	Mar.	Apr.	May	June	July	Aug.	Sept.	Oct.	Nov.	Dec.	Total
EXTERNAL INCOME													
Social Security													
Pension													
Pension													
Disability													
Disability													
Fee Income													
Inheritance													
Other													
Other													
Subtotal #1													

RETIREMENT INCOME BUDGET

INCOME PLAN Month Year ____

Type of Income	Jan.	Feb.	Mar.	Apr.	May	June	July	Aug.	Sept.	Oct.	Nov.	Dec.	Total
ASSET-BASED INCOME													
Savings													
Savings													
Investment													
Investment													
IRA													
Keogh													
Real Estate													
Real Estate													
Contract													
Royalty													
Other													
Subtotal #2													

RETIREMENT INCOME BUDGET

INCOME PLAN Month ____ Year ____

Type of Income	Jan.	Feb.	Mar.	Apr.	May	June	July	Aug.	Sept.	Oct.	Nov.	Dec.	Total
EARNED INCOME													
Earning/Position													
Earning/Position													
Earning/Position													
Business/Earning													
Business/Earning													
Other Earned													
Other Earned													
Subtotal #3													
+ Subtotal #1 ____													
+Subtotal #2 ____													
TOTAL INCOME ____													

Total Expenses/By Month _____

Variance _____

(Mark + and $ amount for the income exceeding planned expenses; and mark
– and $ amount if the expenses exceed anticipated incomes.)

Note to the Budget: This will give you a working basis for evaluating your planned expenses and income and for making any necessary/desired changes. Later, as you operate with the budget you will refer to it each month to compare its entries with the facts of your income and spending.

— —

ASSETS of (Names) _____

Date of Preparation :_____ **Draft Number** _____

	Value	Income	Keep/Sell
Home			
Home			
Real Estate			
Real Estate			
Automobile			
Automobile			
Furniture & Appliances			
Jewelry			
Cameras/Other			
Collections			

	Value	Income	Keep/Sell
Other at home			
Business			
Business			
Securities			
Securities			
Securities			
Securities			
Savings Account			
Investment			
Investment			
Other Asset			
Other Asset			
Other Asset			

Total Value of Assets _____

Mortgages/Loans against the Above_____

Net Value of Assets _____

Notes on Assets: Following are my/our considerations and decisions regarding our assets.

— —

SUMMARY STATEMENT REGARDING
FINANCIAL PLANNING FOR RETIREMENT

I/We agree that this retirement/financial plan will be in effect on or before

(date)_____

I/We commit to this financial plan for retirement, and will effect the following changes/steps in order to make it happen:

1.

2.

3.

4.

5.

6.

7.

8.

9.

10.

Signed _____ Date _____

Signed _____ Date _____

MAKING MONEY/
SAVING MONEY

Here are two ways to have more money available to do what you want when you want to do it:

- Save more money

- Make more money

There really are no limitations on either or both of these methods. By that statement I challenge any assumption that mature people must accept "fixed income" limitations in retirement years. You can save money in scores of ways without scrimping, and without having to cut back your lifestyle. The process can even be fun, and you don't have to wait for retirement years to start.

At the same time the ways to make money are virtually unlimited. All of the ideas in this chapter have been proven to be workable and effective, but are only samples of the many opportunities open to you. Think of these suggestions as thought-starters. Try them on for size, think about them, amend them, shape them, change them to fit your own talents and situation. Some ideas might produce "fun money"—others just might exceed your expectations in financial gains and satisfaction.

Only you can determine what fits your own needs, opportunities, and expectations. It is what you choose to do with these ideas that will determine how much more money you have to spend—by paying less for what you buy and/or producing more money through your own efforts.

More Money to Spend by Paying Less

How would you like to spend 20 to 30 percent less at the supermarket, without purchasing any less than you are now? How would you like to save

119

10 to 50 percent on your travel? How about paying less for your banking services?

If you could reduce your overall spending by 10, 20, or 30 percent, again without depriving yourself, what more could you do with the money? How much could you put away for a vacation, for a new car or boat, for investments or gifts, or whatever you want?

Try some of these money saving ideas now, to learn how unlimited you are, and how much more you can do with the money you have.

Saving at the Supermarket

There are three ways to achieve significant savings at the supermarket: by planning your shopping, by shopping sales, and by using discount coupons.

Planning Your Shopping is the first important step: to determine what you want or need to buy, to save on the products you buy most frequently, to avoid having to buy at higher-price convenience stores, and to provide the products and abundance of selection you want in your pantry and freezer. You can do it all and save 10 to 30 percent from your supermarket bill, even while buying the brand names you know and trust.

To start the planning effort make a list of all of your regular supermarket purchases. Make two columns: one for perishables (fresh produce and dairy products), and one for non-perishables (canned, packaged, and frozen items). For example, your perishable purchases each week might include bread, milk, eggs, fish, meat, lettuce, celery, carrots, etc. Your non-perishable list may be comprised of frozen vegetables, coffee, canned tunafish, tomato sauce, bath soap, laundry detergent, and the like. These are "stock shelf items" and your list will be used as reference when developing your weekly shopping list, and for scanning for sale prices in supermarket advertisements. When the non-perishable items are available at reduced or sale prices, you'll buy a supply for several months. When we discuss discount coupons you'll see how to increase your savings on the sale-priced items.

Make another list for each week or two-week period when you will do your supermarket shopping. Have your calendar or datebook available, so to note your planned meals, and to plan your shopping for the special events you have already listed. Include the foods you will want for the bridge party, the potluck dinner, and the drop-in visit by relatives. Do your meal and supermarket list planning only after you have eaten a good meal. You will find the planning easier.

List fruits and vegetables, baked goods and staples first, so that your selection of meats, fish and/or chicken is made to augment these less costly and better-for-you foods.

120

Consider meal planning that allows a large hot dish or salad for one meal to be used later for another meal or two. There's an economy of scale in most supermarkets where larger sizes cost less by the ounce—so by planning extended or re-use dishes you'll save on the price, and the time and cost, too, of the later preparation. Check the value of the items you are considering by the cost per ounce. If the store does not post such, I carry a small hand calculator (under $10) to compute the cost per ounce for comparing values.

Compare the regular and sale prices for brand name products, after calculating any saving you will have by using discount coupons, with the price of the store's generic or "house brand" products. If the generic brand is lower in price you might try a package or two as a trial, comparing it for quality with your regular brand product. In many cases, the generic is actually produced by a brand name manufacturer. From my own shopping experience, though, I have found the combination of sale pricing and discount coupons to offer a lower price than the generic alternatives.

Plan your fruits and vegetables by season. Asparagus might cost near $2 per pound when out of season, and 47 cents in season. In that one example, there is a 75 percent saving by buying in-season foods. Apple and orange types vary significantly by season, as do most other fruits and vegetables. Your County Cooperative Extension Service (find them in the government listings in your telephone directory) should be able to provide you with the seasonal list of produce for your area.

Identify the supermarkets that offer the best prices, accept manufacturer's coupons at the declared or double value, offer good sale prices, and are near enough so that you don't waste time or transportation costs.

If you have a choice of supermarkets, check their sale ads each week, for your listed products and produce, and for the items you buy regularly. Allow some flexibility in your purchase list if the supermarket advertisement has a sale price on an item where you may easily make a substitution.

Always shop with a prepared list, with intended purchases grouped according to the arrangement of the store. This will make your supermarket visit more efficient, and coincide readily with your use of discount coupons. As in food planning, go grocery shopping only after you've eaten a meal. If you plan your weekly supermarket shopping effectively, you may avoid ever having to shop at a convenience store where prices may be some 30 percent higher.

Plan your shopping for the low business times of the day or week at the supermarket—in many parts of the country, weekdays between nine in the morning and three in the afternoon are the best. You'll spend less time searching for a parking space, and you'll be able to get assistance from the butcher, clerks, or the manager if you have a special need or request.

Your trip to the supermarket can become an adventure to be anticipated—planning is the key and savings are your incentive.

The Check Is in the Mail—Discount Coupons

Your local newspaper, the magazines you read, and the mail you open all
deliver discount coupons for purchases in the supermarket. The coupons
range in value from 10 cents to more than $1, and are just like checks for
you to use when buying the specified products. When there is competition
between supermarkets, some of them may double or even triple the value
of a discount coupon.

Most adults do use discount coupons—but most do not use them in a
planned and continuing program to reduce their supermarket bills by 10 to
30 percent. Such discounts are possible and combine with the sale price
shopping to produce even greater savings.

Discount coupons are promotional offers where the manufacturers hope
you will try their products and become regular customers. The shopper who
collects discount coupons actively—even aggressively—should be able to
find coupons for the majority of his or her supermarket purchases. You don't
have to switch brands if you seek out coupons wherever they can be found.
Your local newspaper should have two or three Free Standing Insert (FSI)
sections each week, and there are probably additional coupons printed in
the regular food section. Check the magazines you receive, and even "junk"
mail. Several promotion companies are mailing these discount coupons,
and include a consumer survey form. Complete and return every one of
these survey forms, as your response will trigger added mailings of even
more coupons. Many libraries and senior citizen clubs and centers have
"coupon exchanges"—where members bring in coupons they will not be
using and get, in exchange, coupons that they want for discount shopping.

If you make a personal commitment to the collection, sorting, consideration, and then use of discount coupons, the effort should take about one
hour each week. You will need a pair of scissors and your list of regular
shopping purchases, plus some method of filing the coupons for use. You
may buy a checkbook-size cloth file for a few dollars, and this will work if
you save a small number of coupons. I prefer a check-size expanding
cardboard file with 15 to 25 pockets. Each of the sections is labeled by
section of the store or type of merchandise—such as "meat/fish/poultry,"
"baked goods," "pasta/rice," etc.—for easiest sorting and retention.

Save up all coupons received and tackle this project once each week, and
on a regular basis. I recommend clipping and considering each of the
coupons for possible use now or even months in the future. Those to be
retained then will be sorted and placed into the pertinent file sections.
Coupons that you will not use may be shared with friends or forwarded to

a senior citizen club or center. Once each month discard coupons that are no longer valid.

As you plan your supermarket shopping each week you'll want to access your discount coupons, placing those to be used in an envelope, arranged in the same order as your shopping list. This system should increase the number of coupons you use when shopping, and multiply your cash savings significantly. I, for one, do our family shopping, and clip and maintain our discount coupon file. Our savings on discounts alone average 15 to 18 percent of our gross supermarket bill, while buying only the items and brands that we really want. Our savings increase to more than 35 percent— at least $1,500 each year—when the discount coupon and sale price savings are combined. In our case the savings approximate almost $30 for each hour of the planning and coupon clipping effort.

Many people advocate and use rebate certificates when they make purchases of some items. I have found these worthwhile when buying larger items offering rebates of $3 to $5 or more. The cost of the time and effort, envelope, and postage can then be justified. Rebate programs are used by many manufacturers of small appliances, furniture, and other products.

How much will you save by planning your supermarket shopping and by using discount coupons? It is up to you. Keep track of your savings and reward yourself for your successful effort. For example, if you save $20, treat yourself to something that costs $5; or give yourself a cash bonus each month or each year from a percentage of the savings.

Keep track of your progress each week, with a simple scorecard, like the one on the next page.

Buying at a Discount

If you're age fifty or better there are many discounts available, increasing in number as you qualify at age sixty or sixty-five.

Whenever and wherever you shop, ask if a quoted price includes the senior citizen discount. Don't be afraid to ask, because many businesses that offer senior discounts do so without promoting the fact. If you feel uncomfortable asking about a discount, practice in front of your mirror for a few minutes. You'll find it gets easier every time you ask the ten-second question, and it may save you from 10 to 20 percent of the regular bill. That's not bad pay for a ten-second effort.

Most all visitor attractions, such as theme parks, have nonposted senior discount rates, averaging up to 20 percent from what younger people will pay. Most hotel chains have senior discounts. When asking, compare the discount rate to other promotional rates that might be available. Most motion picture theaters now offer senior discounts—at ages ranging upward from fifty-five.

123

The Supermarket Savings Record of: (your name(s)

Week: _____

Overall spending in the supermarket and/or
for groceries   A $_____

Items purchased on sale at retail value: $_____

Sale price of those items: $_____

Net saving from cash paid/sale items: B $_____

Discount coupons used/total value: C $_____

SAVINGS THIS WEEK: Add B & C =   D $_____

TOTAL PURCHASE VALUE THIS WEEK: Add A,B,C = E $_____

Percentage of savings: Divide line D by line E = _____

Cumulative savings to date this year: $_____

Isn't it great to be paying less? Congratulations!

If you're not driving in peak traffic to and from work each day and are over age fifty, ask for a senior discount on your auto insurance. In fact, ask about all your options when insuring your car. For example, if you raise your deductible to $500, you may find a worthwhile saving on the premium. Consider the real and replacement value of your car, against the premium cost for insuring the vehicle itself. When buying a new car, ask your insurance broker in advance to provide a list of typical rates for various makes and models of cars. Predictably, rates will be higher for smaller and sporty cars, and for those that are most often stolen. Avoid duplicated coverage if you're a member of the American Automobile Club—don't pay your insurance company for towing coverage or for their own version of an "auto club." Ask your broker how to save money on the insurance premium, and before you buy or renew your coverage "shop" the same coverage with two or three other brokers.

Ask for discounts on your home owners insurance, too. If you are retired, and therefore are at home more often during the day, ask your insurance broker about a discount. Many burglaries happen during daylight hours, so if you are home, the chances of such thievery go down. Ask for a discount at the pharmacy. Ask everywhere that you do business. And, if one fine business offers you competitive prices and a discount and another fine business only offers you the competitive prices, consider the discount saving when choosing the store that will get your business.

Many businesses will offer cash discounts. After all, credit card usage costs the business between 4 and 7 percent, and installment sales may cost them even more. You may save money when spending cash, when you ask this ten-second question: "What is the discount for cash?"

How many other ways can you find a discount? Can you combine a discount with a sale price when buying merchandise or services that you want? In many cases, yes. Scan the newspaper ads to learn the regular and sale prices of items you are considering purchasing and defer buying until the "price is right." And watch the ads in newspapers and magazines, too, for announcements of senior discount cards, offered cost-free by merchants.

If you're in control of your time, you can dine out when restaurants need the business. Many establishments offer early diner discounts to those ordering, say, before six or seven in the evening. Some offer senior citizen discounts in addition. When making your reservations, ask about these discounts, which can save as much as 30 percent.

You can even get a discount on car servicing. Offer to bring the car in on the day and time when the auto service facility needs the business. For example, most shops are very busy first thing in the morning and on Mondays, Thursdays and Fridays. Offer to have the service done on Tuesday or Wednesday afternoon in exchange for a discount. You still get the same quality service—and you will pay less for it.

A dentist in San Diego, California, offers a discount on the same basis. Make an appointment at your convenience and pay the going rate. Make an offer to have your appointment at his convenience or on a short-notice call, and he offers a significantly-discounted price. Other dentists—and many other professional practitioners—are sure to follow this concept. You get what you want and need at a saving; the professional gets business at a time when he or she might have none. Everybody wins.

Saving at the Bank: If the rate of investment return is the same, consider the discount/savings advantages of different banks. Can you get cost-free checking; free safe deposit box, free photocopying, added percentage points on your invested funds (even one-quarter to one-half percent may make a significant boost to your income)? Banks and savings and loan associations are in a very competitive business, and mature adults have most of the available money for nonbusiness deposits. In presentations to preretiree groups and senior organizations I recommend that mature adults visit several banks or savings institutions, presenting a simple statement and a question: "I am (name) and I have $_____ to put in one or two financial institutions. I am _____ years of age. Now, what advantages do you offer me to bring my business to you?"

Many of the advantages offered are not in the published brochures. For example, will they handle note collections for you at no cost? Will they provide cost-free traveler's checks? Will they (name any other service for which you are paying now)? You never know until you ask.

Keep notes and then compare. You will find savings that you never knew existed. And, when you find them, you will have more money left in your account to earn more interest. When you complete this comparison and decision process and find real savings, give yourself an extra special treat—for you will have the bankers coming your way.

On Saving Money

When flying from San Francisco to New York years ago, I did a survey for one of my newspaper columns, asking every passenger (who was awake) if I could see his or her airline ticket. On that single flight I found seven different airfares being paid for the identical airplane seats. The passenger with the lowest fare had paid barely 40 percent of what the highest-fare passenger had paid. With deregulation of the airline business, the fare structures have splintered all the more. It is fascinating to be able to get the flight you want at 60 percent less than the published fare, while the airline gets what it wants—a paying passenger. (See Chapter 10, on travel, where we present many more ways to pay less and travel more.)

There are countless added ways to have more money through saving on what you do buy. Warehouse clubs are proliferating, where you can buy at near wholesale, and they are producing added competition for retailers. How will the retailers compete? With reduced prices, sales, and discounts, of course.

Chart all of your expenditures and commitments and analyze them monthly. Are the expenses necessary? For example, do you have a continuing balance due on your credit cards? The monthly interest charge may be more costly than you realize, and your best step may be to pay off the balance soon. Are there beneficial prepayment or annual payment discounts for your insurance or property taxes? Are you making lump-sum payments where no discount is offered, where you would gain by keeping the funds invested for a longer time?

How much will you save this week, this month, this year? How will you track your savings? And, importantly, how will you reward yourself from a percentage of your newly found savings? The benefits are yours to anticipate and enjoy.

About Making Money

You have the opportunity to make more money now no matter what age you are. It's true: The potential is virtually unlimited. Lest you get the wrong impression, this is not a Get Rich Quick scheme or program. It is a presentation of ideas you may want to consider and use in your future direction.

If you want to retire from one career and start another, it is possible. If you want to be your own boss after leaving someone else's payroll, it is possible. If you want to remain active, working part-time, full-time, or in your own venture, it is possible. It is your call.

For too many years the universal attitude has been that people worked for a certain number of years toward the single goal of not having to work. For politicians and labor bosses the concept fit the bill. But the concept does not fit most of the population. Most people—perhaps you are one of these, too—don't want to retire and just do nothing. Most, according to research, would prefer to shift careers or work patterns—perhaps being the boss instead of the employee, the business manager instead of the accountant, the stockbroker instead of the computer salesperson, the travel agent instead of the secretary.

In this section you'll find ideas that should aid your thinking with proven ideas and possibilities.

Earlier I told the true story of the housebound lady on welfare who gained a good income, new friendships, and a more interesting life from her telephone wakeup service. In producing this solution we did not look at what she could not do; we did not assume that she was limited to a welfare existence; we did not grant that she was to be pitied. We went beyond the traditional attitudes and assumptions and looked at what she could do, what she wanted in her life, and what satisfactions and opportunities she desired. There are many opportunities open for you, too. The following pages should help you in choosing new directions.

Go Into Business

Full-time or part-time, on-site or absentee, there just might be a business for you—if that is what you want in your future. Businesses range from something you operate from your kitchen table to ventures that eventually employ hundreds or even thousands of people. The size of a business in no way determines how much profit the ownership can or should make. A cruise-only travel agency might be started with just a few thousand dollars and involve only a couple to operate it, yet produce $40,000 a year income, plus perks in the form of free or low-cost travel. On the other hand, a restaurant franchise might cost $500,000 or more, employ fifty, gross over a million dollars a year, yet earn its owners no more than $50,000 a year. Of course, the value of either business may increase for added gain when sold later.

A part-time consultancy based on your career experience or specialty might pay three or four times your earlier hourly earning rate. A sales representation operated from home can be full- or part-time, producing a respectable income in addition to community activity and involvement.

A retired police officer I once interviewed tripled his retirement income soon after establishing a small business to sell water-filtration systems. Rather than go door to door, he works near dispensers of bottled water outside of supermarkets. His simple system is to help people lug the water jugs to their cars, reminding them of the weight and that they were paying 25 cents a gallon for the bottled water, while he offers an in-home system that requires no heavy toting and costs only 2 cents per gallon. He works only the days and hours he wants, yet sells enough in this low-key, helpful way to earn an added $40,000 a year. He supports no employees, and has time to go fishing, travel, or to romp with his grandchildren.

If you want to generate a small business of your own, consider some of the following ideas:

Representation: Whether selling for a firm like Amway or Fuller Brush or as a representative for a product line sold to businesses or stores, there are thousands of marketing opportunities. What field do you know or like where you can sell someone else's product line in your area or by mail to identified prospects?

With grown children on their own, a couple wanted, finally, to do some project together, rather than head to different jobs every day. The man knew printing well but did not want to be tied down to operating a print shop. They both wanted some freedom to choose the hours and days they worked. So this couple set up shop as graphics and print representatives, operating from a bedroom once occupied by one of their children. With a personal computer and representative relationships for several quality printers and graphic services around the nation, they developed their own customers from a prospect list of local businesses and organizations. Their business is now booming, as they maintain telephone and periodic in-person contact with their clients. With control of their time and the ideal of sharing a project together, they now net far more income than they did when working for others. They provide real solutions for the businesses and organizations they serve—better pricing, quality supervision and counsel—and the printers and services they represent must do all the work of fulfillment.

Are you knowledgeable in any field where there are a number potential buyers for similar services? Most effective "selling" really isn't a "hard driving, beat them into buying" job. It is establishing a credible relationship and providing sensible and advantageous solutions to the clients or customers you serve.

"Nothing happens until somebody sells something" is a truism accepted in business. Might there be that field or product that you know or like where you might structure a sales representation business in your preretirement or retirement years? Think about it.

Consulting: Do you have a skill or expertise valuable to other businesses or organizations? One of the fastest growing fields in service businesses is in consulting. Many companies today are motivated to bring in experts when necessary, rather than to retain them on staff. Consultants may be retained throughout a year to provide regular service, or be called in to lead or assist on a special project, a "turnaround" program, or at peak business times.

The consultant earns fees at an hourly, weekly, or monthly rate two to three times the salary received for a staff professional, but is on the job only when necessary. If there is a market of several or many companies that can use the particular type of consulting, the rewards can be positive, and the professional can take as much or as little work as he or she wants.

To be a consultant in any field takes knowledge and experience, an ability to look at new situations and evaluate them, and then to shape, or help shape, positive results. Depending on the subject field, you'll need a full range of research materials and other publications so that you can be "up" on your subject. The cost to create a consultancy is generally small, just for business cards, letterhead, a business phone and answering machine, and a simple brochure detailing what services you offer and the results you produce.

You don't need a Ph.D. degree to be a consultant: Harriet Schecter of San Diego is a lady who thrives on transforming chaos into order. So she created a consultancy to do just that, and her customers include businesses who need to organize an inventory system to others that need to bring order to their records before the Internal Revenue Service auditor arrives. Individuals retain her service to organize medical and payment records, bring order to family tree information, or to sort estate information and properties. Harriet works from her home and is on the go actively, with a new "mess into order" challenge each day. She has a waiting list of customer requests.

There are many other examples of consultancies that make sense. Retired firemen have the credentials to advise businesses on fire safety, make periodic inspections, and train staff. Retired policemen have expertise to show businesses and organizations how to improve security methods and devices, in addition to providing staff training and counsel to management. How about some of these, not so evident in concept:

The Bank Viser: As a businessman, I sure would like to have retired bank personnel available actively as consultants in establishing and maintaining banking and financial relationships, to help evaluate the development of loan and credit line requests, to advise on coordinating negotiations with banks to get the best arrangement for the business. Banking is an ominous mystery to most business people, and the individual BankViser might find a dozen small to medium-size businesses willing to pay retainers to have such expertise available. I know that I would.

Public Relations/Publicity Consultant: There are firms in this field, but the business and organization need is, generally, underserved. Having a background, expertise, or keen interest in community affairs, journalism, broadcasting, psychology, and/or governmental affairs is necessary. Many companies have someone who can crank out a news release, but most small companies have no idea how to structure a community or public relations program based on the need to achieve specific goals. The opportunity is open for more than just career journalists.

FindersPlus: Businesses spend thousands of hours trying to find the right sources and then handling the negotiations for purchases of goods and services of all types. Do you have a broad knowledge in any particular field where you could assist several companies with instant answers, better pricing, and other advantages? This concept could be embraced as a consultancy—or as a consultancy/service business combined—in any of a thousand fields. This is not an idea that has been developed into a standard business format or that is being franchised, so if it fits for your own, individual area of expertise, go to it.

Your Secretary: A business might be structured by one or several mature adults to provide executive secretarial services for clubs and organizations, businesses, and business groups. What you have done for years as a volunteer is today a salable commodity: maintaining membership lists, preparing a newsletter, coordinating meeting sites and agendas, taking and publishing minutes, handling correspondence—and more. With several clients for variety—and so that no single one controls your fate—you can probably operate this business from home.

Swap Meets and Flea Markets: Deal with a private school, drive-in theater, or other facility with a lot or yard area that is not used on Saturday or Sunday. You can pay a negotiated rent or give them a percentage of the profits. Start by clearing out your own garage, and get others to do the same. Then get collectors or part-time dealers to join the group. Your overhead cost is low, and you generate income by renting the sales spaces and/or by taking in merchandise for sale on consignment. One person, a couple, or a small company involving several mature adults can make a fine income from this type of venture, perhaps even expanding it.

A GetItThere Service: Most businesses run into insurance and staff cost problems in making their own deliveries, so there may be an opportunity for you to do them on a route basis. This company concept/name is one of my own creation, and it says what the venture does as its service—

deliveries, post office box pickups, supply pickups, other errands. If you drive the route yourself, you might set a fee by the month per business or store, with an additional small fee per delivery. If you manage the business and have others drive, they should be independent contractors and share in the volume of business they handle. How many customers would it take? Perhaps twenty to thirty—not many to develop when you consider the income, activity, and independence you'd have.

Service business needs are all around you in your own community or field. Do you want a business to remove the limits from your income? Use these ideas to start your thinking. There is a business analysis chart later in this chapter for your use when considering the possibilities.

Franchise Businesses: The late, great Ray Kroc made the world believe in the franchise business when, at age fifty-five, the former ice cream machine salesman bought a small drive-in restaurant called McDonald's. He took the concepts of quality preparation and predictable service methods and perfected them, and then instead of operating just one restaurant, he taught others to make, market, and serve hamburgers and other fast foods in identical fashion. Thus, he was not limited in what he or his company could finance and manage. Using the concept of franchising, McDonald's established a phenomenal growth rate unmatched in the field. Other businesses had franchised operations before—from Radio Shack and bookkeeping services to pizza parlors—but it was Kroc who set new standards of quality control and success. Before Kroc, franchising had developed a questionable, if not bad, name, as slick operators marketed unproven and even failed business ventures. To counter the then rampant practice, new legislation and governmental oversight were established in the franchise field.

Today you can purchase franchises in fields as diverse as advertising agencies, financial services, car washes, auto dealerships, janitorial services, quick printing, auto painting, travel agencies, transportation services, clothing boutiques, appliance stores, as well as fast food restaurants. Not all of these operations are viable, operable, or predictably profitable. The franchise concept might work for you if you do not already have another direction chosen, based on your expertise or interest. At the library, look into the *Franchise Annual* and the *Wall Street Journal* listings. Read *Inc.*, *Money*, *Success*, and *Venture* magazines regularly—a good idea for anyone in a small or medium-size business.

Before purchasing any franchise have an accountant analyze their financial figures, have a knowledgeable attorney check their contract, and have your banker or a marketing consultant analyze the concept to see if the product or service is viable in your community.

Operating a franchise business is taking someone else's ideas, methods, research, product or service lines, and accepted name and reputation as your own, and working as an independent branch manager. Is that what you see yourself doing for the next ten or more years? This, too, is something to think about as you create your future.

What to Avoid in Business Possibilities

When considering a business to develop, buy, or to franchise from another, know that there are a few ventures and possibilities to avoid. Starting a restaurant is probably the most predictable business failure known, yet purchasing a good fast-food franchise has a high predictability for success. Operating the food and beverage concession at the local youth athletic field is often a sound idea because there is less startup cost, you have most of the year off, and little or no added staff is required.

There are no valid and viable "thousands of dollars to be made from mailing envelopes from home" and similar schemes advertised in the classifieds. Mass mailing houses do the direct mailing effectively and efficiently. These types of "get rich quick" schemes take your money and tell you to place similar ads to take money from others. And, if you do get into this type of "mail envelopes from home" business, get ready for a serious visit from the postal inspector or the local authorities.

Another scheme to avoid is that which offers to put you in the direct-mail business. You buy their catalogs and lists of names, "already on labels, ready to affix," which you send to "customers ready to buy from you." If the catalogs and merchandise were any good, and the names as valid as they claim, why should they split the income and profit potential with you, a stranger?

Take a long, hard look before jumping into the typical offers in business-opportunity type publications. Think hard if you really want to sell a product like matches door to door (even if they claim that "everybody needs matches, and you can make millions each year!") Question whether you want to try selling something where you have to "make the market"—that is, where a product or service is not known or accepted, not advertised, or even of questionable benefit to the buyer or user.

"Get rich quick" schemes are all around us, each sounding too good to be true. (They are!) Operators of these fraudulent schemes make more money selling their "secrets" than can ever be realized from the venture itself. There is a saying in the law enforcement business that "if it sounds too good to be true, it is probably a fraud."

The Form of Business

Before starting a business, you need determine the form you will use. Businesses can be sole proprietorships (by a single person or a couple), partnerships, joint ventures, or corporations. Each form has advantages and disadvantages. One of the advantages of a business is that many of the costs involved are tax deductible as valid business expenses—purchase or lease and operation of an automobile, office and telephone expense, memberships, entertaining, and more.

The decision on the best form for your business should involve your attorney and an accountant—but read seriously on the subject first. A $20 book can give you a fine background and provide the questions you need to ask and the subjects you need to consider when meeting with the attorney and accountant. And, because you will be more prepared, you'll pay far less in fees than if they, at $40 to $200 each per hour, use professional time to teach you the same information.

The advantages of a sole proprietorship are that it is easy to set up, it works for most people, and generally offers the simplest form of accounting. However, if you make a mistake, if there's an accident in the business and you are sued, or if a claim is filed that is larger than the company can handle, you are personally liable. As the business is your personal property, all of the profits are yours to keep, and all of the losses are yours to pay.

In a partnership two or more persons own the business, with each bringing to the venture a representative share of duties, responsibilities and skills. Ideally, the partners should team well—perhaps one of the partners strong on sales, the other on operations—so that the duties and sum of abilities adds up to more than what the partners could achieve individually. You need to know that you are mutually compatible and that you respect each other's ability and performance. You must agree on performance standards and expectations. It is exciting when partnerships "work," for the teamwork produces a far stronger venture in operation and potential. Like sole proprietorships, partnerships involve personal liabilities for losses suffered by the business.

A joint venture can be any joining of forces and in any combination. This form is used often by two or more established businesses to fund and operate yet another business. Real estate developers create joint ventures for specific projects and then close out the venture when the project is completed and sold, hopefully at a profit.

The corporation form of business is traditional for most large businesses, as either closely held or as public corporations. Accounting procedures become more complex and there are both added governmental regulations and compliance programs involved; many business decisions must be approved by the board of directors—resolutions made, seconded and voted on—and more detailed records kept. Legally, the corporation is "another person" with a legal life of its own. Thus, owners and management have only limited liability for the corporation's debts and other obligations, in most cases. The price for such protection might include double taxation—

of both the corporation and the owners, instead of just the owners—but the S corporation offers the owners of small businesses both limited liability and tax liability roughly equal to that of sole proprietors and partners.

Which is the right form for you? It depends on what you want from the business. Again, the best advice is to read up on the subject, with recommendations from your bookseller and librarian, and then to consult with the appropriate professionals.

Getting a New Job

Your new horizons for the next twenty or thirty years might involve switching careers or moving your life into a new direction. For instance, a career housewife might want a new life experience and enter (or reenter) the employed workforce. If you're close to, or in, retirement, you might want to change careers—perhaps to a job that you don't have to take home with you, as has been the case for thirty or forty years.

One way or another, there are jobs available in most parts of the country for all who are willing to work. We have all seen the negative news stories that report mature adults being forcibly retired early, "with no hope that anyone will ever hire them again," because they happen to be fifty, sixty, or even seventy and eighty years of age. The stories assume the worst—and the stories are wrong.

Know that there is an employment crisis developing that will get more severe over the next decade. The crisis is created not by disappearing jobs but by an increasing number of jobs and a shrinking workforce available to fill them. This is fact not only in the United States and Canada but throughout the developed nations. European countries are actively importing workers today, and some plan to accelerate that practice and pace in the future.

Are there jobs for mature adults? You bet! Businesses, labor organizations, government, and social service agencies are finally recognizing that mature adults are the most loyal, best performing, and most reliable employees they can have in their companies.

Where are the jobs? Almost everywhere you look. For example, the fast food business has recognized the workforce shortage caused by declining numbers of teenagers—their traditional source of employees.

One fast-food chain was working its managers from morning, when they opened the doors, to late at night, when they locked up, read the cash registers and did the cash count, and tried to catch up with staff scheduling. In between, the managers did everything else, from training an everchanging staff to filling in at the counter when one of two of the younger persons just did not arrive for work. The average tenure in a fast-food restaurant is under six months, so many units have 300 to 600 percent staff turnover each year.

When the restaurant chains turned to mature adults as employees, they got an unexpected gain in the bargain. The presence of the adults brought more maturity to the staff; positive relationships were built between the younger and older staff; the mature adults had much lower absenteeism and sick days than the younger; and managers found that the mature adults could assume responsibilities such as opening in the morning and closing at night; they could also handle problems with customers better than the younger employees. Minimum-wage jobs for the mature adults, in many cases, were upgraded to assistant managerships at higher salaries.

Professional employment services like Kelly Girls have long recognized the shortage of qualified personnel and have created separate operating divisions for finding, training, and assigning mature adults for full-time and part-time work. Another example of a firm that employs mature workers is PowerForce, which provides local product representatives for companies selling through supermarkets and grocery stores. They hire field representatives to work part-time, mainly on their own schedules, directly with store managers on behalf of brand name products.

Dr. Donald Monaco, a psychologist and vice president of Drake Beam Morin, an international outplacement firm headquartered in New York City, stated emphatically that "there are jobs for people at any age, if their skills and physical abilities are still present." The assumption that "there are no jobs" is the major impediment to finding a job at any age, he told me. "If you believe there are no jobs, you're beaten before you start."

Drake Beam Morin works with executives who are being retired by large companies, early retirees resulting from corporate mergers, restructuring, or cutbacks. "The first block is esteem, or the lack of it, caused by the realization that there will be a change.

"Whether a move is caused by a corporate change or personal decision, the employee should use the opportunity to reassess where he or she is, the skills and experience possessed, and the career direction—past, present, and future. It is a unique opportunity to change directions to something more satisfying, more rewarding, closer to home, with shorter hours or whatever is important by personal choice."

The level or type of position you desire determines the representation you make in seeking out the right employer. If you have been employed for decades by the same company, there's no doubt that change can be unsettling, the task of finding new employment seemingly awesome. But the situation is far from impossible. In fact, after an initial, inevitable period of doubt, the opportunities for positive change become apparent.

The first step is to get busy planning for the future. Prepare sheets of tablet paper, drawing a line down the center—as in the earlier suggested charts. List the frustrations you have had in your most recent job or in jobs past on the left side; on the right side, list the rewards and satisfactions of what you have been doing. As earlier, do not try to edit these as you do them, but list them as they come to mind.

On the left side of another sheet list your real interests and what you would like to find in a job; on the right side, list what you would prefer to avoid. Perhaps you want to avoid commuting, early or late hours, overtime, smoke-filled rooms, loud people—list them all.

Then put the two sheets of paper side by side. In one position the two "negative" columns will be together—study them. Then switch the positions of the sheets, so that all of the positive ideas and goals will be together—study them, too. What you learn might be very surprising. On another sheet of paper write your condensed thoughts, to be used as your guide in the preparation of your resume.

Even if you're seeking a simple job, you must prepare a proper resume. It is the document that will control the interview; thus, at least part of the interview will be on your terms. Present the resume in this fashion:

RESUME
Your Name
Address
Telephone Number

Background Information: (Here show your background, responsibilities, growth and promotions in jobs, and how you produce success—but in only two or three sentences.)

The Position I Am Seeking: (State the type of position, type of company or opportunity desired.)

Digest of Experience: (List pertinent positions and assignments, either in outline or prose form.)

Personal Achievements and Activities: (Marital and family status, education—unless very limited—community, church, or other activities. Hobbies, if interesting. Health status, if good to very good or excellent.)

Skills, Licenses, Recognitions: (Any licensed qualifications for what you have been doing or want to do? List here.)

References: (On request only, following the interview)

Availability: (Immediately? Or the date when available.)

The first sample resume is for a bookkeeper who wants, instead, to seek a position in the restaurant business.

R E S U M E
George V. Simpson
9999 Fulton Avenue
Arklington, Minnekansan 99999
(555) 555-1212

Background Information: A career member of a management team, experienced in cost and personnel analysis, with unique ability to handle details and responsibility and to maintain profitability.

The Position I Am Seeking: Assistant manager of a quality restaurant, which allows my growth in management and opportunity.

Digest of Experience:
Thirty years as office manager and bookkeeper in the machine screw industry, with active involvement in personnel, payroll, profitability analysis, supply ordering, bookkeeping, and record keeping. Promoted four times; managed my department at or under budget most recent ten years: promoted to management of six staff members.

Four years in the restaurant business, learning it from the ground up while in high school and college. Food and bar service, relief duties as host, and handled some special projects for the manager.

Three years in United States Army as clerk, assisting the company commander, stationed at Fort Leonard Wood, Missouri.

Personal Achievements and Activities:
Married, 34 years. Wife's name is Helen.
Three grown children: Henry, 32; Abby, 30; Toby, 27.
Active in the Church of Perpetual Responsibility, where I coordinate the ushering for all services.
Attended Moline City College, majoring in business.
Hobbies include cooking, travel, occasional golf.
Health: Excellent.

Skills:
Operate ten-key calculator for doing dinner check audit and cash reconciliation.
Familiarity with computers and information that can be secured from them.

Licenses and Recognitions:
Achievement Award, Accounting Club of Arklington
Best Chili Award, Arklington Chamber of Commerce Contest
Bookkeeping Certificate, State of Minnekansan

References: On request, following our interview.

Availability: I am available for the right position now.

Thank you.

George wants to shift careers, so he is identifying the possible needs of the field he wants to enter, while presenting experience and credentials to show how he would be an asset to the right employer. His only restaurant experience was in busing and waiting tables while in school—as so many of us have done—so it is added to show some exposure to, and understanding of, the business. In the resulting interview the resume will be the control document for the discussion, focusing on how many ways George can fit the needs of the job, not on what he does not yet know or the experience he does not yet have.

George is totally fictional as is the resume, but a similar one that I wrote in response to ten classified ads for assistant restaurant managers drew three positive requests for interviews. The concept is to match the skills and abilities you have, honestly, with the anticipated needs of the job.

George's resume, and Mary's on the next page, are based on my own experience, what has worked for me and for people I have advised.

Do a rough layout of your resume, leaving lots of space between the headings. Think about the field or job you want, the skills necessary in the job, and the assets that might be important for you to have. Think about how you have grown in whatever your jobs or assignments have been in the past, the responsibilities given you, the success you have managed or been part of in those assignments, your promotions, skills and more. You will find that you have a lot going for you. Thus, it is evident from George Simpson's resume that he was a loyal employee who did not set the world on fire in the machine screw business—yet, he has a right to aspire to what he wants to do, and he does bring some talents and abilities to the possible job, even if he has no experience in that particular management field.

Another resume? I'm glad you asked. What if you're a housewife wanting to launch a career after raising a family? Try this for an example:

RESUME

Mary Todd Jones
4444 Hill Street
Lowland, UpState 99998
(444) 555-2121

Background Information: I present a background of success in managing the financial and operating affairs of a household, the ability to lead and work with others, through my community work with the Girl Scouts of America, the Community Town Council, and as an officer of the Bay State Little League.

The Position I Am Seeking: I am seeking a retail sales opportunity, particularly in women's or children's wear, with an opportunity to advance in position and with responsibility for the success of the store.

Digest of Experience: My successful experience includes management of scores of community organizations and events, the teaching of sewing and dressmaking to girl scout troops, and serving as treasurer seven years for the Little League. I have sold merchandise successfully at garage sales and swap meets and for church and community bazaar events.

Skills, Achievements, and Activities: I type and handle the telephone well. I have taken night school art classes to learn design.
I am active in the Community Town Council.
Hobbies include: reading, writing letters, tennis.

References: On request, following our interview.

Availability: Now, on a full-time basis.

Thank you.

All experience can be applicable to a particular job, if that experience is desired as an asset in that job. Here, the applicant shows that she's responsible, can work with people, accepts leadership, has an ability in sewing and some exposure to design, and that she can work with figures and balance a checkbook—all based on her background as an active volunteer.

The Job Seeking Process

When you figure out what you want to do, the job quest is easier because you are not just looking at classified ads to see if you fit jobs that companies are looking to fill. When you put yourself in that passive position, you are the victim—the potential employer is in complete control, and you are stuck just looking for a job, "hoping that someone will hire you." Change the ground rules to make the game fair to your side.

Remember, you are the asset that a business needs for its success. You have proven experience, proven loyalty, proven promotions, and proven responsibility—even if it was in a different business or field of endeavor.

Check the classifieds, of course. But check the yellow pages and the display section of the local newspapers and any trade publications in your desired field. Make a list of the businesses in the fields you are considering. Phone each one of them to find out the name of the president or general manager or, in a large company, the head of the department or personnel manager where you want to work. Then send the appropriate manager a personal letter and resume. This letter opens the door to that company and states your interest in working with them. Try to tickle their interest in some way, and then say that you will phone on a specific date (three to five days after their receipt of the letter), seeking their most positive response and the opportunity of an interview.

You and I both know that the president or general manager—or his or her secretary—will bounce your letter and resume to someone else, but that is okay. When you phone on the stated date, say, "I'm (your name) and I sent a personal letter and resume to (name) on (date), and in that letter I stated that I would follow through today by telephone. Is (name) in, or is there someone else who was given my personal package?" When you state your introduction and question in this way, you will get an answer. (Practice the lines ahead of time so that you don't have to read them, but can deliver them without stopping for a breath.) The answer might come from the secretary, stating the name of the person who now has your letter and resume. If so, ask to be transferred, and start the next conversation with: "(name—catch the name of the secretary or other person who first answered the phone) or (name of the president or general manager that you wrote) asked me to follow through on my letter and resume that he/she forwarded to you this week. Have you received and reviewed it, and with whom should I speak regarding the opportunity with your company?" (Practice this line, also. Be natural, not staged or stiff . . . If you deliver the line positively, you will get a positive response.)

The person answering the phone will have to respond on your grounds. They have either reviewed the package or not. They might have an opening or not.

You say: "I have admired your company, and in my professional relocation I want(ed) to talk with you as one of the very first. When is that possible?" (What can they do but arrange an interview?)

Assume a negative option "close," if you think you would enjoy an assignment with this company. You say: "I'll be in your area next Tuesday. Will it be more convenient for you to meet at ten in the morning or two in the afternoon?" Make up your own time options, but don't pause in asking the question, not even for a breath. The other person will respond by accepting one of these times or by suggesting an alternate. You have your interview.

Here are some "do's and don't's" for the interview:

• Do arrive early for the interview, dressed just a bit above their expectation for the level of position.

• Do have extra copies of your resume. Have these prepared in a quality way and quick-printed or photocopied on tinted paper. (They'll find the resume easier on a paper-laden desk.)

• Do be aware that they have invited you to visit with them. Your resume will be the focus of the interview discussion, but rebrief yourself on your entire background and interests.

• Do not apologize for your age.

• Do focus on today and the opportunity for both you and the company if you were to begin working there. Forget about "how it was done in the old days." Think about solutions for today. You don't need all of the answers, so back off from straining too hard.

• Don't have a chip on your shoulder about "equal opportunity."

• Don't forget that the interview is for your evaluation of the company and the opportunity as much as it is for their evaluation of you as a potential employee.

• Do have paper and a pen or pencil with you to make notes as pertinent during the interview. If you agree to provide additional information, establish with the interviewer an agreed date when it will be provided.

• Don't give up if the openings they have don't fit your needs or desires. Say right out, "I want to thank you for the opportunity of this visit and I understand that you don't have a position that we should be discussing right now; but with whom do you think I should be talking or discussing the right opportunity?" The interviewer just might name competitors with jobs you are seeking. If possible, get the name of the person you should call.

• Do get as many such leads as you can. Follow up by phoning the prospect and stating, "I was recommended to you by (name) of (company)

141

when I met with him/her yesterday. Do you prefer that I send my resume in advance, or might we set an interview appointment right now?" Then, "I'll be in your area on (name the day, soon). Would ten in the morning or two in the afternoon be better for you?"

• Do continue talking with people directly involved in the work you want to do; they can be of help to you.

• Don't try to "power drive" your message—let the resume take you forward.

• Don't take just any job, because you don't need to. If you haven't interviewed for a job in a number of years, answer some ads for jobs that you know you don't want just to get into the swing of the interview process.

• Do send a thank-you note to the person who interviewed you, expressing your pleasure in learning about the company and how your talents, abilities, and experience might be of great assistance to them now and in the future. Also indicate any agreed or promised date for your follow-through with them or their follow-through with you. Include your telephone number immediately under your name and signature at the bottom of the letter.

• When you have that right opportunity and company in front of you, and only when you feel that they have accepted your candidacy for the job, you ask the closing question: "Shall I start this Monday or next Monday?"

You are on your way!

About Making Money and Saving Money

Mix and match these concepts and more as you build your mature years plan and direction. We have only scratched the surface here, in giving some directions and examples for making money and saving money in mature years. (Perhaps that will be the detailed subject of my next book.) There is no such thing as a limit in income or in spending ability if you apply whatever fits your desired lifestyle from the above recommendations.

If you want to work, you may. If you want to be in business, you may. If you want to get more for the money you have and spend in mature years, you may. This book provides a variety of recommendations that work. Now the fulfillment is up to you.

A CHART FOR MAKING MONEY AND SAVING MONEY

The Plan for: (name) _____

Date of this Plan: _____   **Revised Date** _____

Fill in these blocks:
FOR MAKING MONEY in my mature years, I will produce the following income, or will explore the following ideas now, for producing added income:

	Monthly	Annually
Business:		
Type to explore		
Capital needed		
People needed		
Location		
How I feel about the potential		
When will I launch/purchase this business?		
Consultancy:		
Possible to do?		
What subject/field?		
Define the customer base.		
Earlier hourly earnings		
Consulting hourly earnings		
Earnings possible		
Startup costs		

	Monthly	Annually
Operating costs		
Income projections:		
How do I feel about doing this type of work?		
Action plan to establish		

Secure a Job:

	Monthly	Annually
Full-time or part-time:		
Desired field(s):		
Desired position:		
Desired salary to start:		
Desired salary after one year:		
Resume prepared? When?		
Job seeking program defined:		
Potential employers identified:		
What do I need to be ready to seek the job?		
What do I need to be ready to work?		
My timetable for securing this position:		
How do I really feel about continuing to work?		
My refined decision, in writing.		

Other Income Ideas: The following ideas have been in my head in the past or present, and I want to explore them as part of this plan: _____

_____

_____

_____

_____

_____

For me/us I want the following good things/people/events/income in my/our life (lives):

_____

_____

_____

_____

_____

_____

_____

I/we agree to the above, and will target the development of the following income and asset building, starting (date) _____

    Income, as defined above, $ _____ per month/year

    Asset building (such as a business) from $ _____ to $_____

    within _____

ON SAVING MONEY, I/we project a saving of $_____ or _____ percent in expense

    levels per____ month;____year.

    Our "treats" or rewards for this saving will be:
    (list them—travel, clothes, dine out, whatever)

This plan fits our overall mature lifestyle as I/we desire it now and in the future:

Signed: _____ Date: _____

Signed: _____ Date: _____

— —

CHAPTER 9	PERSONALLY YOURS IN THE MATURE YEARS

There's good news and bad news about being a mature adult.

The bad news is what you hear on broadcast and read in the press about aging, as some "experts" claim it to be a time of loss—declining abilities, faculties, and estate. Attend any gerontological conference to see and hear the many sessions based on some claimed and newly-identified debility or problem. If you believe their assumptions and discussions, you would not look forward to the future with anything but fear and trepidation, concern and uncertainty.

The good news is that, for most mature adults, these "experts" are wrong:

• There are frail elderly, of course, but most older adults will never be frail.

• There are adults who lose mental capacity or ability—most for the same reasons that younger people lose mental capacity or ability—and some because of Alzheimer's disease or senility. The odds are in your favor that as an older adult, you will never contract Alzheimer's or be afflicated by senility. "Regardless of what you may have heard, organic brain damage affects less than one percent of those over age sixty-five," according to the *Medical and Health Encyclopedia*, edited by Richard J. Wagman, M.D., F.A.C.P., of Downstate Medical Center in New York City

• Some mature adults are poor, but statistics show that they were also on the poverty rolls in earlier years.

• Some mature adults are ill in advancing years, but most are not, and there is no assumption that you or your spouse will be ill or ailing. Re-read Chapter Four on health for the facts.

Nearly two-thirds of Americans age sixty-five-and-over are pleased

147

with their lives, according to a May 1989 survey reported by the *Los Angeles Times*. Only about half of the people between the ages of eighteen and forty-nine expressed satisfaction with their lives, in this survey of 3,050 adults.

You are in control of your transition through life. As you faced challenges in earlier years, there may be new challenges or changes in the future. We address many of those possibilities in this chapter.

About the Aging Process

Aging is a transition process started at birth. You grew in size, strength, and ability; you learned to assimilate and reason, calculate and communicate. You learned to use and interpret your senses, and how to feel emotion. You learned from teachers, and from trial and error; and this lore and experience was collected in a miracle brain bank that allows recall as a basis for evaluation, reason, decision, and action.

As a child you fell many times before standing. As a youth you made mistakes from lack of knowledge and experience. As a younger adult you had to learn a profession or trade, how to establish and handle relationships, how to be a parent, how to handle personal finances, and how to face up to fire, famine, floods, and wars. Through the years you have grown through experience, challenges, good times, and tough times.

You have said "hello" to tens of thousands of people, and have also said tearful (or welcome) "goodbyes" to others. People, events, experiences, achievements, challenges—all have been building blocks in your transition from yesterday to today. The next 20 or 30 years will be no less a continuation of that transition.

In this chapter we look at the personal side of mature years, with briefings and suggestions for your possible use.

Transition: Freedom Time

You have a new freedom of time and choice in your retirement years. Your obligations and constraints of younger years are now, or soon will be, behind you. Choose exciting new directions and challenges and your next 10, 20 or 30 years may prove to be the very best of your life. Choose, instead, to do nothing in retirement years, and the odds are that you'll have little satisfaction, and that, from inactivity, your physical condition will deteriorate. The choice is yours.

I call these the "freedom years," instead of the "leisure years." *Webster's New World Dictionary* defines "leisure" as "free, unoccupied time during which a person may engage in rest or relaxation." For too long the common assumption has been that people work to a certain age and then stop for rest, doing nothing, "at leisure" until death. It was a neat way to process people out of the work force, creating job opportunities for younger persons, but a horrendous waste of human minds, ability, and potential. Government, business, labor, and even churches have taught this philosophy for years—never recognizing the individual accomplishment, rights, and potential of the mature years. It was easier to put non-working people on a shelf, send them to "rest homes," and assume the senior years to be those of illness, limitations, and problems. The stereotypes that led to "pity the poor senior" were fostered and accepted. Unfortunately, many older adults accepted this role and fate, fulfilling the conventional assumption. In creative retirement planning you, not others, are in control of your life, your direction, and your new adventures and accomplishments—and there is virtually no limit to what you can do.

The great George Abbott is still creating hit Broadway productions in his one hundredth year. George Burns won his first Academy Award at age eighty. At eighty Albert Schweitzer was operating a hospital in Africa. George Bernard Shaw was doing some of his best writing at ninety-three, and Grandma Moses was painting successfully at one hundred. On college campuses throughout the country mature adults are earning advanced degrees in their seventies and eighties and even launching teaching careers.

This time of transition should be one *to* a new direction, as you make full use of your new freedom of time and choice. You may release obligations or imperatives that earlier dictated or put restrictions on your life. You have a calendar of days which you may fill most any way that you desire, designating the dates and times to accomplish what you want. Your planning should start now for the next five years. Plan goals and activities, trips and events. A computer or word processor program will also have a calendar, projectable for years into the future. When you sit with five years of calendar pages or a computer calendar, you will realize the magnitude of your opportunity.

Start planning your freedom time as you complete the sections of this book. As you identify what you want to do, resolve the accomplishment dates in writing. This works well when considering the opportunity of travel one and two years in advance—the better for preparation for the trips and for attaining discounts in the pricing. It works for planning career changes, for back-timing your education and research projects, and other aspects. If you later change your mind, you can always adjust your calendar. Even if you elect to continue working, you will now be able to identify more freedom time than you ever had in earlier years.

The point is that the choice is yours, provided that you assume a "take-charge" position and do what is best for you.

Transition: Taking Charge

You're the boss in choosing where you will go and what you will do from here. This means that, as you determine, you may make all the changes you want, including where you live, with whom you associate, and what you do with your time. You may decide to continue working in your current position, even if it is based on a need for added income in mature years.

Your children do not and should not control your lifestyle. They are now growing or grown and need to learn and experience just as you did. If they are married with families, it is all right not to be always at their beck and call for assistance, cost-free baby-sitting, and house repairs. In fact, you may find it better to give them space and time on their own. They "commanded" a lot of time as children and as you supported them, even into or through college. That time was good and right as a family. Now, though, you need not be their continued servant, and you need not feel guilty about it.

Consider carefully the people you want in your mature years. If you want to be active and creative, choose to be with other active and creative people. You need not continue relationships that drain your energies or pull you in other directions. In working years we are many times captive to relationships that drag on us—people who are always complaining, people who demand that we support or buoy them up, or people who exist in negativity. You may choose to put these relationships behind you, being alert to avoid similar people in the future.

Each of us has a quantity of energy each day which we may put to good and creative use. But nothing will sap your time or creative energies more than negative people or problems. When you identify those people, events, or problems, you may put them and the resulting stress out of your life. Or, you may face them head-on and effect changes. To some this seems to be a callous position; but you must be in charge of your own fulfillment, accomplishment, and plan forward. Of course, you will continue to help family and friends in times of distress. This is creative use of your energy. But you need not feel obligated to continue in relationships and circumstances that are exclusively and consistently negative.

I address this subject in retirement lectures and workshops: "When are you the most tired?" I ask. The audience members think for a few minutes and then answer:

• "On Friday nights as I return home from work," is a typical response. "Why?" I ask. The response: "A group of us will stop for a drink, and the talk is always complaints about work." "Are you unhappy with your work?" I ask. "No, I like it, but the others need to unload their complaints." "If you wanted to feel great Friday evenings on returning home, what would you change?" "I would stop going to the gripe session," comes the response.

"Will the world stop if you did not participate, if you just planned something with your spouse each Friday night? Would you have the stress of those complaints draining on you if you just quit taking part in the Friday evening sessions?" I ask further. "No, the negative drain would be gone," is the typical response. "Who is now in charge?" I ask. The reponse is positive: "I can choose to do something different and be in charge of my own life. Now I feel good about it!"

• "When are you the most tired," I ask of another participant. "After our regular bridge games," is the response. "We have our games three times each week, and if I didn't participate they would not have the fourth to play." "Do you enjoy the game?" I ask. "Well, yes, I guess so. It is something to do as none of us get around a lot." My response: "Why don't you get around some or a lot? You seem to be healthy and mobile." "We all are, but we have been playing bridge three times a week for years." "What do you talk about and why do you think you get so tired after the games?" "We're getting on in years—in our sixties—and each of us have our aches and pains, and we hear about others who have their own aches and pains." "What do you solve or create in these bridge and ailment sessions? Is that what you want to do for the next 20 years three times a week? What would happen if you took charge of your life and went out and did the things you really wanted to do, rather than committing yourself to something that is exhausting you emotionally, is giving you no exercise, and is solving nothing that you need in your life?" I challenge in return. "I guess they would have to find another person who wanted to talk about the same things, or they'd have to get active, too." "Then ," I ask, "what will you do for the best in your life?" The answers vary from "I'll change what I am doing," to "I don't think I can let the others down, but perhaps some day in the future . . . ." Each respondent has made a decision based on himself or herself, some for the better, some for no change at all.

• "I don't really have the energy to get going in the morning. I'm so exhausted each night after the eleven o'clock news on television that I fall asleep during Johnny Carson." I love this typical question when it is asked. "Why must you watch television each evening? What new things have you learned from the reruns; what culture have you gained from the situation comedies; what positive things have you learned from the evening news? The late news is rife with reportage on disasters, murders, accidents, world conflicts, political rhetoric and charges. What's there to feel good about? What does any of it change in your world?" There is generally a pause before any answer. "Because . . ." and there is a defensive attempt to justify being a couch potato, as if there is an absolute need to watch television. I press further: "Have you other interests which provide satisfaction for you? Have you considered conversation? Have you considered hobbies, taking a walk, working out with a video exercise tape, reading, going out dancing or volunteering to help at a homeless shelter? Any of these activities—and more—will make you tired, honestly and physically so. But, watching an average of forty mayhems each evening on so-called entertainment television programs, and then accepting all of the carnage and conflict of the late news, provides yet another emotional drain. Is that what you want to do for the next 20 to 30 years? If not, change it now. You're the boss, and depending on which direction you choose the result will be more drain and pain, or active participation in something beneficial and rewarding."

You are in charge of your personal renaissance in the mature years. You have the freedom of time and direction to create the continued life transition that you desire.

Transition: Relationships

There will be changing relationships in each step of your mature years transition. Despite all good intentions and promises otherwise, you will drift away from those friends and associates affiliated with your job or profession after you leave. That does not make it wrong; nor does it mean that you are suffering a loss. Those relationships may be considered part of the transition as you move on to new opportunities.

If you're in the early phases of retirement planning, evaluate your present relationships. Are they all business based? Are they all church or neighborhood based? Will they hold you back when you want to go forward, or will they become a positive part of your yesterdays as you take advantage of the freedom and opportunity of your mature years?

Are there relationships which will hold you back if you allow them? Are you draining on others in relationships? If so, isn't it time for you to identify the problem and correct the practice?

Your relationships with your spouse may crash drastically unless you shape your life direction forward. There is the oft-told story of Sam, who had gone to the same job five days each week for 40 years, and then, without planning, he retired—with nowhere to go. Home seven days each week, Sam and his wife, Betty, were at each other's throats. She complained bitterly to her friend: "Alice, I can't stand it. Forty-two years ago I married Sam for better or worse—but not for lunch, too!"

Successful mature years planning involves both partners in a marriage, individually and jointly. This is why most every planning chart in this book calls for you to make individual entries first, and only after that do you compare and resolve your direction as partners. Your relationship must recognize individuality and independence as well as the joint or team program and goals.

Your relationships will change, and that is not all bad. In most cases, you will have the time and opportunity to make them better. Relationships with sons and daughters may be newly-approached on an adult rather than mainly on a parental basis. If you're well satisfied with yourself and your direction, you'll serve as a greater role model for them and for your grandchildren.

If your individual, personal life is directed and rewarding, you will have all the more to offer to your partner and to family, friendships, and other relationships.

Transition: The Retirement from Work

For many persons the transition from working to retirement is an emotional and stressful event, identified by sociologists as the "first trauma." If you are uncertain about the future and your direction in retirement, the transition may catalyze fear and concern. The fact that there is an increase in arthritis in some women at specifically this age and time of life is significant and pertinent. Planning for the retirement transition becomes vitally important. It is more than just a financial concern or plan. It encompasses the entire range of subjects in this book, for it may be an entirely new direction and program for 24 hours a day, 365 days a year. You must be in charge of the retirement transition.

There have been proposals for "phased retirement" and "shared job creation" for mature adults, so to ease the change from a full-time work commitment over months or years to a non-working status. Theories and demonstration programs do not create fact in the real world, and other than a few companies, like Traveler's Insurance in Hartford, Connecticut— which offers both opportunities—any such transition is one that you will have to create for yourself.

Answer the questions again: Do you really want to retire from the work force? And if so, when and how? Do you want to change careers? Do you want to move? Do you want to do nothing or something, and if so, what? Do you have the ability to approach retirement, knowing that you will not have financial or other problems?

If you are being pressured to retire from a company and you do not agree to the move, know that you may challenge it. Mandatory retirement is invalid by law, except for certain high risk fields. If you want to challenge a retirement mandate, your local office of the Equal Opportunity Commission and/or your state department of labor are ready to answer your questions and be of assistance.

You may have other reasons to retire: a medical or a financial condition which would mitigate any desire to do otherwise. Even if that be the reason, know that you have the same freedom of opportunity and time as all other mature adults.

Have you created your mature years plan, knowing where you want to be headed and what you want to do for the next 20 or 30 years? Are you ready to make the next giant steps? If you have any question, don't rush into retirement—take more time and thought so that you are in control of the transition and your direction forward.

Transition: Grandparenting

There is no more privileged role in mature years than being a grandparent. You have inalienable rights to build the best of human relationships with these second generation offspring and a right, too, to spoil them. They will learn from you about age and opportunity; you are the living role model representing mature years as a positive or negative time of life.

As you have had the challenge of being teacher, disciplinarian, provider, and supporter of your own children, you must now grant them the right to that role and responsibility with their children—your grandchildren. That opens to you the opportunity of a remarkable relationship with both children and grandchildren that may go beyond blood lines: a real friendship.

Retailers already know that you will buy the better or best grade of clothing and quality toys for your grandchildren. Cruise ship companies have added pull-down berths in staterooms for grandparents and grandchildren traveling together. Insurance companies have created special policies so you may endow their college educations.

As a mature adult you may have added challenges regarding your grandchildren, as 40 percent of new marriages end in divorce. Children become the victims of the parental discord often assuming themselves responsible for the breakup. At such a time the grandparental role is all the more vital, as you should assert your continued rights of visitation.

There is a need also, I suggest, for you to learn a lot about the challenges in the lives of children and teenagers today: drugs, the effect of broken homes of their associates (creating a fear of a similar fate in their lives), questionable educational values and training, crime, and the threat of war and, therefore, death. Few adults really communicate with children about these fearful subjects. That may be your vital role as a grandparent: taking the time to go fishing, and talking; taking a cruise, and talking; doing a project, where you both may talk if there is reason to do so. I suggest that you read and learn in each of these areas, so you have meaningful answers. Learn how to recognize the signs of drug use—for you might be the very first to recognize a problem. And, if there is a problem, you may deal with it positively, productively, and without shame or guilt.

If you and I are concerned about crime, imagine its impact on a child not big enough to protect herself or himself. If we are concerned about drugs, put yourself in the place of the youngster facing peddlers and ruffians at the very doors of the schoolhouse. Consider international conflicts and talk about nuclear weapons. Our experience tells us that these arguments have been going on for years. But the child doesn't have this experience, and can be frightened when hearing only of nuclear weapons and witnessing more national and international bloodletting nightly on the television news. Your communication role may be one of sharing without lecture, for listening and teaching.

There is a special human bond possible between grandchildren and grandparents. It is something you should find opportune and rewarding as you go forward in your mature years. It does not mean that you must never be more than one block away; in fact, it might mean just the opposite— such is yours to determine. It does call for you as grandparent to be that special person to your grandchildren. Your reward? The biggest, most unselfish hug you'll ever receive, and a bond that may transcend miles as well as years.

Transition: Your Parents

If your own parents are still alive, they may have an increasing inability to take care of themselves. Today, we may have four and five generations of family alive at the same time, with those generations separated by thousands of miles and very different lifestyles.

If your parents can continue to live in their home, are there support services needed? If they are frail, will you invite them to live with you? Or will other family members make the invitation? What needs do they have that you can provide? Are they financially able to care for themselves? Are their own affairs in order? Are there other sons and daughters with whom you should coordinate in the interest of your parents? Or, are your parents as fiercely independent as you would want to be at whatever their age?

You may find your relationship with your parents very special today, without the dominant/subservient roles as parents and children, sharing today and tomorrow in a new friendship.

When operating the GLADventurers senior citizen travel club years ago, my wife, Marcia, and I learned much from mothers and daughters— in their seventies and fifties, and eighties and sixties—who traveled together. They found new discovery in destinations and in each other. Long unsaid thoughts and feelings were shared; even long-standing conflicts or misunderstandings were resolved and set aside.

If my own father were alive today, I'd shoot a real game of pool with him—where he didn't let me win as he did earlier; or play that game of poker for match sticks or beans, where he did not bend the rules for me; or find time, finally, to learn the real story of the San Francisco earthquake, when his father's Ansgar Lutheran Church was the high ground refuge for those who fled from the devastation. I guess I never had time to listen before; and I want to do so now, if I could. There is a heritage that is uniquely our own, not written in history books, but vital in our understanding of who we are and how all of today came to be.

Perhaps, if parents or uncles and aunts are still with us, this is the time to listen and savor—for we are the progeny of their possibility and perseverance. Such is our own history to be shared, in turn, with sons, daughters, and grandchildren.

Our parents and kinfolk also are going through their own transitions—from an entry into the world to a time of passing from it. Each has his or her role, performance, and success—and has made possible the life we have. They have been a part of our lives, and at the right time for each of them, will move on from this life—hopefully satisfied, having completed a role and a mission.

Our own transitions through life will have these events and relationships. We recognize them for what they are and for what they have meant to us, as we go forward in carrying our own lives and their heritage forward.

Transition: Sexuality, Touching, and Caring

There are two hypes perpetrated on mature adults. One is by churches which insist that the practice of sex is intended solely for the procreation of children. The other is by younger people who cannot envision a loving, caring, sexual relationship between mature adults. After all, advertising and television, motion pictures and the popular press have presented sex as the domain of the young. But the sexes are still distinct and mutually supportive. Both have sensualities and needs that span entire adult lifetimes, not just a limited number of younger years.

Life conflicts and strains may produce major hindrances to sexual relations for many persons—from job, business, and financial pressures, from a loss of exclusive "time together," and from one's personal concerns about ability to fulfill a partner in the sex experience. Being overweight "from the good life," and reduced mobility from a lack of ongoing exercise, may also inhibit the sexual relationship. The time of menopause for women and uncertainty of status in retirement additionally become factors inhibiting sexual contact. Current research shows that the human body retains most of its senses through life, and the ability to respond in a sexual situation continues possible, even if a bit slower.

Swedish scientists found that sexually active mature adults are more vital, have higher levels of sex hormones in the blood, and have better memories than their celibate counterparts, as reported in *Prevention* magazine. Bernard D. Starr, Ph.D., writing in the *Starr-Weiner Report on Sex and Sexuality in the Mature Years*, estimated that for 97 percent of those 60-79 years of age sex was a crucial part of their lives, and for the 80-plus group, 93 percent called sex vital.

Sexuality in mature years may take on new dimensions, with more time and opportunity for sharing. Sexuality in aging may involve the sex act or may not. Feeling comfortable sexually and rewarded by the relationship may take on new importance and satisfaction, and may be a rediscovery for many mature adults. It is something to talk about. Psychologists report today that the lack of open communication about sex and sexuality is the cause of diminishing relationships between husbands and wives in the mature years. Dr. Joyce Brothers teaches, in her lectures, that sexual fulfillment is possible for most people, including those with arthritis or other limitations. It only takes a consideration of the limitations, and imaginative approaches for maintaining the physical relationship.

There will be more time in your mature years for a meaningful sexual relationship—a return to it, a modification of it, or a redesign of it. Even touching and caring may take on added meaning.

This transition in life path is one of continued opportunity even if different than in your twenties. You have more experience now, more ways to enjoy, more ways to share than ever before. Dealing with your own sexuality is important for your life's best and most satisfying years today and tomorrow.

Transition: Mortality or Morbidity

All of us, at some point, will complete our lives on this earth—a point in time called mortality. Some will be ill for years as they head for death—and that illness path is defined as morbidity.

The ideal, according to Dr. Thomas C. Namey, is to live a very healthy and active life, and then, when the time is appropriate, to die quickly. We know how to keep our bodies healthy—through nutrition, exercise, and activity. But both birth and death are facts of life—it is what we do with ourselves in between those two events that makes the difference.

Contrary to earlier assumptions, most mature adults don't worry about dying—and you shouldn't have to, either, if you think now about the eventual fact and resolve your planning for it. A death is a terrible time for the survivors, particularly if they must deal not only with the loss, but also with the arrangements, financial affairs, and other decisions.

In a comedy routine Steven Wright claims to be the only person to know when he will die: "My birth certificate has an expiration date." If each of us similarly knew when death would happen, we could defer any thought

157

about it until near the last minute. But we don't know, so should think and resolve about it now, so we don't have to think or worry about it in the future.

The best living gift we can offer those who survive us is to have all affairs in order and all arrangements made in advance. Here is a check list:

The Will and/or Trust: Are these documents prepared, updated, and with copies easily accessible at the time of need? Never put the only copy in a safe-deposit box.

Records: Are all financial and historical records also accessible, inventoried and in order? This is a worthy project which may take two days of personal effort now, or possibly years of work by your family and attorneys later.

Final Arrangements: Have you pre-determined and arranged for your funeral? You may plan such arrangements and funding through a funeral director. Just one day of thinking about and resolving this now means you never have to think about it again—and neither will your family and friends.

Titles and Deeds: Are home and property deeds in proper title for easy and effective transfer to survivors? One day of collection and inventory, and a one hour appointment with your attorney, should assure this for you and your survivors.

Insurance: Have you properly insured for possible, necessary, or anticipated medical care and, if needed, nursing home costs? Have your property insurance policies been reviewed, considering inflation and replacement values, so that these, too, are current and appropriate?

Living Will: Have you resolved personally whether you want to be sustained by life support systems in a hospital? Consider this question with action now, particularly if you prefer that no life support system should be used if, at the time, the only predictable eventuality is death. In most states you may enact a Living Will that will provide your own legal direction, relieving your family or friends of that traumatic decision.

One week is about all the time necessary to accomplish all of the above. If you're married, take the time now to talk about the eventuality so you have a mutual understanding and resolution in each of the areas of concern. Once they have been addressed and resolved with action, you can go forward without question or concern.

Transition: Death of a Spouse

The most caring thing you can do for your spouse is to resolve and enact all of the steps defined as part of mortality and morbidity—removing those eventual needs at a time of stress. You may also make a commitment to maintain the very best of health throughout your mature years so to assure, in every way possible, mortality instead of morbidity.

And, you may prepare each other with the knowledge necessary to carry forward in the event of death. In many older households, the man handled the financial affairs, and if he died first, the widow was awash in financial problems and concerns. Confidence men prey on older widows, assuming their financial naivete. Your spouse might need to learn more about financial affairs, or about the household, food preparation and service. The process is definitely not a "countdown to mortality," but instead a new sharing of information and responsibilities. The financial information, for example, may be shared as an ongoing process as a matter of positive living.

In death it is far better to be remembered for the good times and sharing, rather than for the mess you left for the survivor to figure out.

Death of a spouse is the "second trauma" identified by sociologists, and statistically, men have shorter life expectations than do women. We may deny that it will ever happen and be unprepared for it, but if your spouse were to die in an accident, how prepared are you to carry forward? That's a question for any age, and not only for mature adults. What do you need to do or provide for such eventuality? Is there estate value and insurance coverage to provide financially for the survivor?

If your spouse were to die, would you be able to take your own life forward, and not be bound up in memories and loss? It is natural to grieve. It is natural and healthy to combine grief with positive resolution to go forward actively. It is easy to say; a personal challenge to accomplish.

Transition: The Physical

Assume that in the aging process you will have physical changes. Your body has been changing throughout your life, and certain body parts and functions may slow down. Each has its own time line; they don't all break down at one time because of age. Our bodies are designed to work well throughout our lives, if we keep ourselves healthy.

For most people, eyes reach a peak in performance before age forty; and therefore eyeglasses are the order of the day for many or most mature adults. Through life we have strained our eyes, overworked them, and made them work in too little or too much light. Diminished hearing ability is possible, even as early as age thirty, from both environmental (noise) and natural causes. Remedial steps are available, though, either medically or by using an appliance. Hearing aids today are small—many almost invisible to the eye—and very effective. Your decision should not be based on vanity ("I don't want people to know that I can't hear them."), but instead on maintaining your maximum ability to hear for communication, learning, and socialization. "Correcting" eyesight and hearing, as needed, is the most positive way to handle any physical change in these senses.

But what if there is another physical setback? Let's draw an analogy to the glass containing water at a 50 percent level. The glass is half full, to the positive person, who is anticipating the benefit of the water. To the doomsayer or complainer, however, the glass is half empty as he or she focuses on the void. That remaining water will never satisfy the person who is focused on "what I don't have" or on what is not there. When stationed at Letterman Army Hospital during the Korean war, I met patients of both convictions. Sergeant Herb Rhodes manipulated hooks instead of the hands he lost to a field mine explosion. There wasn't a task that he avoided; there wasn't a time he shied away from meeting or sharing with people. But there were others with lesser physical problems who focused on what they had lost. They demanded the most attention because they assumed helplessness based on what they assumed could not be done—and so they increased their invalidity.

Many physical problems in mature years may be deferred or alleviated through exercise, nutrition, and activity. You have a choice of approaches if you do experience a difficulty or limitation: by getting the best and most out of what you can do; or by giving in to the limitation for more than it is, reducing your aims and expectations severely.

The physical body is wondrous in its ability to compensate. We found at Letterman Army Hospital that where one arm or leg was disabled, the alternate and supporting limbs would produce more muscle and strength. Later private and government research showed that arthritic joints actually gained through use, in most cases, and that muscles above and below the affected knee or other joint could be increased so to reduce the strain. Giving in to the affected joint through non-use actually worsened the condition, increasing the debility.

An eighty-year old man once taught me a neat fact of life and living in his statement: "No, I don't run or move as fast as I used to or as younger people do—but I don't have to. I know where I am going and from experience I know the shortcuts. I get there at the same time and I ain't winded when I come through the door."

By knowing more about your body and mind you may keep both functioning to their fullest. Through activity you also keep the body working and the mind alert for any opportunity you choose.

How do you consider the water glass representing your own health and physical being? Is your mind set on what you have as an asset or on what you don't have? How and why you choose your direction will determine, similarly, the fullness or emptiness of your mature years today and tomorrow.

Transition: Making It Happen

Your direction in retirement years is up to you. You have the sheets of paper and the calendar, and you may determine your plan. You need not put into that plan anything that you don't want: no millstones previously carried, no relationships that have been sapping your energies. Even bad habits may be discarded in a new plan for the best of your mature years. Sharpen your focus on what you want to do in the future and not what you had to do in the past.

There will be personal challenges and changes as part of this life transition. When we recognize them as such and plan for them, they can fit into the plan instead of destroying it.

Contemporary composer and singer David Pomerantz advises in song: "It's in every one of us to be wise. Find your heart. Open up your eyes." Your mature life transition *is* as he sings it: a very personal thing.

A Personal Planning Chart

Do copy the following chart onto tablet paper, leaving lots of room between the subjects. Complete these forms individually; and if a couple, then compare notes to prepare a consolidated list.

———————————————————————————————————————

PERSONAL PLANNING CHART FOR:

(Name) _____

My/Our age today is: _____.

If I/we take better care of myself/ourselves I/we should live to be _____ years of age.

My/Our lifespan(s) may be _____ more years.

If I/we don't change personal health care, I/we should anticipate the following problems:

_____

_____

_____

For my/our freedom time as mature adults I/we want to do the following:

(list them) _____

_____

_____

For the best of freedom time and mature adult years plan I/we will change the following things, people, or events which are draining on me/us, and will put behind me/us:

_____

_____

_____

I/We will purchase or prepare calendars for the next five years: _____ Yes? _____ No? _____

Perhaps when I/we think of it sometime in the future;

_____ other: _____

Date of this purchase: _____

The start of entries for this mature lifespan calendar includes: _____

_____

_____

_____

The kind of relationships and people I/we would like to have in my/our life forward are:

_____

_____

_____

I/We define my/our role and opportunity as a grandparent to include: _____

_____

_____

_____

For my/our own parents, I/we project that: _____

_____

_____

_____

On sex and sexuality here are the steps and changes that may or should be made:

_____

_____

_____

Here is how I/we have prepared for mortality, as an important accomplishment for those who survive me/us:

The will: _____

_____

The trust: _____

_____

Records: _____

_____

Final arrangements: _____

_____

Titles and deeds: _____

_____

Insurance: _____

_____

Living will: _____

_____

Other: _____

_____

_____

_____

Here is how I/we have prepared others (each other) to carry forward in the event of my/our death: _____

_____

_____

For my/our physical well-being here are the adjustments to be made: _____

_____

_____

_____

This is the date when all of the above will be accomplished or be underway for accomplishment: _____

My/Our added comments and commitments:

_____

_____

_____

Signed: _____ **Date:** _____

Signed: _____ **Date:** _____

CHAPTER 10

THE TRAVEL ADVENTURE

Travel is one of the grandest adventures and opportunities available for the mature adult. You are able to plan your time better, and may pay less for travel than people who are tied to strict work and family schedules.

In every recent marketing survey, travel places at or near the top three mature adult desires and activities. According to studies by the U.S. Travel Data Center, 80 percent of all pleasure travel is by persons over age fifty, and mature adults take more trips per year, spend more days away from home, and travel longer distances than younger people.

Therefore, as a mature adult you're a sought-after traveler, and the airlines, hotels, cruise lines and other travel businesses will provide incentives to gain your patronage. That sounds like a "good deal" for all involved.

Considering Travel

Name anywhere you'd like to go in the nation or the world. There's a way to get there economically and comfortably—if you plan actively and correctly.

There is adventure, too, in researching how and when to travel, in deciding where you would like to go, in reading up on what to do and discover there, and in planning your trip to meet or exceed your expectations. Whether your goal is to stretch out on a tropical beach (doing nothing more difficult than reaching for that tall, cool glass refilled periodically by the local waiter or waitress), or whether you want to take your own version of the grand tour (visiting every museum and historic site in Europe), you will fulfill your desires better if you plan ahead.

Professionals in the travel business find that the most disappointed travelers are those who just "took a trip" because it was advertised, without planning for what they were going to do or discover while there. Their expectations were nonexistent, so most of the travelers spent most of each morning reading tour brochures or local directories to find "something to do" that very day. Only when it's time to leave do most of these people realize what they've missed.

Travel is an investment of your time and your money. As you invest in a security on the anticipation of a financial return, you may consider travel an investment with a return in personal gratification and in the pleasures of sharing and of education in discovering another part of the country or the world. In travel as in finance, planning is the key to success. In addition, there can be as much fun and sharing in the planning for travel as there is the fulfillment of the actual trip.

Smart travelers consider their longer and more important trips as many as one, two or three years in advance. Shorter trips can then be blocked around the longer trip dates, and planned for variety in travel experiences. By starting your thought and discussions early, you will have time for research, comparison shopping, and—most significantly—for taking advantage of early booking discounts and advantages in price and benefits.

On Travel Planning and Purchasing

The best place to start and conduct your travel planning is through a professional travel agency, particularly one that is a member of the American Society of Travel Agents (ASTA). This organization has high membership standards regarding the professional level of management and staff, financial ability and performance. For cruise travel, your agency should also be a member of the Cruise Lines International Association (CLIA). The membership requirements are not as stringent as those of ASTA, but CLIA membership does signify acceptance of the travel agency for booking business with international cruise lines.

As an additional recommendation, if you're considering tour travel, the travel agency should recommend member tour operators of the National Tour Association (NTA). There are performance and financial standards necessary for membership in NTA, so that if you book with a member company, you are not likely to be stranded somewhere in the world, and your tour will be operated as advertised. There are other warranty and protection programs for air carriers, tour operators, and other travel providers—all in place to assure the value and performance of your trip investment. Ask your travel agent about them.

It comes as a surprise to some travelers that almost all services and counseling by professional travel agents are free of charge. Their income is derived from a commission paid by the airlines and other travel carriers, cruise lines, hotels and motels, tour operators and even auto rental firms. Your patronage of a particular firm should be determined by the quality of their service, the value/pricing you get in your travel, and your agent's attention and follow-through on your behalf if there is a problem.

Could you do this planning for yourself? Sure, but consider just one fact: In the travel business there are thousands of price changes—particularly in air fares—every day, and only through the travel agent's computers can this information be accessed so as to obtain the most advantageous fares and arrangements at any given time.

I, personally, would never book a cruise trip without going through a professional travel agency. There are too many considerations and arrangements to handle. There are differences in ships and their accommodations, fares, itineraries and more. The professional travel agent will reserve your dinner seating, arrange your connecting air and ground transportation, suggest and book pre- and post-cruise tours, and advise on passport and visa requirements—and more.

A travel agency should be chosen for its area of expertise. Some specialize in cruises, some in general pleasure travel, some in business travel, and some in travel to a specific part of the world. The travel agency, basically, shops the travel vendors to determine the "right" arrangements to meet the desires and expectations of its clientele. In their area of expertise they will probably have personal experience with the vendors— the travel "packagers," the cruise lines, airlines, hotels, motels and attractions. When interviewing travel agencies, ask about their particular area of expertise, looking for one that meets your own needs. When you find an agency where the staff is responsive to you, asks you questions about your desires in travel, about your flexibility in scheduling when price becomes a consideration, about any health requirements or concerns, about your preferred seating on airplanes, about your past travel experiences, and about your expectations from travel, you have found the right agency for your travel planning and arrangements.

Just as an accountant is unable to make recommendations without knowing your financial status, concerns, and goals, travel counselors cannot create the "best" trip for you without knowing your personal desires, budget, and experiences, Prior to visiting a travel agency, write your thoughts on paper, so that you can share them easily. Be candid about your budget—there is, generally, a way to solve a travel need within most budgets. In New York City, for example, there are hotels for $400 per night, and others where you will sleep just as well for $90 to $100, and delightful Bed and Breakfast Inns for $70 or less.

We all know that the front of the airplane, with the highest-price first class seats, arrives at the airport at the same time as the back end, where the economy and discount-priced seats are located. Unless you're six foot three inches or taller, as I am, or well over two hundred pounds, which I am not any more, you might travel acceptably well in the economy section, and pay far less for the ticket if you plan and buy it advantageously. Aboard a cruise ship there are inside cabins available at a fraction of the cost of suites or outside cabins—but they are all on the same ship, their occupants dine in the same restaurants aboard ship, share the same swimming pool and sun deck, and enjoy the same show each evening in the lounge. So, be candid with your travel agent about your goals and your budget. There's probably a way to have the best of travel experience and have some money left in the bank, too.

Make a list, also, of the activities you enjoy and of those things you don't like to do. For a visitor to London there might be fifteen tour programs from which to choose, but only one that includes visits to bookstores or curio shops. If such were your particular interests and your travel agent didn't know, his or her recommendation might be made for a tour that spent a lot of time in castles or museums. Your list of "likes/don't likes" helps determine the trip selection. In order to foster your interest and considerations, pick up a selection of brochures at the agency for your consideration of where and how you might like to travel. Considering ideas for your travel wish book can be an adventure all its own.

As long as your travel agent continues to be responsive, continue your relationship. You'll find yourself welcome to drop by and discuss travel and ask questions even when you are not planning a trip that would mean business for them.

About Cruising

How about a luxurious trip where you unpack once and your resort does the traveling from one destination to another? Travel by cruise ship offers the choice of most parts and ports of the world, and a range of ships, pricing, and amenities to fit most pocketbooks.

Once the cruise travel opportunity centered on the Caribbean, the Mediterranean, and Southeast Alaska, but today you can find a ship—or even a selection of ships and itineraries—in almost every navigable waterway in the world. New opportunities include the South Pacific, the Orient, Hawaii, the Mexican Riviera and Baja California, South America, New England and Eastern Canada, Scandinavia and the British Isles, and Africa—in addition to a greater selection of itineraries in the Caribbean, Alaska and Mediterranean. You may cruise inland in the U.S. on the Mississippi and other rivers, through England, the wine country of France, and on the Rhine in Germany. You may cruise for a week or a month, two or three days, or even take a one-day cruise to "nowhere."

Prices range from as little as $100 per day per person to as much as $500, depending on the ship and its itinerary. That price includes just about everything aboard ship—room, lavish meals, entertainment, pool, gymnasium and programs. Additionally, your airfare from home to the port city might be included or be available at a discount.

Tipping for service aboard a cruise ship will prove to be far less than when traveling on shore. Some cruise lines do not allow tipping at all. On other lines, you'll recognize your waiter in the dining room and your room steward, probably at $3 each per person per day. Other services you might recognize are the maitre d', wine steward or for on-deck or bar service. Your travel agent will advise you on this.

There will be all kinds of activities and cultural programs aboard, and you may partake of any or all of them—or none of them. There is no pressure—this is not like going to camp or the company picnic where you are "expected" to do everything. Physical education classes will be available and include on-deck exercise, walking, and jogging sessions. Other classes might be offered in financial affairs, bridge playing, classic movies, current affairs, or a briefing on the culture and shopping opportunities in the next port of call. At night, there are varied entertainment programs in the main lounge. Simultaneously there will be music for dancing elsewhere, perhaps a late-night disco, a motion picture theater, and strolling musicians on deck.

Most ships will have "dress-up" evenings every other or every third night, so that men would wear a tux or dark suit and tie on the more elegant ships, or just jacket and tie on a more casual ship. For the ladies it means formals or other evening wear on the luxury ships to pantsuits and cocktail dresses on other vessels. Your travel agent will be able to advise you on what type of clothes to bring, or will book you aboard a ship that fits your wardrobe and clothing preference.

Dining will be special on most every cruise ship you choose. The chefs aboard rank with the best in the world, presenting gourmet choices at breakfast, lunch and dinner, mid-morning and mid-afternoon snacks, and a late-night buffet supper. You choose whatever you desire from the menu—without ever having to consider a price tag. Only your drinks and/ or wine will be charged as extra.

There are several ways to save money on cruising. By booking and paying a deposit as much as a year in advance, or by booking close to the date of the sailing, you can save as much as fifty-percent of the listed ticket price. Work with your travel agent on either of these alternatives, but for the "fire sale" discounts, you may purchase the ticket through a cruise discounter. In the latter case, you must be knowledgeable about the cruise ships and itineraries offered, cabin location, and more. I still prefer the travel agent, who provides more complete and responsive service—and who is, after all, your local neighbor—whereas the cruise discounter might be thousands of miles away. Special values in cruising are also available in "shoulder" and "off" seasons. The cruise is the same, but the price is less if you can travel when the demand is less, that is, before or after the prime season.

The cruise experience is a special way to see yet another part of the world in a quality environment. Service, generally, is superior, equal to that found in only the best hotels and resorts ashore. It is even a great environment and opportunity to bring grandchildren.

About Tour Programs

The tour operator is like a cruise company, though dealing with a different type of travel product, and most quality tours are sold through travel agents. Tour programs today come in many varieties—from complete, door-to-door, escorted excursions with just about everything planned and included, to individual programs where you are more or less on your own.

The original tour concept was to take two weeks and "do" ten or eleven cities, as exemplified in the movie, *If It's Tuesday, This Must Be Belgium.* You can still find tours of the whirlwind style, but today's tours are generally less frantic. Many use the "hub" concept, where travelers settle into a hotel for two, three, or more days, and venture out daily by rail or charter coach on tour programs. Other tour programs put the traveler in one or two resort areas for one week each, and include transportation, sightseeing programs and more, on an individual basis.

Tours, like cruises, provide you with a travel package where all or most arrangements are handled and paid for in advance. Some tours will be completely escorted, with most meals, transportation, and other activities included. Others allow for individual travel, with airfare, hotel arrangements, airport transfers, and some meals, admissions, etc. provided in the package. By dealing in volume the travel tour operator can negotiate much lower rates and still market the programs through travel agents at rates lower than you would pay if buying the elements separately.

When considering a tour, make your list of "likes and dislikes" as in general travel, and then study the brochures to see if the tour program matches your interests, or has enough free time so that you can structure your own added adventures.

Senior citizen discounts are offered by some tour operators; these vary by company, season, and other considerations. Every time you discuss a tour, ask if there is a senior citizen discount, and at what qualifying age.

Tour operations take a lot of the guesswork and expense out of travel. If you don't mind traveling with a group of others and at their pace, you might find this a sociable way to see the world.

There is no structured form for tour brochures or presentations, so I recommend you make your own comparison chart. Take sheets of large paper, one for each day of the tour, and prepare them as follows. (Write in only what is specifically included, not what is presented as an option.)

Tour Comparison Chart For Tour of:_____		
Day/Part/Event	**Tour One (Name)**	**Tour Two (Name)**
Day (one, two)		
Start City:		
Hotel/Class:		
Breakfast:		
Lunch:		
Dinner:		
Other Food:		
Tour to:		
Tour to:		
Free Time:		
Escorted/Not:		
Special Program:		
Attraction:		
Attraction:		
Attraction:		
Other:		
_____		
_____		

My Desires/Items—Included?

On to the next day plan.

Then after listing the various tour programs, by listing only what is included you can see easily what is and is not included.

Prepare a summary sheet, in this format:

— —

TOUR SUMMARY/COMPARISON SHEET   Tours to: _____

Item:	Tour One (name)	Tour Two (name)	Etc (name)
Number of Days:			
Price from brochure: Added (see the small print for port charges, taxes, etc.)			
Price for travel, round trip from/to home to join this tour			
Net estimated cost:			

ESTIMATED ADDITIONAL COSTS:

For tours not included:			
Meals not included:			
Sightseeing not included:			
Admissions not included:			
Added accommodations: (such as overnight prior to start and following final day of tour)			
Other costs anticipated:			
Total of added costs:			

Item:	Tour One (name)	Tour Two (name)	Etc (name)
REVISED GROSS COST (all costs, included and non-included)			
Number of tour days:			
Cost per day (divide tour days into the Revised Gross), per person:			

Comments: (Here comment on the validity of each tour, on what is and is not included, based on your desires, likes, and dislikes. You will want to share this comparison chart with your travel agent for his/her analysis and authentication of pricing/considerations.)

DECISION: (Write here your decision. Pick one tour, or resolve to buy none of them, and to seek other possibilities or other ideas.)

About Airlines

Airlines can get you anywhere in the world—and you can fly at the regular fares or at one of the other, lower fares available to those in the know. Air fares fluctuate by the day and by route. They are adjusted to meet competition, tending to increase in markets where an airline has little or no competition. Some airlines offer senior citizen discount fares on all flights, generally 10 percent off the regular coach fares, but this discount level is far less than the price you can get by working with Supersaver, Maxsaver, and Excursion fares, where discounts may be at 50 percent or more. Other promotional fares are offered, too, at special times when airlines are looking to fill seats.

A list of airline discounts compiled as of this writing would be out of date before this book reached your bookseller or library. But there are some general principles to follow in seeking and finding the lowest airfares available.

On the Supersaver and Maxsaver fares, a number of seats will be available, generally, on each airline flight, particularly those flights through a "hub" where you must change planes. (Unfortunately, there will be few, if any, on nonstop flights across the continent.) The actual number of seats is "capacity rated," meaning that if the demand is high for a particular flight, the capacity rating determines that there will be few tickets at deeply discounted prices.

Some of the discount fares will have restrictions, such as not allowing changes or rebates or having cash penalties for changes. On these tickets, predictably the best of discounts available, only a serious emergency—provable by letters and other documentation—will be recognized for refunds or adjustments without penalty. These fares will also have advance purchase requirements, such as thirty days prior to the first flight.

Excursion fares are advance purchase tickets that also have a length-of-stay requirement, such as over a Saturday, and perhaps with other restrictions to include the allowable days and times of flights. Discounted evening fares are offered by many airlines, if you don't mind flying the "red eye" to your destination. From personal experience, I have found these flights to be used by families with children, thus often quite noisy with crying babies.

As in other travel, the earlier you can plan your flight with your travel agent, the better. Discount fares may be available, and if not, you may be placed early on the "wait list" for lower fares as other travelers cancel their arrangements, or as the airline expands the capacity rating on the specific flight.

If you plan any air travel at all, I recommend that you join the frequent-flyers club for all airlines you might to use. While you might not build up enough mileage to earn free tickets, their monthly mailings offer special discounts for flights, hotels, auto rentals, and more. Membership in most of these clubs is free, and your travel agent will have membership forms. The other benefit with membership is that, on most airlines, you will be able to secure preferred seating for a flight at the time of reservation, so that you won't have to stand in line to get seat assignments at the airport.

My travel agent's computer has each of my frequent-flyer membership numbers, my preferred seating specifications, and more. When handling my reservation, she also logs the pertinent membership number for earned mileage credit and makes my seat reservations. Does it work? In the past fifty flights, including some where reservations were made close to the flight date, my preferred seating—far forward on the aisle in nonsmoking—is where I sat on forty-eight of those trips.

When dealing with your travel agent, insist that you want the lowest airfare possible. I do not recommend running to three or four travel agents to get them in competition, because they are all working with the same computer access. And such an action is shortsighted when your best relationship should be with a primary agent where you can seek counsel and ideas that you trust.

When flying, it is best to hold down liquor consumption, to drink more water, and to eat more lightly. Get up and walk around every hour or so—you can generally stand in the back of the section for a few minutes—to keep your circulation system in good working order. Even while sitting you can stretch your limbs and muscles to prevent stiffness. You'll get off the airplane feeling better, more ready to tackle the adventures at your destination.

Special meals for a flight may be ordered at no added charge, at the time of reservation or at least forty-eight hours ahead of the flight. Such special meals might be Kosher, low-cholesterol, vegetarian, or a fruit plate. Many travelers find these special meals to be more palatable than the standard airline meals.

Flying is the surest gateway to travel adventures. As just one traveler, I make 30 to 40 roundtrip flights each year—150,000 to 200,000 miles aloft, and with connecting flights counted, that adds up to more than 200 takeoffs and safe landings. Some 450,000,000 air trips are taken in the United States each year—a doubling of the number of travelers since the airline deregulation in 1978. There are more flights—to just about anywhere you'd want to go—and most of the trips operate on schedule. Airliners are clean and efficient travel (even if the rows in tourist class seem a bit closer together these days). I, for one, feel much safer aboard a jet than I do in the taxicab or jitney bus which will carry me to and away from the airport.

About Hotels and Motels

As a mature adult traveler you'll find a greater selection of hotels and motels available today than in years past—and most everywhere you'll find a senior citizen discount at some qualifying age.

The best general rates will be found at the times when business people or family vacationers are not traveling. In New York City, for example, you will readily find 40 to 50 percent discounts on weekends and in the summer. In Las Vegas the lowest rates are for Sunday through Wednesday nights. In business traveler hotels, your best rates will come on Friday and Saturday nights and in holiday seasons.

For senior citizen discounts the qualifying age ranges as low as fifty. When you or your travel agent make the reservation, ask for the best available room rate and then for their senior-citizen discount. The savings are, typically, 10 percent, but may be as much as 50 percent. Have a membership card in a national senior-citizen organization and/or proof of age for presentation when you register to assure your discount advantage.

Many hotels will have promotional packages, which traditionally offer a lower room rate for a stay of more than one night. Breakfasts, dinner, and other benefits may be included in the deal. Most business travelers stay in a hotel or motel only one night, so it is to the management's advantage to secure travelers who have the ability to stay two, three or more nights. You'll find these benefits in their senior citizen traveler or promotional programs. Your travel agent should also have this information.

Many hotels also operate their own jitney bus service to the airport—providing a real saving on ground transportation costs. Ask about this possibility when making your reservations. Members of airline frequent-flyer clubs will find special discounts, which may be advantageous. Read about these discounts in the club newsletters.

Traveling for Free

How about traveling for free? It will take some qualification and development time on your part, but it is possible to see the world at little or no cost.

Take tours by putting together a group of fifteen to thirty people who want to go to the same destination as you. Working with a travel agent or tour operator, you may be able to earn your free participation for having organized the group. If you are active with a club or other group and want to put the effort into "selling" the tour to a large enough number of people to earn your free passage, chat about the possibility with a travel agent. There are mature adults who travel somewhere each month on this basis—and at no cost. Some cruise tours can also be packaged in this way.

The number of qualifying tickets necessary to earn free passage as an escort varies by tour operator, airline, or cruise line; this will take some specific discussion with a travel agent or tour operator. Generally, they'll be glad to listen to your ideas. Bear in mind, however, that without certification you cannot deal directly with most tour operators, cruise lines, or airlines.

Another opportunity for cost-free travel is to serve as a tour escort for a local tour company or travel club. In these assignments you need not be an expert on the areas to be visited, but you will have to serve the participants and the operation of the tour as a traveling manager. Explore this opportunity with professional tour operators, travel agencies which operate tours, and with local senior citizen clubs and centers with member tour programs.

If you have an expertise that would be of interest to a number of people, you may qualify to lecture aboard a cruise ship. Lauretta Blake operates Working Vacations, Inc., in Sunnyvale, California, booking lecturers aboard ships of several cruise lines. In exchange for two to four lectures each week, you may have your cabin and all meals without cost. Lauretta does charge a booking fee of 10 to 15 percent of the value of the cruise ticket, but you would have the opportunity to travel for two or three weeks, or even for extended periods.

For single men, Royal Cruise Lines, based in San Francisco, offers a seagoing opportunity to serve as dance, bridge, and game partners for single ladies on their cruises. The relationships must be completely platonic, of course, and candidates are screened before being contracted for the program. A mature single man with social graces and the appropriate wardrobe may sign aboard a Royal Cruise Line ship and travel the world, with all of the advantages of a paying passenger.

You will find contact addresses for both of these companies in the "write for" section in the back of this book. Other cruise lines are now following Royal in the social partner program. You may secure a list of the cruise lines from your travel agent, your library, or by writing the Cruise Line International Association, also listed in the "write for" section.

Other travel-free opportunities are offered to those working for travel agencies. Many mature adults train as travel counselors and take full-time or part-time positions in travel agencies. Both low-cost and cost-free travel are available to professional travel agency personnel. Discuss this possibility with travel agency operators and travel training schools in your area.

Those Telephone Offers

Mature adults have become the targets for telephone offers of "bonus" and "discount" travel. Bogus operators are active throughout the continent, phoning mature adults, and announcing that "you have won a travel contest," "you have the special opportunity of free travel," or "we are looking to bring some thoughtful people to (resort name) for just the cost of the airfare." If you fall for their offer, you will pay "service charges," "just the price of the air tickets," or for a special discount book that, predictably, is not worth the paper it is printed on.

Tens of thousands of persons have been bilked by these offers that sound "too good to be true." The fact is that if a deal sounds too good to be true, it is almost surely fraudulent. No reputable travel operators solicit by telephone with such offers.

If you're tempted to respond positively to such calls or to a mailing with a similar offer, ask yourself these four questions: "Did I really enter the contest they claim I have won?" "Why do they insist they must have an answer right now, this minute, this week?" "Do they want my credit card number to run up bogus charges against my account?" "Why should I send my money to someone I don't know, who is only a voice on the telephone?" Your best response to phony offers will be to hang up the phone or to toss away the form letter. (Of course, if you enter sweepstakes or contests actively, you will want to check to make sure you don't toss away a valid prize announcement. But such announcements are not made in form letters.)

In travel, I recommended that you deal right at home, with a professional business, where you can deal face to face. It is in this way that you will have the service and attention that you need and the very best and most predictable of arrangements. Don't be fooled by disembodied voices with blue sky pitches. They are perpetrating scams intended to bilk you. If you buy what they're selling you the first time, they'll mark you as a sucker who might also buy the Brooklyn Bridge or swamp land in Florida.

Traveling with Grandkids

One of the greatest opportunities and pleasures you have as a mature adult is spoiling grandchildren. That is your right. And it is also an opportunity in travel.

Consider taking a cruise with your grandchildren. The environment is one of quality and safety for them, so that they have a measure of freedom and independence aboard ship. Most ships will offer daytime programs for the children, so that you don't have to watch them every minute of the day. They can dress up for meals and discover what fine food can be—quite different from the stuff in plastic cartons, cardboard, and paper wrappers served at the fast-food restaurants ashore. For children as the third or fourth person in a cabin, the cruise fares might be as low as $50 to $60 per day, each, and that includes meals and, on many ships, special programs.

In this fine environment you may have very special times with your grandchildren, seeing them at their best in a grownup world. As a last tip on this subject, remember, the children use the pull-down bunks—that is part of their adventure and your privilege of mature age.

Education Programs

Mature adults are returning to university and college campuses around the world as part of the Elderhostel program. These one- or two-week (sometimes longer) programs are typically held on the campus, and participants stay in dorms. Mornings include classes in local, cultural, historical, or other subjects; afternoons and weekends are free for other personal or small-group tours and programs. For information write to Elderhostel, 80 Boylston Street, Boston, Massachusetts 02116.

Many universities are arranging their own mature-adult or senior programs, particularly in summer. See Arthur Frommer's *New World of Travel* book for hundreds of good ideas.

The Last Word on Travel

Welcome to the world, anywhere and anytime you choose, as a mature adult. Capture the freedom that is yours—to explore, to discover or rediscover, to learn, to frolic, to reach out, to expand your horizons. You now have more control of your time and more freedom, too, from previous limitations.

This chapter details many of your opportunities as guidelines for your considerations and planning. What, where and why you explore is yours to determine as the fulfillment of your own interest and desire.

The travel industry of the nation and the world invite you to share their best, offering you discounts and other advantages to make travel the very best part of your retirement years lifestyle.

CHAPTER 11

OPPORTUNITY IS YOURS IN THE MATURE YEARS

Opportunity is a major advantage of your mature years—and most of the opportunities are yours for the asking. Return to school, join a club or senior center, receive a discount on your purchases, have your tax returns done, and ride the transit system for less.

In Chapter Eight we discussed discounts as part of making and saving money. In this chapter we define many added opportunities you should anticipate and use.

The Club Opportunity

There's a social organization for mature adults meeting most any day and at any time in your city or town. This does not mean that, as an older adult, you must run to join a club now or ever. If you have been a "joiner" in earlier years, where the social programs have been a part of your lifestyle, the mature adult—or "senior citizen"—clubs are presented for your consideration.

Most mature adults are not involved in any local senior clubs or centers—surveys show that less than one-third of the senior citizen population participate in them.

Some of the largest clubs are national, such as the American Association of Retired Persons (AARP) and the Canadian Association of Retired Persons (CARP). Each has a network of local area chapters where programs range from business meetings to card games, and dances to travel trips.

The **American Association of Retired Persons** (AARP) charges national dues of $5 and offers a bi-monthly magazine, a monthly newsletter, membership recognition discounts for auto rentals and for some hotels and motels, and exclusively-contracted vendors for prescriptions by mail, health, auto and property insurance, investment programs, travel tours and an auto club. The $5 annual dues cover a married couple as members, with a qualifying age at fifty. When you enroll, be ready for an aggressive direct mail program to sell you the contracted services, but you are not obliged to buy any of the offerings. Less than five percent of AARPs national membership is involved in local chapter activities or programs.

The **Canadian Association of Retired Persons** is patterned after AARP, and the CARP News is its quarterly newspaper. You will find addresses for AARP and CARP, and all other referred organizations in the "write for" section in the back of this book.

Other "national organizations" have been created for special interests:

National Alliance of Senior Citizens (NASC) operates for politically conservative mature adults, has an active newsletter and member mailings, and offers some discount programs. NASC has a few local area chapters, and a main thrust of its activity is in political lobbying in Washington, D.C. and state capitals. Membership dues are $10 individuals; $15 for married couples.

National Council of Senior Citizens (NCSC) operates as an adjunct to the AFL-CIO and does have local membership chapters throughout the United States. Its political lobbying positions reflect those of organized labor. There is no age qualification for membership, and NCSC offers a list of member benefits, insurance and discounts for annual dues of $8.

National Association of Retired Federal Employees (NARFE) offers local chapter organizations and a national lobbying program to protect their specific retirement benefits. Annual membership is $12 for retirees and present employees of the federal government.

Catholic Golden Age provides discounts and a list of benefits to members age fifty-plus affiliated with the church. Its bi-monthly publication is the CGA World.

Gray Panthers is probably one of the most visible senior organizations, and its members include people of all ages. Local chapters are active in cities with university and college campuses. The Gray Panthers are issue oriented—to advocate more government and business provided services for persons age sixty-five and older—and you'll find its members carrying picket signs, and active in rallies and other public events.

Older Women's League is a parallel organization to the Gray Panthers, focusing their efforts specifically to the interests and needs of older women in the United States. There are local chapters for this small but active national organization. Membership fee is $10 annually.

Do Your Taxes?

The **Volunteers In Tax Assistance (VITA)** is a program coordinated by the federal Internal Revenue Service (IRS), offering income tax preparation assistance cost-free to mature adults. The service works well for simple returns. For complex returns or tax planning, continue to retain the best professional counsel you can find. For information, contact your local office of the IRS.

Back to School

Doors to colleges, universities and adult schools swing wide open for mature adults, with many offerings at little cost. The opportunities involve both admission to the regular classes and curriculum and to special classes and programs for mature adults. Most campuses offer the opportunity to monitor or audit classes, when there is a seat open, for an entire semester. Other schools will register mature adults for degree programs at lower tuition and fees. Administrators in higher education have found that younger students work well alongside and gain from mature adults in the campus programs. Mature adults, concurrently, have found that they can more than hold their own when they participate and are graded in classes shared with the younger students.

Community colleges and adult schools have developed special curricula in financial planning, physical fitness, hobbies and recreation for mature adults.

What did you miss in earlier school or college days? What new subjects or skills do you want to learn today? The doors are open wide and the campus beckons. Start your consideration by contacting the colleges and adult schools in your area, or in the area to which you intend to move. You will find them most responsive.

As mentioned earlier, **Elderhostel** has one- and two-week sessions in more than 1,100 college and university programs around the world. The programs are very inexpensive—$200 to $300 per week—and include accommodations in college dorms, classes, meals and activities. You need only buy your transportation additionally.

Elderhostel classes concentrate on local history and culture, or diverse subjects such as archaeology, the sciences, literature and art. Each day there is time for class sessions and for afternoon planned tours or personal explorations.

To the Sports Field

Some of the best bowling time available is during the day, when lanes are less crowded. For mature adults this presents a special opportunity as bowling business organizations and equipment manufacturers have pushed for the development of "senior" leagues and tournaments. Participation fees are reduced from those charged younger age groups. Want more information? Just contact your local bowling center or the American

Bowling Congress.

Softball: More than 200,000 persons age fifty-five-plus are participating on softball teams in special leagues. The Amateur Softball Association will provide information on local leagues and opportunities, and information, too, on how to start a league in your own area.

Major League Sports: Many major and minor league baseball teams offer "senior discount" clubs and days. The concept started with the San Diego Padres and the Senior World Senior Padres program, where six Sunday baseball game admissions are offered in a $6 club membership program. Now, many baseball teams offer similar programs and/or special discount ticket pricing.

Serve Around the World

If you're an executive and willing to travel to another country as a volunteer—but with expenses paid—consider the International Executive Service Corps. This program provides managerial and technical assistance to private enterprise in the less developed countries of the world. The assignments may prove most rewarding.

Transportation

Most local transportation and transit systems have special or discounted rates for mature adults, and the qualifying ages range from a low of fifty-five to a high of sixty-five. Contact your transit systems to check for their advantages and special rates. It might be more advantageous, at times, to take the transit bus or trolley and leave your automobile at home.

Senior Centers

In most every community there will be some sort of a facility identified as a "senior center," offering a variety of programs and events, such as dances, pot luck meals, lectures, entertainment, bridge and other card tournaments, group travel and more. Age qualifications vary widely as do the type of programs and advantages offered.

In most senior centers you'll find someone on staff who is most knowledgeable on specific advantages and opportunities in your local community or region. Many centers offer facilities for hobbies, such as workshops and equipment for sewing and other skills.

Before you say,"I'm not a *senior* citizen," drop in and look around. The "senior" name on the door might be a drawback, but the offerings might be very advantageous to you.

About Opportunities

There are opportunities everywhere for mature adults, either as special programs or as advantages in recognition of your maturity. If you retire and have complete control of your time you will want to assess what you desire in your new lifestyle—and then look at all that is available to fulfill those dreams as specific opportunities for mature adults.

If you choose not to retire, the opportunities are still yours as you make your decision and take time to take advantage of them.

Mature age really does have its advantages!

YOUR COMMUNITY
IS WHAT YOU
MAKE IT

You have a remarkable opportunity in your mature years to better the world around you—your community, the nation, the earth, for others, for safety or sanity, for any good reason that you believe in.

You have attained experience. You have seen the results and problems that arise when people are not involved; you have also seen the positive changes and benefits when people face up to challenges and go to work to solve them. You may choose your own level—from national leadership or to working in a very important project just down the block.

In the freedom of your mature lifestyle, consider most positively your active volunteer involvement. You can make a difference.

The Political Challenge

In our modern democracies we elect people to represent us in government. Too often, we then let them do as they will, and their executive and legislative directions differ from our own. Special interests lobby, and many times prevail, even when it is not in the best interests of the electorate.

Bad legislation happens when elected officials have not heard our voiced concerns or requests. Special interest lobbyists, therefore, are heard more often and more effectively.

In the mature years you have the opportunity to gain better representation at all levels of government. You have or will have the time for "participation," taking the time to learn the issues, communicating and sharing those thoughts with others, and then, individually or as a group, making those opinions known effectively to those elected to "represent" you. Define your own concerns—and they don't have to be just "senior citizen" issues or programs.

A 1989 survey by Waldenbooks, a major book retailer in the United

States, asked a sample one thousand members of their Sixty-Plus Book Club to define their major concerns. The issues identified:

- drugs and drug abuse in the nation, 58 percent;

- the budget deficit, 51 percent;

- crime, 49 percent;

- the homeless, 33 percent;

- illiteracy, 31 percent;

- the cost-of-living, 28 percent;

- AIDS, 19 percent;

- gun control, 18 percent;

- child care, 11 percent;

- teenage pregnancy and human rights issues at 9 percent.

What are your concerns? Are you ready to "participate" by motivating your representatives? Are you ready to put your concerns in the forefront to better your local and national communities? What your community will be for you and your neighbors, and what your country will be in its direction, will be determined by how you and other mature adults become involved.

Let's take a look at the jobs to be done, and the opportunities you have in shaping your nation and communities for today and tomorrow.

Legislators often vote based on the weight of mailbags. First, they weigh those which support a position, and then weigh those which express opposition. The heavier bag or stack of mail should influence the vote.

Legislators really don't have all of the answers. Most of the best solutions for problems and best ideas for innovative steps forward come from others. If the solutions and ideas come from constituents, then the legislators can vote as you direct, as your representative. If the suggestions, instead, come from special interests, the result is legislation and governmental action that evokes complaints from the electorate.

The mission, therefore, is to make your ideas and solutions heard—in writing and by speaking out, and in communicating to others and the media. In the legislative business this is called "grass roots" communicating and campaigning. "Vox Populi"—the voice of the people.

Here's how it is already working:

In Indianapolis, Indiana, Genevieve Riley was concerned about the direction of state and national legislation, and concerned, too, that there was an unfilled need for communication among mature adults. She founded the Federation of Older Hoosiers as a watchdog and advocacy organization, and runs it most effectively. Lynn Cantu, editor of the *Senior Beacon* in Indianapolis, told us: "People in government listen when Genevieve speaks. She does her homework and knows the issues. She is producing results."

Airline pilot Daniel Hawley had retired to Las Vegas, Nevada, to "play with his toys"—a fifth-wheel trailer for traveling, a home near the golf course, a computer and other electronic gadgets. For 35 years he piloted for American Airlines, and had earned recognition for his abilities with a committee appointment by the Federal Aviation Agency. But his concern over Congressional legislation in 1988 evoked more than just his complaint—it brought him to action. He put together a voluntary organization that rallied more than 400,000 mature adults as a driving force to have the legislation changed.

Jim Osman was concerned about communication to, with and for mature adults in eastern Washington state, so when he retired as circulation manager of the *Spokane Spokesman-Review*, he started his own newspapers, *Senior Times* and *Senior Power*. In each issue he details news and issues to more than 60,000 readers. He voices his concerns through regular commentaries in the newspapers, in volunteer appearances at government hearings, and in public speaking and television appearances throughout eastern Washington and northern Idaho.

Virginia Aubrey had retired but was concerned about the direction of the federal government and its policies and programs on aging and general federal spending. She shared her thoughts and concerns everywhere she could, and the result was strongly positive. The National Alliance of Senior Citizens was created, with Virginia as its first president. A dozen years later, she is still at work, discussing issues, testifying to Congress, and working with mailing lists and letters on the computer system. Her work has created a voice for mature adults who prefer more conservative philosophies and actions by government.

Elsewhere in the United States and Canada, mature adults are discovering their real interests and concerns, and that they can and do make a difference.

The issues are as you determine them—environment, education, crime and safety, welfare or any other concern. The scope might be in leading or supporting a national campaign; or it might be in identifying the need for an electric stoplight down the street. In each, someone has to be concerned enough to do something about it.

187

Can You Affect or Effect Legislation?

Yes, you can. We have discussed the "weight of mailbag," and that is a first step. Rallying others to the cause is important. Writing letters to elected officials is an important part of the program. Contacting and writing media of your concerns and opinions works, too, in the form of letters to the editor for publication, and in suggestions for coverage to the news editor. Participation in community meetings is important at many levels, and town hall meetings of elected national officials provide yet another forum. You may become active in an existing organization; or if none exists in your area of interest or concern, start your own.

With more freedom of time in your mature years, you have a unique opportunity to participate in deciding what happens in government, and not just relying on someone else to guess how you should be represented. When you speak out in concern then others may respond. When you speak out actively you can produce changes for the better. In many ways the furture depends on the good people, like you.

Your Time and Volunteerism

During World Wars I and II, volunteers rolled bandages for the Red Cross, sold defense and war bonds, collected metal and fats for recycling, served as block wardens for national defense, and staffed the USO facilities. Volunteers have aided at the time of disasters, taken in and fed the homeless, and have helped raise barns where a previous one had fallen in a fire.

Volunteers meet a human need in a very human way, providing what no one can buy: their personal involvement and commitment. Today's needs and opportunities for volunteers abound in their range of involvement, variety and scope and are no less important.

Our *Senior World* newspaper regularly surveyed charitable and service organizations, asking the questions: "What percentage of your volunteers are mature adults?" and "If you lost all your mature adult volunteers, how would it affect what you are doing in your organization?" The answers were almost shocking in their reality and universality:

"What percentage are mature adults?" Two thirds for most organizations.

"What would happen if the organization lost mature adults as volunteers?" More than 90 percent of the non-profit organizations said they would be out of business. This percentage was consistent in every survey over a seven-year period.

Depending on the type of project or program you choose for involvement, you will probably find greater satisfaction and reward than in earlier working years.

In San Diego, California, retired magazine editor Marion C. "Maggie" Small had a very deep concern about literacy among all age groups. As a columnist for *Senior World* newsmonthly, he advocated his concerns and ideas—and he gained response from other mature adults, and better yet, a commitment to do something about it. Maggie structured literacy classes in the area and promoted financial support. Other mature adults became his teachers of children and adults who had not learned to read, and of immigrants who knew little English. That commitment and program has been recognized nationally, and a larger volunteer organization was created in the area. But for his concern, leadership and action, thousands of people in Southern California would still be unable to read or write.

Jack Bunis retired from a New York City teaching career to West Palm Beach, Florida, a land of golf courses, tennis courts and bridge games. Instead of games and sports for his retirement years he chose current affairs—teaching and drawing other mature adults into discussion groups. The result is a large current affairs organization he leads in weekly meetings, and an active schedule of lectures on local, national and international issues to all types of organizations and all age groups.

In Arizona, the Sun City Lions Club holds the national record for collecting aluminum and old newspapers for recycling, raising more than $300,000 annually to support youth, medical and community programs. The successful program has been managed and staffed for 15 years by mature adult members of this service club.

Chicago resident Jules Klowden retired from a career in the insurance business, and had a deep concern over the quality of Medicare Supplement Insurance policies sold to persons age sixty-five-plus. Rather than just complain, he voluntarily devoted 40 to 50 hours weekly to an analysis of all policies sold in the field, charting them for inclusions and marking omissions he thought important. He brought the concept to our *Senior World* newspaper, resulting in the first Medicare Supplement comparison chart ever published. That was ten years ago and an updated chart with accompanying reportage has appeared every year since. He established manuals and training techniques for volunteers to analyze policies held by senior citizens. He secured free office space for the volunteer services from city and county governments. He lectured every where he could find an audience.

Jules Klowden's remarkable techniques and charts were adopted by the federal and state governments: he testified many times to legislative committees, and received many official commendations. Hundreds of volunteers around the national teach and use his analysis and charting techniques.

Jules Klowden's work brought positive change in this field of insurance, benefitting tens of millions of other mature adults now and in the future. He doesn't brag about his accomplishment: "Life has been good to me, and I wanted to do something that was needed, where my work could make a difference for senior citizens. I'm glad it is still working."

Over the years as a journalist I have written hundreds of stories about mature adults as volunteers. In the following I present a number of the ideas that I learned from their own volunteer efforts.

With Youth:

Youngsters have some of the greatest needs, as families are torn by divorce, as parents and the children are affected by drugs, and as poverty conditions continue. There are needs and opportunities, too, in serving with youth in activities, sports and education.

Consider some of the following:

Boy Scouts and Girl Scouts: With more single parent households, and more households where both parents have to work, there is a real need for group and troop leaders. Alternatively, you may find your professional or hobby skills ideal as a teacher in merit badge programs. You might also bring a very important and necessary adult link and influence to some of the children.

Literacy Volunteers perform some of the most important and rewarding service, in tutoring children (and adults) in reading and expressing themselves through writing. You need not have been a teacher by career; but you should enjoy reading so to convey your tutoring with enthusiasm.

Sports Leagues and Teams: Name the type of sport you know and enjoy, and there is probably a league, team or tournament which would be excited to have your involvement. If you have the time for league or tournament management, you will bring a maturity to the job, and find delight in return, as you see the youngsters grow in skills and ability through sport. You may serve as a manager or coach, working one-on-one with the children. Or, you might prefer being an umpire or referee. All are necessary jobs; all are rewarding for mature adults and youth alike.

Special Olympics: For disabled or retarded youth, there are the Special Olympics with events at the local through national levels. In this program you work with children who perform with more determination and grit than youths not so limited. These programs need good, dedicated and caring leadership and assistance at all levels.

In Education, there are many needs for volunteers: assisting teachers in classrooms, in tutoring, in Parent-Teacher organizations. Your local public and private schools will respond most positively when you offer to help. One volunteer we interviewed reads to pre-school classes and then helps teach arts and crafts as aide to the teacher. "I'm a ham as an actress," she told us, "but the children love the way I tell the stories in animated fashion, acting out the roles. I think I get more out of it than they do."

In Junior Achievement. Bring your talents and experience in business to high school youth as they operate their own Junior Achievement companies. This remarkable program teaches youth the theories and opportunities of the free enterprise system, and volunteers staff the organization's board of directors and are advisers to the individual companies. Contact your local high school or check the white pages of your telephone book to secure information on this program.

In human service: There are juvenile homes and social service facilities where children need positive, one-on-one adult attention. The stability you bring to a conversation may help a youngster to a new direction at the time his or her world is otherwise akilter. I have heard mature adult volunteers talk "straight out" with youngsters, perhaps the first time any adult has so addressed them. You may find a spark of life and interest that has eluded the staff professionals, and you may create a relationship of trust that the child will long cherish. Youngsters need role models and, if you're up to the commitment, you may want to contact your local community agencies to ask for the challenge.

Other youth: What other youth organizations exist in your area, and what might you do in a meaningful way to work with them on a part-time or even full-time basis? Is there a new youth service or program that should be started? Consider that, too.

The Role in Your Community

Identify an organization or service in your neighborhood, town or city where you can make a difference. Look around you. You'll find groups and services, founded by people who also want to better their community and serve its people, and you can join in that mission.

Consider active involvement in a social and service organization, taking an active role in their community programs. The Rotary Club, Lions, Elks, Soroptomist, Optimist, Kiwanis, and other service organizations spend more time and effort on community programs than they do on events to benefit their members. They raise funds for hospitals and medical programs, support youth education and sports programs, get involved in community clean-up and holiday decoration programs, and stage community events of their own. There is camaraderie, with a place and time to meet and visit with other people, and, too, alongside each other in working on community projects.

If you have business experience, consider volunteering with the Service Corps of Retired Executives (SCORE), working with small businesses; take

191

your abilities to the Peace Corps somewhere in the world; or teach self-reliance and skills at the Christian Appalachian Project in Kentucky.

How much should you be involved? As much or as little as you desire. It may be hard work, but predictably, you'll love the results.

Senior Citizen Programs

There are needs and opportunities for volunteers in the senior citizen field, from staffing and coordinating programs in senior citizen centers, to assisting in nursing homes. Or, consider volunteering as a driver for Meals on Wheels.

Singer Frankie Laine—he of "High Noon" and "Ghost Riders in the Sky" musical fame—has his own concerns about proper nutrition for housebound and frail senior citizens. Now he takes his concern to countless meetings where he speaks out and to benefit concert stages as a performer, specifically to raise funds for the Meals on Wheels program. Frankie at 76 is going strong after quadruple heart bypass surgery, and is still performing in concert appearances throughout the world.

Federally funded programs, like RSVP—the Retired Senior Volunteer Program—provide regular staff members for charitable and non-profit social service organizations.

Advocacy organizations offer volunteers a role in helping to change or provide services for senior citizens in your community. Consider carefully if you agree with the type and method of advocacy before volunteering.

Other Volunteerism:

How about doing or being a (an):
Docent for the museum or municipal art gallery;

Usher or **usherette**, **stage hand** or **manager** for community theatre;

Library assistant at the local college, high school or community facility;

Fund-raising manager for United Way or another charitable cause;

Tour and Travel Manager/Coordinator for a senior center, club or organization;

Public Relations Person for a local community service organization;

Volunteer Field Representative for an elected official;

Mature Affairs Columnist for the local newspaper;

Manager of Youth or Senior Bowling Leagues in conjunction with local facilities;

Reception Person for a community service facility, free health clinic or town council;

Safety Awareness Lecturer to local clubs and organizations on behalf of the local police department;

Crossing Guard for the school district or youth center;

Information Center Staffer for the town council, or the convention and visitors bureau;

Airport Staff Person for Traveler's Aid services;

Hospital Volunteer in the gift shop or in assisting patients;

Tax Counsel to low-income senior citizens, disabled or foreign speaking persons, in conjunction with the Internal Revenue Service;

Truck Driver for the Salvation Army Toys for Tots winter campaign;

Teacher of classes conducted by community agencies or educational facilities;

Reader to the blind or partially-sighted;

Telephone Volunteer in a local TAP—Telephone A Partner—program in your local area;

Newspaper and Aluminum Collector for local service agencies which sell the commodities for recycling;

Newsletter Editor for a community organization;

Lobbyist, on a volunteer basis, for a cause in which you believe;

Handyman in assisting disabled or poor persons repair or maintain their property;

Or even, the *Nice Person* down the street who fixes kids' bicycles or bakes cookies as afternoon treats.

All of this is being part of your community. It is your opportunity to share, and to gain from it in return. You can make a difference where it counts most.

A Worksheet for Volunteering

Make notes about how you will give back to your nation and community some of yourself as a volunteer, where you may make a difference:

VOLUNTEERISM PLAN FOR: (Name) _____

I(We) like the idea of volunteering time to produce real results in the community as part of my mature years lifestyle plan.

The skills/abilities I would like to use are: _____

_____

_____

_____

I(We) envision the type of national/community organization or service to be (list several if you): _____

_____

_____

I(We) see the volunteer role to be (list a variety if you desire): _____

_____

_____

For me, I(We) would like to receive from this dedication, effort and experience: (Think about this—the reasons you will make a serious and effective effort.): _____

_____

_____

I(We) will start this volunteer program on (Date): _____

The contacts I(We) need make to learn about these possibilities are: (Write these down, and research the telephone numbers) _____

_____

_____

Other research I(We) need do to determine the "right" volunteer effort: (Visits to do, people to interview, reading or other.) _____

_____

_____

Other Comments and Notes: _____

_____

_____

I(We) agree and commit to devoting _____ hours per week(month) to this effort, based on the plan above.

Signed: _____ **Date:** _____

Signed: _____ **Date:** _____

You are on your way—and both you and the world will be better for it!

— —

YOUR RETIREMENT YEARS LIFE PLAN

Meet a few more people as they offer their thoughts and example as you look to your retirement years planning:

Poet of the North Land: Larry Beck is the Bard of Alaska, and he travels the nation, performing his own work and the poetry of Robert Service, telling of the Great Land—the Forty-Ninth State, and its lure to the traveler and adventurer. Larry and I talked about a special kind of retirement where you don't have to drop out of sight, where you can design your life, because you have earned the right to do so.

Larry responded in his own style—in verse—for this particular point in this book. I share it with you now.

It's How You Think
By Larry A. Beck

If you think you're old, my friend, you are,
But a sweeter song is sung
By those who see a different star.
You're young if you're thinking young.

You see, aging has its value too.
Though your hair be streaked with grey,
Your lifelong plan will see you through
If you believe in life each day.

Don't buy it when they tell you
That over fifty means decline,
Don't let the downers sell you,
They're our best years, yours and mine.

They would have you slow and just relax,
They would have you rest each day
"Do not do those things that tax,
Just act your age," they say.

Baloney! Great battalions
Were seldom led by youth.
There were older mares and stallions
That won the day and that's the truth!

And if they tell you otherwise
Just holler "Hey, you're nuts,
You're talking about some other guys
No ifs or ands and buts."

And as each new day is dawning
And the rocking chair appeals,
Take no apologies or fawning,
It's living, friend, that heals.

Find a switch that turns you on,
Find a cause or truth or way,
Your get up and go has never gone,
You must arise and live each day.

The Singer speaks: We have been talking about age and rejecting the stereotypes and assumptions. Singer, composer and actor Kenny Rodgers sees it this way: "Growing older is not upsetting; being *perceived* as old is."

We have been talking about your new and vital role in your community and the difference you can make. I share with you just one more story on volunteerism, not because the lady is a celebrity, but because she is choosing to make a difference in the lives of others.

Volunteering that Moves Mountains: When her late husband, John Douglas French, was afflicted with Alzheimer's Disease, he left a brilliant career as a neurosurgeon and co-founder of the Brain Research Center at the University of California at Los Angeles. She made two major commitments: one to his care (for five years until his death in the spring of 1989); the other to found and gain funding for one of the leading research programs into the disease. Her program, The French Foundation for

197

Alzheimer's Research, has already raised more than two million dollars for work in the field. Her board of directors reads like a *Who's Who of the World*, including First Lady Barbara Bush, and entertainers Carol Burnett, Art Linkletter, Helen Hayes, Jennifer Jones Simon and Jack Lemmon. You remember the lady as Dorothy Kirsten, for 30 years one of the most brilliant stars of the Metropolitan Opera, and from motion pictures, television, radio and the concert stage. Today, her drive and volunteer dedication continues, even after a stroke, and her foundation will open added hospital and research facilities throughout the United States. Dorothy Kirsten has seen Alzheimer's Disease and its effect on her husband; her work will now find better treatment and a cure to save others in the years to come.

The New Career: When we talk about changing careers and launching new directions, Natasha Josefowitz of La Jolla, California, comes to mind most prominently. She worked in other careers, raised a family, and then changed direction professionally. Natasha achieved her master's degree at age forty, and her doctorate at fifty. Today, at sixty-four, she is recognized internationally as a management consultant to business. She teaches in universities, has authored nine books, writes a weekly newspaper column, and hosts her own network radio program. Natasha abounds in energy and looks forward to even greater professional gains in the future. When we appeared together on television, she shared some of her philosophy and counsel to other mature adults.

To The Youth Generation:

"Your skins are taut
Your faces smooth
Like fresh plums.

My skin is wrinkled
My brow is furrowed
Like a prune.

Prunes are sweeter."

Identity Crisis

"When I was young I used to wonder what I would be when I grew up
And now that I have grown up I don't have to wonder what I will be
For I have found out who I am."

Unpublished, © Copyright 1989 by Natasha Josefowitz

On Mature Women and PMZ:

"Our older years are the very best
For we have "Post Menopausal Zest.""

Dr. Natasha Josefowitz is published by Warner Books, with volumes including: *Natasha's Words for Families*, *Natasha's Words for Friends*, and *Natasha's Words for Lovers*.

You can continue to perform and accomplish as you have done in your earlier years, enriched by experience. Here's a quick story as illustration. When 70-year-old pianist Mischa Elman boarded the plane from the United States for his final European concert tour, he said, "When I made my debut as a twelve-year-old in Berlin, people used to say, 'Isn't he wonderful for his age?' Now, they're beginning to say the same thing again!"

And throughout this book we have dealt with factual stories. It is time to present one bit of humor, and you are free to use it any time those around you deride or assume the worst about the mature years. The story is credited to William Lederer, author of *I, Giorghos*.

An 80-year-old man goes to a doctor for a checkup. The doctor tells him, "you are in terrific shape. There's nothing wrong with you. Why, you might live forever. By the way, how old was your father when he died?" The 80-year-old patient responded, "Did I say he was dead?" The doctor couldn't believe it. So he said, "Well, how old was your grandfather when he died?" The 80-year-old patient responded again, "Did I say he was dead?" The doctor was astonished. He said, "You mean to tell me you're 80 years old and both your father and grandfather are still alive?" "Not only that," said the patient, "my grandfather is 126 years old, and next week he's getting married for the first time!" The doctor said, "After 126 years of being a bachelor, why on earth did your grandfather want to get married?" His patient looked up at the doctor and said, "Did I say he wanted to?"

Reviewing for Your Retirement Plan

It is now time to re-read your notes and charts and write your Creative Retirement Living Plan.

You have read and considered most all aspects of creative retirement planning, a direction and a lifestyle of your own design, based on your own ground rules. Our concept and mission together in this venture is to allow you to move *to* retirement by your own creative plan, and not just *away* from your present job or business.

You can and should be in control of your retirement plan. The amount of money you'll need to retire will be determined by your own lifestyle desire and budget. Develop your own positive health program as a first priority to insure your mortality instead of morbidity in your retirement years.

You can make money and save money, launch a new career or business, travel the world, lead in your community and even change the world around you. You have a remarkable opportunity of 365 days a year and 24 hours each day which you may now shape to your own direction.

Re-read each of the chapters in this book, and then gather in order all of the charts and lists you have made. Reconsider the desires and priorities you have already identified, and add more thoughts. There was a reason you made the many statements; perhaps some were feelings that were earlier unstated to yourself or to anyone else.

Allow your mind to play with the images of what you have selected. See how they "feel" as you experience them. At that point, identify in a new chart or list your resolved and possible directions; identify your added considerations. Re-read and reconsider your thoughts and priorities every morning and evening for at least a month—immediately as you awaken in the morning, and as your very last thoughts before going to sleep. Your subconscious mind will aid your evaluation.

At some point soon, you will resolve your plan. Your financial ability and plan will fall into place. Mark your calendars for each step of your plan.

You will have created your own retirement years program as you have earned it and how you want it to be.

As the final step, here is a guide for your chart of resolutions in your creative retirement planning:

— —

CREATIVE RETIREMENT PLAN OF:

Name(s): _____

Date Resolved: _____ **19** _____

I/We have resolved our desires and plan for our retirement years to include:

Subject:	What I/We will do about it and when:
Health	
Career/working	
Present job/business:	

YOUR RETIREMENT YEARS LIFE PLAN

Subject:	What I/We will do about it and when:
Residence/housing	
Financial plan/feasibility	
Role in community/for others	
Legal/insurance affairs	
Travel/recreation	
Activities/hobbies	
Personal/lifestyle	
Other plans	

Our retirement plan/program will start on: _____

Our date of retirement to new living will be on: _____

I/We reserve the right to make adjustments/changes in this program, but only after the same amount of consideration and planning I/we have put into this overall plan.

I/We endorse and commit to the program above.

Signed: _____ Date: _____

Signed: _____ Date: _____

POSTSCRIPT: THIS IS YOUR TOMORROW

Your retirement years may be whatever you determine them to be. In these pages we have explored your many opportunities, presented suggestions and possible ground rules.

If you really got involved in this process you have also gone through two or three thick tablets and have bulging notebooks. And that is right.

You are the one person who has the right, ability and opportunity to write your own plan for the next four-, seven- or ten-thousand days. I have provided the variety of road signs, avenues and byways you might choose, together with ways to define your ideals as achievable destinations.

Creative retirement planning is far more than having enough money in the bank so you don't have to work. I have enjoyed sharing these planning concepts with you, and I commend them to you—because they work.

In turn I ask you the questions:

"What will be your direction?" and

"How soon will you commit to your creative new plan?"

Your future is as you wish and create it to be. With your planning and commitment now, this really is your tomorrow.

DATA BANK

Where to Write for Information

Throughout this book there are references to people and information. Here is a compendium of those names, with contact information should you want to request information.

Health

American Heart Association offers many reports and brochures on all phases of heart disease and positive/preventive care (exercises, diet and more). Write to request publications in areas of your special interest.

American Heart Association
National Center
7320 Greenville Avenue
Dallas, TX 75231

American Rheumatism Association is a professional membership organization that offers good information, brochures and background publications on arthritis and other afflictions, including gout. For information write:

American Rheumatism Association
17 Executive Park Drive
Suite 4809
Atlanta, GA 30329

Milton Feher, teacher of relaxation, movement, and dance, offers a $3 reprint of magazine articles he has written about his training and techniques, plus a $10 audiotape cassette of his actual instruction. Request one or both, with your payment in advance to:

Milton Feher Studio
200 West 58th Street
New York, NY 10019

Senior Healthtrac: Write for free information on the positive health recommendations in the Senior Healthtrac program. They will provide this as a public service to readers of this book. Mention *Life Begins at Fifty* in your request letter. Address your request to:

Mike Odom/Public Relations
Blue Shield of California
Two North Point
San Francisco, CA 94133

On Respiratory Diseases and Health: the National Jewish Center for Immunology and Respiratory Diseases offers some of the very best informational publications and brochures, cost free, on the subject. Write:

Public Relations
National Jewish Center
1400 Jackson Street
Denver, CO 80206

Information

Consumer Information Center, Pueblo, Colorado 81009, is the simple address to request a catalog of current low-cost and free publications on many subjects of interest and benefit—health, consumer affairs, travel, and more.

The Congressional Handbook lists the name, party affiliation, address, telephone number, and committee assignments of each member of the U.S. Senate and House of Representatives. This is a handy resource for writing Congressional representatives on issues that concern you. Send $3 with your request to:
Publications Fulfillment
U.S. Chamber of Commerce
1615 H Street, N.W.
Washington, DC 20062

Health Resources for Older Women covers a wide variety of health, health-related, and financial concerns. Each section lists the names of organizations dealing with the subject area and selected readings. The 75-page booklet may be requested free of charge. Provide the booklet name and publication number (NIA 87-2899). Address:
National Institute of Aging Information Center
2209 Distribution Circle
Silver Spring, MD 20910

The Traveler's Insurance Company's On-Retirement Program was created specifically to provide seniors with temporary employment opportunities. Placement, as well as some training, is available to qualified seniors. Similar programs have been instituted elsewhere.
The Travelers Companies
On-Retirement Plan
Personnel-Administrative Dept.
One Tower Square
Hartford, CT 06101

Consumer's Resource Handbook is one of the best of publications by the federal government, providing briefings and contact addresses for most every area of consumer concern or complaint. Request a copy from:
Consumer Information Center
Pueblo, CO 81009

Senior Publishers Group will provide the name and contact information for your local area mature market newspapers and/or magazines, when you send a self-addressed and stamped business size (#10) return envelope plus a $1 research and handling fee. The mature market newspapers are published to the specific news and information needs of mature adults, and include discount coupons and more, on a regular basis. Send your request, plus return envelope and fee, to:

Senior Publishers Group
1326 Garnet Avenue
San Diego, CA 92109

AARP Books: Scott, Foresman and Company publishes a number of informational and self-help books for mature adults, in conjunction with the American Association of Retired Persons. For a catalog of the publications available, write:

AARP Books
1900 East Lake Avenue
Glenview, IL 60025

Packet on Aging is a set of 26 booklets that cover many topics of interest to mature people. The full packet costs $11.70; individual booklets are $1.00.

Public Affairs Committee
381 Park Avenue South
New York, NY 10016

Travel

Cruise Line International Association will provide information on all aspects of cruise vacations, through cost-free brochures. Write them:

Cruise Line International Association
500 Fifth Avenue
New York, NY 10110

Working Vacations, Inc., represents experts who can lecture aboard cruise ships, trading services for vacations. Write for information to:

Lauretta Blake, President
Working Vacations, Inc.
1215 McIntosh Avenue
Sunnyvale, CA 94087

Book Passage offers one of the nation's most extensive catalogs of books on travel. Request the catalog free of charge by calling them toll-free at 1-800-321-9785. Or write to:

Book Passage Catalog
51 Tamal Vista Boulevard
Corte Madera, CA 94925

Royal Cruise Line engages mature single men as platonic dance and social partners for women passengers in a unique and effective program. For information write:

Richard Revnes, President
Royal Cruise Line
One Maritime Plaza, Suite 660
San Francisco, CA 94111

United States Tour Operators Association offers a fine informational pamphlet, *How to Select a Package Tour*, including information on what to look for when choosing a tour and a glossary of terms associated with tours and vacation packages. Request the pamphlet by name, free-of-charge, from:

USTOA
211 East 51st Street
Suite 12B
New York, NY 10022

Elderhostel has information on its membership programs and a catalog of its classes for mature adults on university and college campuses throughout the world. Write:

Public Relations
Elderhostel
80 Boylston Street, Suite 400
Boston, MA 02116

In Canada, write:
Elderhostel
Corbett House
29 Prince Arthur Avenue
Toronto, ONT M5R 1B2

Interhostel is an international college-campus based travel and education program for mature adults. For a catalog, write:

Interhostel
University of New Hampshire
6 Garrison Avenue
Durham, NH 03824

Pilot Books publishes a number of paperback directories listing discounts for mature adults for travel. Write for a cost-free catalog, mentioning *Life Begins at Fifty*, this book, to:

Sam Small, Publisher
Pilot Books
103 Cooper Street
Babylon, NY 11702

Barron's Educational Series offers some remarkably effective and reasonably-priced books and tapes on travel and foreign languages for travel. Request the cost-free catalog by writing:

Catalog
Barron's Educational Series
250 Wireless Boulevard
Hauppauge, NY 11788

Golden Age passes may be yours for cost-free entrance to national parks and discount rates for camping. For information, write:

Golden Age Information
National Park Service
U.S. Department of the Interior
18th and C Streets, N.W.
Washington, DC 20240

Hobbies, Activities, and Sports

Amateur Softball Association coordinates leagues and tournaments for age fifty-five-plus players. For information:

Amateur Softball Association
2801 Northeast 50th Street
Oklahoma City, OK 73111

American Bowling Congress has information on bowling for mature adults and where to find leagues and tournaments. Write:

American Bowling Congress
5301 South 76th Street
Greendale, WI 53129

SeniorNet is a computer network that allows modem access to mature adults throughout the nation. For information on the innovative program, write:

SeniorNet
University of San Francisco
San Francisco, CA 94117

Financial

United Retirement Bulletin is one of the very best resources in newsletter format for retirement planning. Subscriptions are $29 per year, but you may request a cost-free sample issue, when you send your request mentioning *Life Begins at Fifty*, together with a self-addressed and stamped (25 cents) business size (#10) return envelope to:

Edith Tucker, Editor
United Retirement Bulletin
210 Newbury Street
Boston, MA 02116

The Retirement Letter is another outstanding resource for information on retirement planning. Editor is Peter A. Dickinson, author of several books on retirement and founding editor of *The Retirement Letter*. Subscriptions are $87 per year, but you may request a sample copy cost-free when you mention the title of this book. Send a self-addressed and stamped (25 cents) business size (#10) return envelope to:

Peter A. Dickinson
The Retirement Letter
44 Wildwood Drive
Prescott, AZ 86301

The Consumer's Guide to Medicare Supplement Insurance is a pamphlet available free-of-charge from

Health Insurance Association of America
Post Office Box 41455
Washington, DC 20018

Nolo Press offers a free catalog of some of the very best self-help books available on personal finance, legal and consumer concerns, and more. Mention your referral by this book when sending your written request to:

Nolo Press
950 Park Avenue
Berkeley, CA 94710

Volunteering

Service Corps of Retired Executives is a very effective volunteer organization and offers information on its program on request. Contact your local office of the federal Small Business Administration, or write:

SCORE/Small Business Administration
1441 L Street, N.W.
Washington, DC 20426

Retired Senior Volunteer Program (RSVP) coordinates volunteer programs for many local charitable and social service organizations. For information, write:

RSVP, ACTION
806 Connecticut Avenue, N.W.
Washington, DC 20525

United Way may be contacted in your local area, or write the national office for information on volunteer opportunities:

United Way
801 North Fairfax Street
Alexandria, VA 22314

The National Center for Citizen Involvement will provide information on local programs where your efforts may make a positive difference. Write:

National Center for Citizen Involvement
1214 Sixteenth Street, N.W.
Washington, DC 20036

Literacy Volunteers of America offers one of the very best involvement programs for mature adults. Write them for information about programs in your local area:
Literacy Volunteers of America
700 East Water Street
Syracuse, NY 13210

Seniors with the necessary skills and experience are needed in all parts of the world to work helping others in the hope of promoting prosperity and world peace. This government program provides transportation and a stipend as well as the satisfaction of a job well done.
The Peace Corps
1990 K Street, N.W.
Washington, DC 20526

Additional information on innovative and valuable volunteer activities may be had from:
National Retiree Volunteer Center
905 Fourth Ave., S.
Minneapolis, MN 55404

Government

President: Write President Bush with your concerns, for he and his office need more wise counsel from mature Americans:
The Honorable George Bush
President of the United States
The White House
1600 Pennsylvania Avenue
Washington, DC 20500

United States Senate: Take your problems, questions, and demands on federal legislation and policy directly to the U.S. Senators you have elected. Write:
The Honorable (name of your Senator)
United States Senate
Washington, DC 20510

House of Representatives: You have also elected a Congressional representative from your local district. Sound off in writing to:
The Honorable (name of Congressperson)
U.S. House of Representatives
Washington, DC 20515

The Administration on Aging provides information on services such as utility and tax assistance to senior citizens who need help in these areas. Write for information:

Administration on Aging
U.S. Dept. of Health and Human Services
330 C Street, S.W.
Washington, DC 20201

The National Institute on Aging conducts research and training related to the aging process and special health problems of seniors. They offer many publications that provide help and information on aging. Write:

National Institute on Aging
NIA Information Center
2209 Distribution Circle
Silver Springs, MD 20901

Crime Prevention

One area in which government at all levels has failed is crime prevention. Mature citizens have often been the target of criminal activity. Two organizations provide information not only on crime prevention but also on programs that assist the victims.

National Organization for Victim Assistance
717 D Street, N.W.
Washington, DC 20004

Victims of Crime Resources Center
McGeorge School of Law
University of the Pacific
3200 Fifth Avenue
Sacramento, CA 95817

Associations

Advocates Senior Alert Process
1334 G Street, N.W.
Washington, DC 20005
(202) 737-6340

Network of national senior organizations for advocacy and information on important issues.

American Association of Retired Persons
1909 K Street, N.W.
Washington, DC 20049
(202) 872-4700

The largest organization in the U.S. for people 50 or older. Offers many benefits at low cost.

American Senior Citizen Association
P.O. Box 41
Fayetteville, NC 20302
(919) 323-3641

Canadian Association of Retired Persons
27 Queen Street East
Toronto, Ontario M5C 2M6
Largest organization in Canada for people 55 or older.

Catholic Golden Age
400 Lackawanna Avenue
Scranton, PA 11850

Gray Panthers
311 South Juniper Street
Philadelphia, PA 19107
(215) 545-6555
An advocacy and action group opposed to ageism and in favor of the extension of senior citizen rights and entitlements.

National Association of Retired Federal Employees
1533 New Hampshire Ave., N.W.
Washington, DC 20036

National Association of Mature People
2212 NW 50th Street
Oklahoma City, OK 73126
(405) 848-1832

National Council of Senior Citizens
925 Fifteenth Street, N.W.
Washington, DC 20005
(202) 342-8800
About 5,000 local affiliates form a network that promotes activism on senior and related issues.

National Interfaith Coalition on Aging
298 South Hull Street
Athens, GA 30603
(404) 353-1331
This group approaches senior issues from a religious point of view.

Older Women's League
730 Eleventh Street, N.W.
Washington, DC 20001
(202) 783-6686

With chapters in almost every state, this group is active on behalf of middle-aged and older women.

Canadian Government Agencies

Department of National Health and Welfare
Income Security Programs Branch
Brooke Claxton Bldg.
Tunney's Pasture
Ottawa, Ontario K1A 0L4

National Advisory Council on Aging
Jeanne Mance Bldg. #1044
Ottawa, Ontario K1A 0K9

For problems with age discrimination on the job, contact the Canadian Human Rights Commission. Their local or regional office is listed in your phone book. Another source of assistance is:

Civil Liberties Association
229 Yonge Street - Suite 403
Toronto M9B 1N9

Department of Employment
Phase IV Place du Portage
Hull Quebec K1A 079

Offers information on unemployment benefits, including special benefits for those 65 years of age and over.

Canadian Government Publishing Center
270 Albert Street
Ottawa, Ontario K1A 0S9

Offers many helpful government publications on health, retirement, and related matters.

Canadian Private Agencies

Association of Canadian Pension Management
2 Bloor Street West
Suite 503
Toronto, Ontario M4W 3E2

Canadian Association of Gerontology
238 Portage Avenue
Winnipeg, Manitoba R3B 2A7

Canadian Long Term Care Association
77 Metcalfe Street
Room 306
Ottawa, Ontario K1P 5L6

Canadian Pension Conference
67 Mowat Avenue
Suite 537
Toronto, Ontario M6K 3E3

Canadian Pensioners Conference
24-830 McLean Street
Halifax, Nova Scotia B3H 2T8

Canadian Association of PreRetirement Planners
10 Chemin Starr
Yarmouth, Nova Scotia B5A 2T1

Canadian Institute of Senior Centres
1003 Steeles Avenue West
Willowdale, Ontario M2R 3T6

National Pensioners and Senior Citizens Federation
3505 Lake Shore Boulevard West
Toronto, Ontario M8W 1N5

State Agencies

Alabama
Commission on Aging
State Capitol
Montgomery, AL 36130
(205) 261-5743

Alaska
Older Alaskans Commission
C-Mail Station 0209
Juneau, AK 99811
(907) 465-3250

Arizona
Aging and Adult Administration
1400 West Washington Street
Phoenix, AZ 85007
(602) 255-4446

Arkansas
Office of Aging and Adult Services
Donaghey Building
7th and Main Streets
Little Rock, AR 72201
(501) 371-2441

California
Department of Aging
1020 19th Street
Sacramento, CA 95814
(916) 322-5290

Colorado
Aging and Adult Services Division
Department of Social Services
717 17th Street
Denver, CO 80218
(303) 294-5913

Connecticut
Department on Aging
175 Main Street
Hartford, CT 06106
(203) 566-3238

Delaware
Division on Aging
Department of Health and Social Services
1901 North DuPont Highway
New Castle, DE 19720
(302) 421-6791

District of Columbia
Office on Aging
1424 K Street, N.W.
Washington, DC 20011
(202) 724-5626

Florida
Program Office of Aging and Adult Services
1317 Winewood Boulevard
Tallahassee, FL 32301
(904) 488-8922

Georgia
Office of Aging
878 Peachtree Street, N.E.
Atlanta, GA 30309
(404) 894-5333

Hawaii
Executive Office on Aging
Office of the Governor
335 Merchant Street
Honolulu, HI 96813
(808) 548-2593

Idaho
Office on Aging
Statehouse Room 114
Boise, ID 83720
(208) 334-3833

Illinois
Department on Aging
421 East Capitol Avenue
Springfield, IL 62701
(217) 785-2870

Indiana
Department on Aging and Community Services
251 North Illinois Street
Indianapolis, IN 46207
(317) 232-7006

Iowa
Department of Elder Affairs
914 Grand Avenue
Des Moines, IA 50319
(515) 281-5187

Kansas
Department on Aging
610 West Tenth
Topeka, KS 66612
(913) 296-4986

Kentucky
Division for Aging Services
Department of Human Resources
275 East Main Street
Frankfort, KY 40601
(502) 564-6930

Louisiana
Office of Elderly Affairs
P.O. Box 80374
Baton Rouge, LA 70898
(504) 925-1700

Maine
Bureau of Maine's Elderly
State House, Station No. 11
Augusta, ME 04333
(207) 289-2561

Maryland
Office on Aging
301 West Preston Street
Baltimore, MD 21201
(301) 225-1100

Massachusetts
Department of Elder Affairs
38 Chauncey Street
Boston, MA 02111
(617) 727-7750

Michigan
Office of Services to the Aging
P.O. Box 30026
Lansing, MI 48909
(517) 373-8230

Minnesota
Board on Aging
204 Metro Square Building
7th and Robert Streets
St. Paul, MN 55101
(612) 296-2544

Mississippi
Council on Aging
301 West Pearl Street
Jackson, MS 39203
(601) 949-2070

Missouri
Division on Aging
Department of Social Services
505 Missouri Boulevard
Jefferson City, MO 65102
(314) 751-3082

Montana
Community Services Division
P.O. Box 4210
Helena, MT 59604
(406) 444-3865

Nebraska
Department on Aging
301 Centennial Mall—South
Lincoln, NE 68509
(402) 471-2306

Nevada
Division on Aging
Department of Human Resources
505 East King Street
Carson City, NV 89710
(702) 885-4210

New Hampshire
Council on Aging
105 Loudon Road
Building No. 3
Concord, NH 03301
(603) 271-2751

New Jersey
Division on Aging
Department of Community Affairs
363 West State Street
Trenton, NJ 08625
(609) 292-4833

New Mexico
State Agency on Aging
224 East Palace Avenue
Santa Fe, NM 87501
(505) 827-7640

New York
Office for the Aging
New York State Plaza
Agency Building No. 2
Albany, NY 12223
(518) 474-4425

North Carolina
Division on Aging
1985 Umpstead Drive
Raleigh, NC 27603
(919) 733-3983

North Dakota
Aging Services
Department of Human Services
State Capitol
Bismarck, ND 58505
(701) 224-2577

Ohio
Department on Aging
50 West Broad Street—9th Floor
Columbus, OH 43215
(614) 466-5500

Oklahoma
Special Unit on Aging
Department of Human Services
P.O. Box 25352
Oklahoma City, OK 73125
(405) 521-2281

Oregon
Senior Services Division
313 Public Service Building
Salem, OR 97310
(503) 378-4728

Pennsylvania
Department of Aging
231 State Street
Harrisburg, PA 17101
(717) 783-1550

Puerto Rico
Gericulture Commission
Department of Social Services
P.O. Box 11398
Santurce, PR 00910
(809) 721-4010

Rhode Island
Department of Elderly Affairs
79 Washington Street
Providence, RI 02903
(401) 277-2858

South Carolina
Commission on Aging
915 Main Street
Columbia, SC 29201
(803) 758-2576

South Dakota
Office of Adult Services and Aging
700 North Illinois Street
Pierre, SD 57501
(605) 773-3656

Tennessee
Commission on Aging
535 Church Street
Nashville, TN 37219
(615) 741-2056

Texas
Department on Aging
1949 IH 35—South
P.O. Box 12786 Capitol Station
Austin, TX 78741
(512) 444-2727

Utah
Division of Aging and Adult Services
Department of Social Services
150 West North Temple
Salt Lake City, UT 84145
(801) 533-6422

Vermont
Office on Aging
103 South Main Street
Waterbury, VT 05676
(802) 241-2400

Virgin Islands
Commission on Aging
6F Havensight Mall
Charlotte Amalie
St. Thomas, VI 00801
(809) 774-5884

Virginia
Department on Aging
18th Floor, 101 North 14th Street
Richmond, VA 23219
(804) 225-2271

Washington
Aging and Adult Services
Department of Social and Health Services
OB-43G
Olympia, WA 98504
(206) 753-2502

West Virginia
Commission on Aging
Holly Grove—State Capitol
Charleston, WV 25305
(304) 348-3317

Wisconsin
Bureau of Aging
Division of Community Services
One West Wilson Street
Madison, WI 53702
(608) 266-2536

Wyoming
Commission on Aging
Hathaway Building—Room 139
Cheyenne, WY 82002
(307) 777-7986

Overview of Pensions

The first private pension plan in North America was established by The American Express Company in 1875. Today, tens of millions of workers in private industry and in federal, state, and local governments are members of pension plans.

In recent years the federal government has taken an active role in protecting the pension rights of workers in private industry. Several agencies have been established in the pension field. To prospective retirees concerned about the safety of their pensions these agencies offer free information and advice. The Coverage and Inquiries Branch of the following corporation offers a free publication, "Your Guaranteed Pension." In addition, the corporation has published "Your Pension: Things You Should Know About Your Pension Plan," available from the U.S. Government Printing Office for $1.00. Write:

Pension Benefit Guaranty Corporation
2020 K Street, N.W.
Washington, DC 20006
(202) 778-8000

The Department of Labor offers a publication entitled "What You Should Know About the Pension Law," in addition to other information and assistance.

U.S. Department of Labor
Pension & Welfare Benefits Administration
220 Constitution Ave., N.W.
Washington, DC 20210

Pension Checklist

- My pension plan is a defined benefit _____ defined contribution _____ plan.
- The name of my Plan Administrator is _____; I can contact him/her at _____.
- I have _____ have not _____ received my Summary Plan Description, Summary of the Annual Report, and Survivor Coverage Data.
- I am now vested _____ or will be in _____ years.
- I presently have earned _____ years of service towards my pension.
- Under my plan, I can take early retirement, with reduced benefits, at age _____.
- I can retire with full benefits at age _____.
- I will receive my benefits in a lump sum _____ or in monthly installments for life _____.
- My Social Security benefit will _____ will not _____ be deducted from my pension benefit.
- My spouse and I have _____ have not _____ declined in writing the joint and survivor option.
- My benefits are _____ are not _____ insured by PBGC.

Source: "Your Pension," published by Pension Benefit Guaranty Corporation.

A Short Glossary of Pension Terms

Accrue: To earn pension credits for years of service under a defined benefit plan. In the case of a defined contribution plan, the process of accumulating funds in a participant's account.

Actuarial Assumptions: Factors that actuaries use in estimating a pension fund's performance and experience as it affects plan liabilities, such as the rate of return on plan investments and the rates at which plan members are expected to leave the plan because of death or job termination.

Actuary: A person who computes pension costs, insurance premium rates, dividends, reserves, etc., according to mathematical probabilities.

Amortization: Periodic payments to reduce the unfunded benefit liabilities of a pension plan.

Annuity: A contract with an insurance company that provides regular income over a specified period of time, often for life.

Basic Benefits: The monthly payments for life provided to vested pension plan participants beginning at normal retirement age, early retirement and disability benefits, and benefits for survivors of deceased plan participants.

Beneficiary: An individual designated by a plan participant to receive pension benefits in the event of the death of the participant.

Defined Benefit Plans: These plans promise a specified monthly benefit at retirement.

Defined Contribution Plans: These plans involve employers contributing to the employees' pension accounts, with benefits depending primarily on amounts contributed and investment returns.

401(k) Plan: Generally, an arrangement under which the participant may elect either to have the employer contribute an amount to the plan or to receive that amount in cash.

Fiduciary: An individual or organization that exercises discretionary control or authority over the management of an employee benefit plan or its assets.

Funding Waiver: If meeting funding obligations would cause an employer "substantial" financial hardship, it can request from the IRS a waiver of part or all of the minimum funding requirement for that year. A maximum of three waivers (five for multi-employer plans) is permitted in any 15-year period, and waived funds must be paid in five equal annual installments (15 payments for multi-employer plans), beginning the year after the waived payment was due.

Money Purchase Plan: A defined contribution plan under which contribution rates are fixed, usually as a percentage of salary; a participant's benefit depends on such factors as the amount of the contributions, investment earnings and appreciation, and expenses.

Multiemployer Plan: A pension plan, collectively bargained, to which more than one employer contributes.

Plan Year: Generally, the 12-month period used in the administration of pension plans. For example, it could be the calendar year, the fiscal year of the employer, or the 12-month period from the anniversary date of the plan's establishment.

Profit-Sharing Plan: A plan established and maintained by an employer that provides for the participation in the company's profits by its employees or their beneficiaries.

Single-Employer Plan: A plan that covers the employees of one employer or a group of related employers.

Summary Plan Description: A description of the principal features of an employee pension plan, written in easily understandable language. It must be provided to all plan participants.

Target Benefit Plan: A defined contribution plan using a formula to set a target benefit for each employee, with the employer's contribution accumulated toward achieving that benefit obligation. However, the employer does not guarantee that the target benefit will be achieved.

Termination: Ending a pension plan, either by means of a "standard termination," under which the plan has enough assets to pay off all its obligations, or a "distress termination," in which PBGC steps in as trustee and, if need be, uses its insurance funds to guarantee the pension payments.

Thrift or Savings Plan: A plan under which employees can contribute on a regular basis. Employers can contribute matching or some fraction of the employee's contribution. (Note: A thrift or savings plan is similar to a 401(k) plan, but there are significant differences.)

Vesting: Completion by a pension plan participant of years-of-service requirements, which entitle the participant to a permanent legal right to receive accrued earned retirement benefits, whether or not the participant continues to work for the company until retirement.

Source: "Your Pension," published by Pension Benefit Guaranty Corporation.

Overview of Social Security

WHO: Any worker who is covered by Social Security—that is, has paid FICA taxes—and who has been credited with the required number of earnings quarters, is entitled to receive Social Security benefits.

WHEN: (1) At any time, if you become disabled so that you are kept from work for at least one year, or if you are the spouse or minor child of a deceased covered worker.

(2) At age 62, but your monthly benefit will be reduced by 20% of the amount you would be entitled to receive at age 65, remaining so reduced for the remainder of time you receive benefits. (Those who retire between 62 and 65 have their benefits reduced by 0.55 percent for each month prior to 65.)

(3) At age 65, with full monthly benefits as determined by your earnings and by the prevailing schedules of payment. In addition, these benefits are raised annually according to a formula based on the rate of inflation for the previous year.

(4) After age 65, with an increase in benefits of 3 percent for each year up to age 70 that you did not receive benefits.

WHERE: You must apply for Social Security; it does not come automatically at age 65. When you visit your local Social Security office to make application, you should bring along any papers or documents that might be useful, including your Social Security card, birth certificate or other proofs of age, recent W-2 form, or proof of kinship if you are applying for survivors' benefits. If you don't have these documents, Social Security officials will help you establish your eligibility for benefits; it will just take a bit longer.

HOW MUCH: The amount of your monthly benefit check depends principally on your age at application, as explained under "when," and your average lifetime earnings record. To get an advance estimate of your benefits, call the Social Security Administration at (800) 937-2000, and request Form SSA-7004. Or mail your request to the Consumer Information Center, SSA, Pueblo, CO 81009. In about six weeks you'll receive a statement of your annual earnings since 1950—take the time to check this for errors—and an estimate of the benefits you will receive on retirement.

The above is only a brief overview of Social Security benefits; there are many individual variations. Local Social Security offices have publications and other informative materials to help recipients and potential recipients figure out the system and how they fit into it. Or write:

Office of Public Affairs
Social Security Administration
6401 Security Boulevard
Baltimore, MD 21235

In addition, the Health Care Financing Administration offers several publications, including "How Work Affects Social Security Checks" (SSA #05-10069) and "Your Social Security" (SSA #05-10035). Write:

Health Care Financing Administration
U.S. Dept. of Health and Human Services
6325 Security Boulevard
Baltimore, MD 21207

Overview of Medicare

Medicare is a federal program that helps people 65 years of age and older to pay for their health care costs. Part A of Medicare is mandatory and comes at no charge to most recipients; however, in 1989 a surcharge was instituted on part of the federal income tax paid by enrollees. Part A covers all basic hospitalization costs for beneficiaries after a single annual deductible (currently $564; subject to change).

Part B of Medicare is optional and helps pay for the cost of physicians' and surgeons' services, out-patient care, and certain drugs and medical equipment. There are deductibles and copayments involved here, but starting in 1990 there will be a cap on a beneficiary's out-of-pocket expenses for Part B charges of $1370.

Thus, Medicare does not pay for all medical expenses, but it does serve as catastrophic insurance. That is, no matter what the illness, a beneficiary's medical expenses are limited, and the program does pay most of the medical bills for people 65 and over.

However, because Medicare does not cover everything, many insurance companies have introduced "medigap" policies to fill in the gaps in coverage. These policies vary in scope and quality. Consumer advocates have cautioned senior citizens not to overinsure themselves by paying for more coverage than they actually need.

For further information write:
Health Care Financing Administration
U.S. Department of Health and Human Services
6325 Security Boulevard
Baltimore, MD 21207

Among the publications they offer are "Your Medicare Handbook" (HCFA #10050), "Health Insurance for People with Medicare" (HCFA #02110), "Medicare and Prepayment Plans" (HCFA #02143), and "Medicare and Employer Health Plans."

Legal and Financial Resources

Legal Assistance

Legal Services Department
400 Virginia Avenue, S.W.
Washington, DC 20024
(202) 863-1820

National Senior Citizens Law Center
2025 M Street, N.W.
Washington, DC 20036
(202) 887-5280

and

1052 West Sixth Street
Los Angeles, CA 90017
(213) 482-3550

American Bar Association
Commission on Legal Problems of the Elderly
1800 M Street, N.W.
Washington, DC 20036
(202) 331-2297

Credit Counseling

National Foundation for Consumer Credit
8701 Georgia Avenue
Silver Spring, MD 20910
Association of agencies that provide free financial counseling services for people who have problems with paying off loans and other debts.

Mutual Funds

No-Load Mutual Fund Association
11 Penn Plaza
New York, NY 10001
Offers information on mutual funds that do not levy any sales charges in commissions.

Investment Company Institute
1600 M Street, N.W.
Washington, DC 20036
Offers the "Guide to Mutual Funds" for $1.00.

Financial Planners

In the 1980s financial planning grew from something used only by the rich to a service that attracted a much broader based and more varied clientele. At the same time some inexperienced and unqualified people entered the field.

The best way to select a financial planner is through personal or professional recommendation. In addition, these two organizations can provide the names of qualified planners in a locality.

International Association of Financial Planning
5775 Peachtree Dunwoody Road
Atlanta, GA 30342
(404) 252-9600

Institute for Certified Financial Planners
10065 East Harvard Avenue
Denver, CO 80231
(303) 751-7600

Complaints about financial planners may also be addressed to:
Office of Consumer Affairs
Securities and Exchange Commission
450 Fifth Street, N.W.
Washington, DC 20549
(202) 272-7440

and

Better Business Bureau
Consumer Information Services
1515 Wilson Boulevard
Arlington, VA 22209
Offers "Tips on Financial Planners" Pub #24-225 A401286.

Banks and S&Ls

Savers who are concerned about the safety of their funds on deposit in a savings and loan (S&L) association may write for a free informational booklet, "There Ought to Be a Law . . . There Is." Address:
Consumer Division
Federal Home Loan Bank Board
1700 G Street, N.W.
Washington, DC 20552

Additional information about insured deposits at commercial banks with FDIC insurance may be secured from the corporation, which offers a free booklet, "Your Insured Deposits." Write:
Federal Deposit Insurance Corporation
550 17th Street, N.W.
Washington, DC 20429

"The Magic of Compound Interest . . ."

is financial writer Andrew Tobias's phrase for the results of a regular program of saving. As the interest earns interest on to infinity, a savings account can grow into a sizable nest egg. In the chart below, saving a dollar a year for twenty years at 7% yields a total of $41. Thus, $1,000 a year—$83.66 per month—for the same period would yield $41,000, and in 30 years, $94,461. Combined with the use of a tax-advantaged IRA, a program of regular savings offers an opportunity to achieve financial security and independence.

Year	6%	7%	8%	9%	10%	11%	12%
1	1.000	1.000	1.000	1.000	1.000	1.000	1.000
2	2.060	2.070	2.080	2.090	2.100	2.110	2.120
3	3.184	3.215	3.246	3.278	3.310	3.342	3.374
4	4.375	4.440	4.506	4.573	4.641	4.710	4.779
5	5.637	5.751	5.867	5.985	6.105	6.228	6.353
6	6.975	7.153	7.336	7.523	7.716	7.913	8.115
8	9.897	10.260	10.637	11.028	11.436	11.859	12.300
10	13.181	13.816	14.487	15.193	15.937	16.722	17.549
12	16.870	17.888	18.977	20.141	21.384	22.713	24.133
15	23.276	25.129	27.152	29.361	31.772	34.405	37.280
18	30.906	33.999	37.450	41.301	45.599	50.396	55.750
20	36.786	41.000	45.762	51.160	57.275	64.203	72.052
25	54.865	63.249	73.106	84.701	98.347	114.413	133.334
30	79.058	94.461	113.283	136.308	164.494	199.021	241.333

Housing

"Housing Options for Seniors Today" is a series of 13 Cornell Extension Service factsheets on housing alternatives and services for older adults. Some factsheets are aimed at service providers, others are directed to the general public, and several include lists of selected books and articles on housing alternatives. A descriptive brochure listing the individual factsheets and prices is available from:

Distribution Center
Cornell University
7 Research Park
Ithaca, NY 14850

Home Equity

National Center for Home Equity Conversion
110 East Main Street
Madison, WI 53703
(608) 256-2111

This organization can provide detailed information about home equity loans or conversions, though it is advisable to retain a lawyer familiar with negotiations of home equity contracts.

ECHO Housing

Coastal Colonial Corporation
Box 452-A, R.D. 4
Manheim, PA 17545
(717) 665-6761

This company can provide information about ECHO housing—Elder Cottage Housing Opportunity. Small, self-contained cottages have been designed to be erected on the property of the senior's family to facilitate care while stressing independence.

Travel

Airline Discounts

Airline	Discount	Eligibility Age
American (800) 433-7300	10% on all flights	62
Braniff (800) BRANIFF	15% discounts within U.S. and to Nassau	60
Continental (800) 525-0280	10% on all flights within mainland U.S.	62
Delta (800) 221-1212	Senior Citizen booklets offer 4 one-way tickets for $384 or 8 round-trip tickts for $640.	62
Eastern (800) EASTERN	10% discount on fares within U.S. and to Puerto Rice & Bahamas	62
Northwest (800) 225-2525 (dom) (800) 447-4747 (intl)	10% discount on all fares	62
Pan Am (800) 221-1111	10% discount on all flights except to France & Russia	62
TWA (Call local number)	10% on all domestic flights	62
United (800) 628-2868	10% discount on all flights; also KLM, Alitalia, Iberia	60
U.S. Air (800) 428-4322	10% discount on all flights	62

Also inquire about clubs for seniors who are frequent flyers.

Insurance

Access America
600 Third Avenue
New York, NY 10016
(800) 851-2800
Provides information on medical coverage outside the United States.
(Medicare does not provide such coverage.)

Travel Insurance Programs Corporation
243 Church Street West
Vienna, VA 22180
(800) 237-6615
Provides information on medical coverage outside the United States. (Medicare does not provide such coverage.)

International Association of Medical Assistance to Travelers (IAMAT)
417 Center Street
Lewiston, NY 14092
(716) 754-4883
Directory of English-speaking doctors throughout the world includes a 24-hour emergency number.

Sources of Information on Health and Fitness

Center for Science in the Public Interest
1501 16th Street, N.W.
Washington, DC 20036
(202) 332-9110
Publishes and distributes many materials on proper nutrition and other scientific approaches to better living.

Elder-Ed
P.O. Box 416
Kensington, MD 20795
Free booklet: "Using Your Medicines Wisely: A Guide for the Elderly."

High Blood Pressure Information Center
120/80
National Institutes of Health
Box AP
Bethesda, MD 20892
Free booklet: "Questions About Weight, Salt, and High Blood Pressure."

Johns Hopkins Hospital
Hearing and Speech Clinic
(301) 955-3434
Offers a free hearing screening test over the phone, 24 hours a day. Follow up of any problem with your doctor is recommended.

National Digestive Diseases Education and Information Clearinghouse
Box NDDIC
Bethesda, MD 20892
Offers general information to the public.

National Institute of Allergy and Infectious Diseases
Box AP, Bldg. 31, Rm. 7A32
Bethesda, MD 20892
Free booklet: "On Flu."

Surgery HHS
Washington, DC 20201
Free booklet: "Thinking of Having Surgery?"

American College of Surgeons
Office of Public Information
55 East Erie Street
Chicago, IL 60611
Free Booklet: "When You Need an Operation"

Vision Foundation
2818 Mt. Auburn Street
Watertown, MA 02172
Free: "Vision Inventory List"

National Society to Prevent Blindness
500 East Remington Road
Schaumberg, IL 60173
Free booklet: "The Aging Eye: Facts on Eye Care for Older Persons."

National Associations

Alzheimer's Association
70 East Lake Street
Chicago, IL 60601
(312) 853-3060
(800) 621-0379

American Diabetes Association
National Service Center
1660 Duke Street
Alexandria, VA 22314
(703) 549-1500
(800) 232-3472

American Heart Association
7320 Greenville Avenue
Dallas, TX 75231
(214) 373-6300

American Tinnitus Association
Box 5
Portland, OR 97207
(503) 248-9985

Arthritis Foundation
1314 Spring Street, N.W.
Atlanta, GA 30309
(404) 872-7100

National Kidney Foundation
2 Park Avenue
New York, NY 10003
(212) 889-2210

National Mental Health Association
1021 Prince Street
Alexandria, VA 22314
(703) 604-7722

National Osteoporosis Foundation
1625 Eye Street, N.W.
Washington, DC 20006
(202) 223-2226

National Safety Council
444 North Michigan Avenue
Chicago, IL 60611
(312) 527-4800

Self Help for Hard of Hearing People
(Shhh)
7800 Wisconsin Avenue
Bethesda, MD 20814
(301) 657-2248

Trade Associations

Group Health Association of America
1129 20th Street, N.W.
Washington, DC 20036
(202) 778-3200
Provides information on health maintenance organizations (HMOs).

Health Insurance Association of America
1025 Connecticut Avenue, N.W.
Washington, DC 20036
(202) 223-7780
Provides state-by-state lists of insurers offering long-term care policies.

American Health Care Association
1200 15th Street, N.W.
Washington, DC 20005
(202) 833-2050

National association of private long-term care providers publishes and distributes information on nursing homes for consumers.

National Association for Home Care
519 C Street, N.E.
Stanton Park
Washington, DC 20003
(202) 547-6586

National Hospice Organization
1901 North Moore Street
Arlington, VA 22209
(703) 243-5900

Health Matters

A Patient's Bill of Rights

Promulgated by the American Hospital Association

1. The patient has the right to considerate and respectful care.

2. The patient has the right to obtain from his physician complete current information concerning his diagnosis, treatment, and prognosis in terms the patient can be reasonably expected to understand. When it is not medically advisable to give such information to the patient, the information should be made available to an appropriate person in his behalf. He has the right to know, by name, the physician responsible for coordinating his care.

3. The patient has the right to receive from his physician information necessary to give informed consent prior to the start of any procedure and/ or treatment. Except in emergencies, such information for informed consent should include but not necessarily be limited to the specific procedure and/or treatment, the medically significant risks involved, and the probable duration of incapacitation. Where medically significant alternatives for care or treatment exist, or when the patient requests information concerning medical alternatives, the patient has the right to such information. The patient also has the right to know the name of the person responsible for the procedures and/or treatment.

4. The patient has the right to refuse treatment to the extent permitted by law and to be informed of the medical consequences of his action.

5. The patient has the right to every consideration of his privacy concerning his own medical care program. Case discussion, consultation, examination, and treatment are confidential and should be conducted discreetly. Those not directly involved in his care must have the permission of the patient to be present.

6.   The patient has the right to expect that all communications and records pertaining to his care should be treated as confidential.

7.   The patient has the right to expect that within its capacity a hospital must make reasonable response to the request of a patient for services. The hospital must provide evaluation, service, and/or referral as indicated by the urgency of the case. When medically permissible, a patient may be transferred to another facility only after he has received complete information and explanation concerning the needs for and alternatives to such a transfer. The institution to which the patient is to be transferred must first have accepted the patient for transfer.

8.   The patient has the right to obtain information as to any relationship of his hospital to other health care and educational institutions insofar as his care is concerned. The patient has the right to obtain information as to the existence of any professional relationships among individuals, by name, who are treating him.

9.   The patient has the right to be advised if the hospital proposes to engage in or perform human experimentation affecting his care or treatment. The patient has the right to refuse to participate in such research projects.

10.   The patient has the right to expect reasonable continuity of care. He has the right to know in advance what appointment times and physicians are available and where. The patient has the right to expect that the hospital will provide a mechanism whereby he is informed by his physician or a delegate of the physician of the patient's continuing health care requirements following discharge.

11.   The patient has the right to examine and receive an explanation of his bill regardless of source of payment.

12.   The patient has the right to know what hospital rules and regulations apply to his conduct as a patient.

No catalog of rights can guarantee for the patient the kind of treatment he has a right to expect. A hospital has many functions to perform, including the prevention and treatment of disease, the education of both health professionals and patients, and the conduct of clinical research. All these activities must be conducted with an overriding concern for the patient, and, above all, the recognition of his dignity as a human being. Success in achieving this recognition assures success in the defense of the rights of the patient.

Smoking

Most smokers want to quit, according to a research study conducted at the Federal Government's Centers for Disease Control, but few succeed in doing so—at least at first.

236

The most effective methods of quitting take account of the typical smoker's three-pronged dependency—physical, psychological, and social—and recognize that breaking this addiction is not a one-time effort for most people but a process that occurs over five to ten years.

Smokers who seek professional help in breaking their addiction generally have a higher rate of success than do those who try to do it on their own. However, only about 10 percent of would-be quitters seek such help—from a physician, hypnotist, acupuncturist, clinic, or through a structured program.

In order to give some assistance to the 90 percent of smokers who do not seek professional help, the following is the outline of a program developed by the American Cancer Society.

When thinking about quitting . . .

List all the reasons why you want to quit. Every night before going to bed, repeat one of the reasons 10 times.

Decide positively that you want to quit. Try to avoid negative thoughts about how difficult it might be.

Set a target date for quitting—perhaps a special day like your birthday, your anniversary, a holiday. If you smoke heavily at work, quit during your vacation.

Begin to condition yourself physically: start a modest exercise regimen; drink more fluids; get plenty of rest and avoid fatigue.

Just before quitting . . .

Smoke more heavily than usual so the experience becomes distasteful.

Collect all your cigarette butts in one large container as a visual reminder of the filth smoking represents.

Practice going without cigarettes. Don't think of *never* smoking again. Think of quitting in terms of one day at a time. Tell yourself you won't smoke today and then don't.

Immediately after quitting . . .

The first few days after you quit, spend as much free time as possible in places where smoking is prohibited, e.g. libraries, museums, theaters, department stores, churches, etc.

Drink large quantities of water and fruit juice.

Try to avoid alcohol, coffee, and other beverages with which you associate cigarette smoking.

Strike up a conversation with someone instead of a match for a cigarette.

If you miss the sensation of having a cigarette in your hand, play with something else—a pencil, a paper clip, a marble.

If you miss having something in your mouth, try toothpicks or a fake cigarette.

Avoid temptation . . .

Instead of smoking after meals, get up from the table and brush your teeth or go for a walk.

Temporarily avoid situations you strongly associate with the pleasurable aspects of smoking, e.g., watching your favorite TV program, sitting in your favorite chair, having a cocktail before dinner, etc.

Develop a clean, fresh non-smoking environment around yourself—at work and at home.

Until you are confident of your ability to stay off cigarettes, limit your socializing to healthful, outdoor activities or situations where smoking is prohibited.

If you must be in a situation where you'll be tempted to smoke (such as a cocktail or dinner party), try to associate with the nonsmokers there.

Marking progress . . .

Each month, on the anniversary of your quit date, plan a special celebration.

Periodically, write down new reasons why you are glad you quit, and post these reasons where you'll be sure to see them.

Make up a calendar for the first 90 days. Cross off each day and indicate the money saved by not smoking.

Set other intermediate target dates, and do something special with the money you've saved.

The American Cancer Society also has a 75-minute sound cassette, "Freshstart: 21 Days to Stop Smoking." Write:

American Cancer Society
1599 Clifton Road
Atlanta, GA 30329
(404) 320-3333

Information is also available from:
American Lung Association
1740 Broadway
New York, NY 10019
(212) 315-8700

Alcohol Abuse

Helpful information can be obtained from the following organizations:
Alcoholics Anonymous
Box 459
Grand Central Station
New York, NY 10163
(212) 686-1100
Local chapters of AA are listed in every phone directory.

American Council on Alcoholism
8501 LaSalle Road
Towson, MD 21204
(301) 296-5555
Provides a referral list of treatment centers.

National Council on Alcoholism
12 West 21st Street
New York, NY 10010
(212) 206-6770

National Clearinghouse for Alcohol Information
Box 2345
Rockville, MD 20852

Miscellaneous Information

Living Well

A person may sign a legal document stating that no heroic or extraordinary measures be used to sustain his or her life in a situation where there is little hope for recovery. For a copy of such a Living Will, write:

Concern for Dying
250 West 57th Street
New York, NY 10107

Lifeline
1 Arsenal Marketplace
Watertown, MA 02172
(800) 451-0525

Offers a communications system that consists of an electronic button that the subscriber carries on his or her person at all times. Emergency assistance can be summoned 24 hours a day simply by activating the button.

Physical Fitness

National Institute of Aging/Exercise
Bldg. 31—Room 5C35
Bethesda, MD 20892

American Physical Fitness Research Institute
654 North Sepulveda Boulevard
Los Angeles, CA 90049
(213) 426-6241

Institute for Aerobics Research
12330 Preston Road
Dallas, TX 75230
(214) 701-8001
(800) 527-0362

National Association of Mall Walkers
P.O. Box 191
Hermann, MO 65041
(314) 486-3945

Walkways Center
1400 16th Street, N.W.
Washington, DC 20036
(202) 234-5299
Association that promotes walking for fitness and recreation. Publishes brochures.

American Running and Fitness Association
2001 S Street, N.W., Suite 540
Washington, DC 20001
(202) 667-4150

Fifty-Plus Runners Association
P.O. Box D
Stanford, CA 94309
(415) 723-9790

Road Runners Club of America
629 South Washington Street
Alexandria, VA 22314
(703) 836-0558
Has over 400 local affiliates. Originated "Run For Your Life," a physical fitness program.

Grandparenting

Equal Rights for Grandparents
7408 Ventnor Avenue
Margate, NJ 08402

Foundation for Grandparenting
Box 31
Lake Placid, NY 12946

Grandparents Anonymous
536 West Huron
Pontiac, MI 48053

Grandparents'-Children's Rights
5728 Bayonne Ave.
Haslett, MI 48840

The Grandparents Journal
Nuxoll Newsletters
East 1419 Marietta Avenue
Spokane, WA 99207
Quarterly newsletter; sample copy available for $1.00.
Grandparents: A Newsletter for Grandparents
in Divided Families
Scarsdale Family Counseling Service
403 Harwood Building
Scarsdale, NY 10583

Toll-Free Numbers

Alcohol Helpline .... (800) 252-6465

Alzheimer's Disease .... (800) 621-0379

(IL) (800) 572-6037

American Cancer Society .... (800) 4-CANCER

American Council of the Blind .... (800) 424-8666

Better Hearing Institute .... (800) 424-8576

Cancer Information Service .... (800) 638-6694

Consumer Product Safety Commission .... (800) 638-2772

Diabetes Information Center .... (800) 232-3472

Healthy Older People Program .... (800) 626-5433

Housing Discrimination Problems .... (800) 424-8590

IRS Tax Information .... (800) 424-1040

Medicare Second Opinion Hotline .... (800) 638-6833

(MD) (800) 492-6603

National Health Information Clearinghouse .... (800) 336-4797

National Society to Prevent Blindness .... (800) 221-3004

Parkinson's Education Program .... (800) 344-7872

Social Security .... (800) 937-2000

U.S. Citizen Vital Records .... (800) 551-0562

Recommended Reading

The many books and other references mentioned or recommended in earlier chapters are here presented by categories for your information and consideration, and possible follow-through with your library or bookseller.

Health

American Heart Association Cookbook, presented by the American Heart Association. Ballantine Books, New York; 540 pages, paperback, $10.95 (U.S.), $14.75 (Canada). ISBN 0-345-32819-1.

Aquacises—Restoring and Maintaining Mobility with Water Exercises, by Miriam Study Giles. Mills and Sanderson, Lexington, Mass.; 287 pages, paperback, with illustrations, $9.95. ISBN 0-938179-11-X.

At-A-Glance Nutrition Counter, by Patricia Hausman. Ballantine Books, New York; 226 pages, paperback, $2.95. ISBN 0-345-31183-3.

Columbia Encyclopedia of Nutrition, compiled and edited by Myron Winick, M.D., and the Institute of Human Nutrition, Columbia University College of Physicians and Surgeons. G.P. Putnam's Sons, New York; 349 pages, hardcover, $19.95 (U.S.), $27.95 (Canada). ISBN 0-399-13298-8.

Complete Guide to Symptoms, Illness and Surgery, by H. Winter Griffith, M.D., with surgical illustrations by Mark Pederson. The Body Press, Los Angeles; 896 pages, paperback, $14.95 (U.S.), $19.95 (Canada). ISBN 0-89586-798-2.

Complete Guide to Prescription and Non-Prescription Drugs, 6th edition by H. Winter Griffith, M.D. The Body Press, Los Angeles; 1,170 pages, paperback, $14.95 (U.S.), $19.95 (Canada). ISBN 0-89586-753-2.

The Complete Manual of Fitness and Well Being, Dr. Robert Arnot, Special Adviser. Viking Penguin, New York; 312 pages, with illustrations, hardcover, $25.00. ISBN 0-670-23431-1.

Eating Well When You Just Can't Eat the Way You Used To, by Jane Weston Wilson. Workman Publishing Company, New York; 390 pages, paperback, $12.95. ISBN 0-89480-943-1.

Everyday Health Tips, by the editors of *Prevention* Magazine. Rodale Press, Emmaus, Pa.; 388 pages, hardcover, $27.95 (U.S.), $34.95 (Canada). ISBN 0-87857-774-2.

Heart Facts—What You Can Do to Keep a Healthy Heart, by Norman K. Hollenberg, M.D., with Ilana B. Hollenberg. Scott, Foresman, Glenview, Ill; 274 pages, paperback, $12.95. ISBN 0-673-24888-7.

Mature Health Magazine is a handsome, informative magazine published ten times annually. Cover price is $1.95, and yearly subscriptions are $15 ($18.50 for Canada). You may secure a sample copy for $1.00 when you mention *Life Begins at Fifty*. Send request and remittance to: Mature Health Copies, c/o Ruskin Associates, 171 East 84th Street, New York, NY 10028.

Maximize Your Body Potential—to an Effective Weight Management, by Joyce D. Nash, Ph.D. Bull Publishing Company, Palo Alto, Calif.; 542 pages, paperback, $14.95. ISBN 0-915950-69-3.

Medical and Health Encyclopedia, edited by Richard J. Waynman, M.D., J. G. Ferguson Publishing Co., Chicago; 628 pages, hardcover. ISBN 0-89434-077-8.

Prescription Drugs, by Brian S. Katcher, Pharm. D. Atheneum Publishers, New York; 357 pages, hardcover, $22.50. ISBN 0-689-11915-1.

The Surgeon General's Report on Nutrition and Health, by the U.S. Department of Health and Human Services and the American Nutritionists Association. Warner Books, New York; 171 pages, paperback, $6.95 (U.S.), $8.95 (Canada). ISBN 0-446-39061-5.

Take Care of Yourself—A Consumer's Guide to Medical Care, by Donald M. Vickery, M.D., and James F. Fries, M.D. Addison-Wesley, Reading, Mass.; paperback, forthcoming. ISBN 0-201-02403-9.

Financial and Financial Planning

Medicare Made Easy, by Charles B. Inlander and Charles K. MacKay. Addison-Wesley, Reading, Mass.; 337 pages, paperback, $10.95. ISBN 0-201-17269-0.

Plan Your Estate (Wills, Probate Avoidance, Trusts and Taxes) by Attorney Denis Clifford. Nolo Press, Berkeley, Calif.; 350 pages, paperback, $17.95. ISBN 0-87337-050-3. (Note: This book has sample forms and explanation of laws in every state but Louisiana—highly recommended.)

Your 1989/1990 Guide to Social Security Benefits, by Leona G. Rubin. Facts on File, New York; 240 pages, paperback, $9.95 (U.S.), $13.95, Canada. ISBN 0-8160-1633-X.

Your Ideas May be Worth a Fortune, written and published by Woodie Hall, one of America's most prolific inventors. Order this book for $10, U.S., or $12, Canadian, postpaid, from: Woodie Hall, 963 La Fiesta Way, Lake San Marcos, Calif. 92069.

General

Age Wave—The Challenge and Opportunities of an Aging America, by Ken Dychtwald, Ph.D., and Joe Flower. Jeremy P. Tarcher, Inc., Los Angeles; 380 pages, hardcover, $19.95. ISBN 0-87477-441-1.

Old Age is Not for Sissies by Art Linkletter. Viking Penguin, New York; 352 pages, hardcover, $17.95. ISBN 0-670-81922-0.

Travel

Arthur Frommer's New World of Travel, by Arthur Frommer. Prentice Hall, New York; 380 pages, paperback, $14.95. ISBN 0-13-617408-6.

Travel and Retirement Edens Abroad by Peter A. Dickinson. Order this 480-page paperback for $18.50 from: Peter A. Dickinson, 44 Wildwood Drive, Prescott, Ariz. 86301. Request a catalog sheet on his several books and newsletters.

Pilot Books has many inexpensive travel publications of special interest to mature adults. Write for their catalog: Pilot Books, 103 Cooper Street, Babylon, N.Y. 11702.

AN OFFER TO YOU

Thank you for buying and reading *Life Begins at Fifty, The Handbook For Creative Retirement Planning.*

If you have been able to apply the information and recommendations, or have other comments, please write and tell me.

As an added inducement, when you send a self-addressed and stamped return envelope, I offer you one of the following special subject reports which will be current at the time you write me: A: Travel Discounts; B: New Ideas for Making and Saving Money; C: News in Health; D: Recommended Books and Magazines; E: Ten New Ideas in Mature Living.

Write the letter or name of the requested report on the lower left corner of the return envelope. The reports price at $3 to $5 each, but if you bought this book, you may have the one requested without cost (while supplies last).

Write me: Leonard J. Hansen
Post Office Box 90279
San Diego, California 92109

Thanks for your reading; and in advance for your comments.

INDEX